Robert C Pitman

Alcohol and the State

A discussion of the problem of law as applied to the liquor traffic

Robert C Pitman

Alcohol and the State
A discussion of the problem of law as applied to the liquor traffic

ISBN/EAN: 9783744797740

Printed in Europe, USA, Canada, Australia, Japan

Cover: Foto ©Suzi / pixelio.de

More available books at **www.hansebooks.com**

ALCOHOL AND THE STATE.

A DISCUSSION

OF

THE PROBLEM OF LAW

AS APPLIED TO THE

LIQUOR TRAFFIC.

BY

ROBERT C. PITMAN, LL.D.,

Associate Justice of the Superior Court of Massachusetts.

———

"We are convinced that if a Statesman, who heartily wished to do the utmost good to his country, were thoughtfully to inquire which of the topics of the day deserved the most intense force of his attention, the sure reply—the reply which would be exacted by full deliberation—would be, that he should study THE MEANS by which this worst of plagues can be stayed."—C. BUXTON, M.P.

———

NEW YORK:

National Temperance Society and Publication House,

58 READE STREET.

. 1877.

PREFACE.

THOMAS CARLYLE, in a letter written in 1872, after expressing his wish for the "success, complete and speedy," of the English "Permissive Bill," and acknowledging the receipt of certain pamphlets relating to Intemperance, curtly added: "The pamphlets shall be turned to account, though I myself *require no argument or evidence further on that disgraceful subject.*"

I can sympathize with the bluff Scotchman's impatience. There are times when this subject is exceedingly wearisome to me, and nothing but a positive sense of duty can hold me to its contemplation. I can easily excuse those who are conscious of having well-grounded opinions, *formed upon evidence*, from reading what I have to say in this volume.

But if there are any who have been heretofore prone to dismiss the whole subject as a vulgar one, I beg them to ponder the rebuke given by Dr. Channing, more than a generation ago, to a similar moral indifference, substituting intemperance for slavery, and inebriate for slave:

"There are not a few persons who, from vulgar modes of thinking, can not be interested in this subject. Because the slave is a degraded being, they think slavery a low topic, and wonder how it can excite the attention and sympathy of those who can discuss or feel for anything else. Now the truth is that slavery, regarded only in a philosophical light, is a theme worthy of the highest minds. It involves the gravest questions about human nature and society. It carries us into the problems which have exercised for ages the highest understandings. . . . . I venture to say there is no subject now agitated by the community which can compare in philosophical dignity with slavery; and yet to multitudes the question falls under the same contempt with the slave himself. To many, a writer seems to lower himself who touches it. The falsely refined, who want intellectual force to grasp it, pronounce it unworthy of their notice."

I offer this volume as my contribution to the discussion of an interesting problem connected with the Temperance reform. I venture to hope that some chapters may have value for the student of social science who may not accept my conclusions. I attach special importance to the *facts* herein set forth, and have taken much care to verify them. No one can have a stronger objection than I have to unreliable statistics, and to loose and exaggerated statements. It has been my constant aim, from taste, policy, and principle, to exclude all such.

Throughout this essay my purpose has been to keep close to the subject indicated by the title, to treat it in a calm and argumentative rather than in a rhetorical style, and to present the policy of Prohibition as not a mere corollary from personal abstin nce, but as based upon the broadest grounds of statesmanship.

NEWTON, MASS., *Sept.* 1*st.*, 1877.

CONTENTS.

PART FIRST.

ALCOHOL vs. THE STATE.

PART SECOND.

THE STATE vs. ALCOHOL.

CHAPTER XXIII.

CHAPTER XXIV.

CHAPTER XXV.

CHAPTER XXVI.

BOOK I.

ALCOHOL *vs.* THE STATE.

CHAPTER I.

In entering upon the discussion of the Problem of the Liquor Traffic, we naturally consider what the traffic does to us before inquiring what we shall do with it. The investigation of a disease precedes and then determines the nature and strength of the remedies. This is the logical, and we believe it will be found to have been the chronological, order of thought with those who have been most earnest practical students of the relation of legislation to this traffic.

By the liquor traffic, of course we mean the common sale of alcoholic liquors as a beverage. It is self-evident that the intemperance of the country is mainly due to this traffic. We are, then, to inquire what are the burdens intemperance lays upon us, and then whether the traffic has any benefits to show by way of offset.

To many it will seem an entirely needless task to set forth the evils which we suffer from this cause. Conceded by so many eminent persons of every school of thought, and emphasized by observers from every point of view,

(11)

they might with propriety be assumed at the
outset as the basis of any argument. We meet
such statements as follow everywhere.

Charles Buxton, M.P., the English brewer,
declares that if we " add together all the miseries generated in our times by war, famine, and
pestilence, the three great scourges of mankind, they do not exceed those that spring from
this one calamity."

Richard Cobden, years ago, put on record
his testimony that " Every day's experience
tends more and more to confirm me in my
opinion that the temperance cause lies at the
foundation of all social and political·reform ; "
while John Bright, his compeer, calls the
" love of strong drink the greatest obstacle to
the diffusion of education amongst the masses
of the people."

Mr. Bruce, the Home Secretary under the
Gladstone ministry, confessed that intemperance was " not only a great evil, but the greatest of all evils with which social reformers had
to contend."

The Archbishop of Canterbury, in a recent
visitation charge, gives this solemn warning :
" There is one dreadful evil overspreading the
whole land, which makes havoc of our workingmen—the evil of intemperance ; . . . unless you make distinct and positive efforts

against it, you will be neglecting an evil which is eating out the very heart of so·ie·ty, destroying domestic life among our working classes, and perhaps doing greater injury than any other cause that could be named in this age."

Dr. Temple, the Bishop of Exeter, lately said: "Of all the preventable evils in the world, intemperance is, perhaps, the greatest.".

The London *Times*, as the organ of the general sentiment of observing men, tersely sums up the matter thus: "The use of strong drink produces more idleness, crime, want, and misery than all other causes put together."

Nor have such utterances been less pronounced in our own country.

The common sentiment as to the vice of intemperance was well expressed in the report made to the Legislature of Massachusetts by the friends of a license law in 1866, when they styled it "that ulcer of the civilization of the Teutonic races." And recently, in vetoing the Local Option Bill, Governor Dix, of New York, used this emphatic language: "Intemperance is the undoubted cause of four-fifths of all the crime, pauperism, and domestic misery of the State." So Governor Gaston, in his message to the Legislature of Massachusetts in 1875, recommending the repeal of the "prohibitory law," says "that intemperance has been the most prolific source of poverty, wretchedness, and crime; that it has filled the State and the country with its destructive influences ; and that its progress everywhere heralds only misfortune, misery, and degradation."

But to admit a truth is one thing, and to realize it is another. I have for years had a growing conviction that these general and sweeping statements fail to impress not only the public, but some of the most thoughtful minds. I have often been reminded of the aphorism of Coleridge: " Truths, of all others the most awful and interesting, are too often considered as so true that they lose all the power of truth, and lie bed-ridden in the dormitory of the soul, side by side with the most despised and exploded errors." A careful, though somewhat brief, survey of some of the deadlier fruits of the liquor traffic can not fail to make upon some minds a salutary impression. But it is the reason and not the imagination or the emotions that we desire to impress; and we shall therefore rely only on sober testimony and facts ; the figures we shall use will be those of statistics, and not of speech.

Nor shall we cover any more ground than clearly pertains to the discussion we have undertaken. For, although as a progressive civilization brings us all together more closely in various ways, and a deeper insight into sociology shows us the numberless ways in which the interest of each depends on all, and that of all on each, so that we realize as never before that "we are one body and members one of another"—still it remains true that we may draw a rough, practical line between the individual and the social suffering that flows from this vice. And so we shall say nothing here of the burdens of the heart; nothing here of sorrows or losses that seem to touch the individual and not the community. The field of misery is so large that we are abundantly content with this limitation.

Let us, then, see what burdens the drinking habit (for this more exactly than intemperance describes the evil) imposes upon society.

CHAPTER II.

WASTE.

A PART of the waste of material wealth which the drinking of intoxicants causes us, is not difficult of approximate estimation.

DIRECT COST.

Dr. Edward Young, the Chief of the Bureau of Statistics in the Treasury Department, estimates the sales of liquors in the United States during the fiscal year ending June 30, 1871, at six hundred millions of dollars, distributed as follows :

Whisky, . . .	60,000,000 gallons at $6, retail,		$360,000,000
Imported Spirits,	2,500,000 " " 10,	"	25,000,000
" Wines,	10,700,000 " " 5,	"	53,500,000
Ale, Beer & Porter,	6,500,000 bbls., " 20,	"	130,000,000
Native Brandies, Wines, and Cordials, estimated at			31,500,000
			* $600,000,000

* As this is partly estimate, it may increase confidence in its reliableness to add what Mr. Young says in the letter containing the above calculation. After alluding to the "gross exaggerations" of estimates made by others, based "on the receipts of internal revenue from the sales of merchandise, including liquors, by retail liquor dealers, and not of liquors alone," he writes : "Temperance, in common with almost every good work, has suffered from the intemperate zeal of its advocates, and from no cause to a greater extent, perhaps, than from the exaggerated statement of alleged facts."

(16)

A small percentage of this vast sum may have been profitably used in the arts and in medicine, but I fear, however liberal an allowance is made for such use, the increase in sales since 1871 greatly overbalances it; * so that the total sum given above must be esteemed an under-estimate of the present annual wasteful consumption. Well may Dr. Young say: "These figures are sufficiently startling. . . . . The minds of few persons can comprehend this vast sum." Some assistance in gaining an impression of it may be derived from a comparison with the value of some useful products of universal need.

The United States census for 1870 gives these annual values of manufacturing industries:

Flour and Grist-mill Products, ...	$444,985,143
Molasses and Sugars (raw and refined), . .	119,325,279
Cotton Goods, ...	177,489,739
Woolen "	155,405,358
Boots and Shoes, ...	146,704,655

Or, to vary the comparison, it appears by the same census that the aggregate of wages paid

---

* Dr. Hargreaves, basing his estimate on the amount of liquors paying tax, as shown by the Reports of Internal Revenue, and of Commerce and Navigation, makes the cost to the consumer, in 1872, to be $735,720,048. ("Our Wasted Resources," p. 51). I may remark that this book has been published since this chapter was written, and the reader who desires to pursue this topic farther, will find abundant information in the voluminous tables which Dr. H. has industriously compiled.

by all the manufacturing establishments of the country for the year preceding, was only $775,584,343, not thirty per cent. in excess of our drink bill.

Let us look a moment at what we spend for enlightening our intellects in comparison with what we spend for muddling them. The total income of all the schools of learning, public and private, from every source, for the year, is given as $95,402,726, not one-sixth of what we waste on liquors.

Our whole printing and publishing bill is but $66,862,447.

All the libraries in the country, both public and private, are said to contain 45,528,938 volumes; if we reckon the average value at $2 a volume, it will give as the worth, $91,057,876; so that we drink up our books in less than two months.

The total value of church property in the United States is put down as $354,483,581. If it were all to burn up, about six months of abstinence would replace it.

Once more let us attempt to realize our figures. The census gives the total aggregate of *State* taxation in 1870 (including therein all Territorial, State, County, and Municipal taxes), as $280,591,521; not one-half the direct tax the liquor consumers lay upon themselves;

while the whole "Public Indebtedness" (exclusive of the National debt, of course) is set down at $868,676,758; which could be swept off by the direct saving from less than a year and a half of abstinence.

It may be interesting to compare our expenditure with that estimated from data given in the Government blue-book for the same year by Mr. William Hoyle, of Manchester, as the consumption in the United Kingdom. Mr. Hoyle (who has devoted great attention to the economical aspects of the traffic) makes a detailed statement, aggregating for the year 1870, £119,082,-285. This is a somewhat less sum than ours, but it represents a considerably larger consumption at a much less price per gallon. The cost for 1873 he reckons at £140,014,712.* (The population of the United Kingdom was 31,817,-108 in 1871, and that of the United States, 38,558,371 in 1870). Who can hesitate to say with Mr. Hoyle :

" It would be acting a wise and Christian part if we paid the money to avert the evils; but to buy them, and at such a price, is madness that is inexplicable, except by taking into account the moral blindness that inevitably results from a continued course of evil."

In 1872 there were 161,144 persons paying

---

* His estimate for 1875, from the excise returns, is £142,741,669.

to the U. S. Government a retailer's license to
sell liquors. If, now, we consider the number
who evaded, the bartenders who served employers, and the yearly increase, we shall con-
clude that 200,000 is a moderate estimate of
the number who are now solely or mainly employed in this business. We, then, are adding
to the folly of a waste of six hundred millions
of dollars in poisoning ourselves, another folly
of withdrawing from all useful industry an army
of two hundred thousand persons to incite and
to furnish us facilities so to do.

INDIRECT COST.

Some statisticians estimate the indirect cost
of intoxicating liquors to a people as equal
to the direct. But this is a mere guess.
We have to leave our figures when we ponder the pecuniary losses and burdens which
the accidents, the impaired power of production,
the pauperism, the disease and death, and the
crime which result from alcoholic drinks impose
upon us. They are not the less grave because
they elude computation.

We shall have occasion hereafter to introduce,
in connection with certain vital statistics, an
impressive view of the loss of productive capacity which society suffers from the shortened life
of drinkers.

Let us turn for a moment now to the loss of production by the living. In 1868, Oliver Ames & Sons, who carried on at North Easton, in Massachusetts, one of the largest shovel manufactories in the world, wrote as follows :

"We find that the present license law has a very bad effect among our employees. We find, on comparing our production in May and June of this year (1868) with that of the corresponding months of last year (1867), that in 1867, with 375 men, we produced eight per cent. more goods than we did in the same months in 1868, with 400 men. We attribute this large falling off entirely to the repeal of the prohibitory law and the great increase in the use of intoxicating liquors among our men in consequence."

Now we do not make use of this statement in this connection for any purpose of argument as to the prohibitory law. That is to be considered hereafter. But mark this : There is exhibited (taking into account the increase of men) a falling off of production of fourteen per cent., stating it roughly. And this difference does not show the whole difference of production between an abstinent and a drinking population, but only the difference resulting from a certain greater prevalence of drinking consequent upon a change of law. Yet even if we take this per cent. as the full average measure of losses to the industries of the coun-

try, the waste appears immense.*   I am aware
of no reason for considering this an exceptional
instance.   Indeed, the Secretary of the Massachusetts Board of State Charities, whose duties
caused him to become familiar with such matters, says in his Fifth Annual Report (p. 36),
after alluding to the experience of the Messrs.
Ames : " I mention this conspicuous instance,
because I feel authorized to do so ; but were I
to use the names of other employers of labor,
who have testified to the same state of things
in their establishments, it would appear that
the evil is general."

The value of · the labor of the country in
dollars and cents it is not easy to estimate, because returns are of the value of products, and
the proportion of value in the raw material is
very variable.   But if we take the return of
wages paid by *manufacturers* alone in the
single State of Massachusetts, as given in the
U. S. census of 1870, it reaches the enormous
sum of $118,051,886 a year.   If we assume as
a rough approximation that the loss of production heretofore stated measures the loss of
wages, we should have a loss of sixteen and a

---

* The Massachusetts census of 1875 gives the yearly total
products of industry as the enormous sum of $639,877,465 in
that State alone.   This, of course, includes the value of raw
material used.

half millions of wages in this single department
of industry, though the leading one in the
State of Massachusetts, in a year — a sum
nearly four times as large as the whole public
expenditure for educational purposes in that
year.

The workman's drinking not only squanders
the wages of the day, but creates an incapacity
to earn wages for the morrow, and ultimately
deteriorates and depreciates the value of his
working power.

But sad as is this double and self-repeating
waste of resources, it has relations still graver
than those which pertain to Political Economy,
of which we shall speak in the next chapter.

CHAPTER III.

DESTRUCTION OF HOME.

"Whoever handles the subject of Massachusetts industry, is dealing not only with potentialities of wealth, but of civilization, of popular happiness and virtue, beyond the dreams of philosophers."—F. B. SANBORN.

POLITICAL ECONOMY grieves over a loss of fourteen per cent. in production, and the Messrs. Ames have a private grief and a personal loss from the annoyance and injury they suffer from the disorganization of labor following an increase of drinking. But this typical fact has far sadder significance when we trace its relation to the home of the laborer. Such an average percentage of diminished ·production means to the individual laborer whose intemperance causes it, a variable diminution of earnings, running from a small percentage to nearly or quite a hundred of loss.

But how disastrous the loss of even a small portion of customary wages to the laborer is, will be impressively shown by the conclusions drawn by the "Massachusetts Bureau of Statistics of Labor," from very carefully collected and tabulated returns. In their Sixth Annual

Report (1875), they state as among their established conclusions (p. 384) :

"*First.* That in the majority of cases, workingmen in this Commonwealth do not support their families by their individual earnings alone."

"*Third.* That fathers rely, or are forced to depend, upon their children for from *one-quarter* to *one-third* of the entire family earnings.

"*Fourth.* That children *under fifteen years of age* supply, by their labor, from one-eighth to one-sixth of the total family earnings.

"*Fifth.* That more than *one-half* of the *families* save money ; less than one-tenth are in debt, and the remainder make both ends meet.

"*Sixth.* That without children's assistance, other things remaining equal, the majority of families would be in poverty or debt."

"*Ninth.* That the average saving is about *three per cent.* of the earnings."

The report of the same bureau for 1876 contains tabulated returns from about 50,000 workingmen, obtained in connection with the decennial State census of 1875. From these it appears "that the average annual income derived from usual daily wages, other earnings, earnings of wife and children, and garden-crops, was $534.99. The average annual cost of living was $488.96. This leaves a possible saving of $46.03 yearly, or 8 per cent." The Report goes on to say: "The returns from

1875 were entirely from *married* men having families dependent upon them, while the returns of 1876 are, in a great many instances, from *single* men. This fact may account, in part, for·the increase in percentage of possible surplus or saving" (p. 342).

The average saving possible, then, to the *home* which avails itself of the labor of wife and child, is somewhere between three and eight per cent., perhaps we ought to say nearer the latter than the former. I suppose no one will doubt that Massachusetts will compare favorably in this respect with her sister States.* Accepting, then, these results as approximatively correct as to the condition of the mere "wage laborer," we are the better prepared to see how the loss of an appreciable per cent. of wages or the gain, becomes a matter of life or death, figuratively, and sometimes literally, in the homes of these people. It is well to look more closely than many of us are accustomed to do at the connection of the industrial prosperity with the higher life of a community. Wendell Phillips has said that the civilization of a people often

---

* Gov. Tilden did hardly more than call public attention to an accepted truism, when he said in his letter of acceptance of the Presidential nomination : "Even in prosperous times, the daily wants of industrious communities press closely upon their daily earnings. The margin of possible national saving is, at best, a small per cent. of national earnings."

depends on the use made of the surplus dollar. A related truth is that the home of the laborer rises or falls as you add a dollar of surplus or a dollar of debt. And it is to be borne in mind that the drinker is losing doubly : by a wasteful expenditure and by diminished earnings.

Let us look into contrasted homes, where the only variable element is the drinking habit of the head. The full wages of the temperate man brings from year to year better food, better clothing, and better shelter. Improved sanitary arrangements tell on the health of father, wife, and children. The house becomes more and more a home. The passer-by notices the vines that cluster about the doorway, and the little flowers that peep through the windows. Upon the inside walls the picture speaks of a dawning taste, and the piano or some simpler musical instrument, shows that the daughter is adding a charm and refinement to the family circle. Books and periodicals show the surplus dollar. Every influence is elevating. Introduce the element of drinking, and you reverse the picture. Year by year the physical comforts of the house lessen. The tenement must narrow to the means,* and locate itself in noi-

---

* A decent home is needed for a decent life. Says Mr. Brace, in the Report on Juvenile Crime : "The source of juvenile crime and misery in New York, which is the most formidable, and at

some neighborhoods. The wife first pinches
herself in food and clothing, but the time soon
comes when the children, too, must suffer. The
scanty clothing becomes ragged. The church
and the school know the children no longer.*
No flowers of beauty adorn, no sound of music
cheers such a dwelling. The fire goes out
upon the hearth, and the light of hope fades
from the heart. Soon the very form of a family
is broken up, and public charity cares for the
scattered fragments. An American home has
been blotted out. Now, it is not with the private
misery that we are here concerned, but with
the effect upon the State. If the chief interest
of the State is in the character of its citizens,
then no agency is more destructive to its interests than the dram-shop, because the dram-shop
is the great enemy of the home, and it is the
character of the home which is not only the
test, but the efficient factor in an advancing or
a falling civilization.

the same time the most difficult to remove, is the overcrowding
of our population. . . . . Overcrowding is the one great
misfortune of New York. Without it we should be the healthiest
large city in the world, and a great proportion of the crimes which
disgrace our civilization be nipped in the bud."—*Proceedings of
International Congress at London,* 1872, p. 232.

* It is very curious and suggestive to observe in the detailed
report upon the individual homes of hundreds of laborers in the
Statistics of Labor in Massachusetts, to which I have heretofore
alluded, how frequently occurs this sentence: "Family dresses
well, and attends church."

CHAPTER IV.

WE are now to look a little further into the hell of intemperance. A very poor man may still be a very wise man, a very happy man, and a very useful man ; but a pauper is, in general, an object of deserved pity and contempt. He has lost, or is fast losing, all the characteristic qualities of industry, independence, and self-respect essential to manliness. The familiar line of Homer tells us that

> " Whatever day
> Makes man a slave takes half his worth away."

But the slave is still a worker. He is self-supporting, at least, and has that title to manhood left. If the slave has lost half his worth, the pauper may be said to have lost it all ; nay, more, so far as the State is concerned, he is worse than a cipher. Not only does the Commonwealth rightly disfranchise him and strike him from the enrolled militia, but he is a burden and an element of disgrace and degradation to the community.

But intemperance is manifestly the chief pro-

ducer of pauperism. I might fill a volume with
the proof. It suffices to look at the official
records and reports of Massachusetts.

The Pauper returns, made annually for a
long time to the Secretary of State, show an
average of about 80 per cent. as due to this
cause in the County of Suffolk (mainly the city
of Boston). Thus, in 1863, the whole number
relieved is stated at 12,248. Of these the number made dependent by their own intemperance
is given as 6,048 ; and the number so made by
the intemperance of parents and guardians at
3,837 ; making an aggregate of 9,885.

The Third Report of the Board of State
Charities, page 202 (Jan., 1867), declares intemperance to be " the chief occasion of pauperism ; " and the Fifth Report says : " Overseers
of the poor variously estimate the proportion
of crime and pauperism attributable to the vice
of intemperance from one-third in some localities up to nine-tenths in others. This seems
large, but is, doubtless, correct in regard to
some localities, and particularly among the
class of persons receiving temporary relief, the
greater proportion of whom are of foreign birth
or descent."

In the Sixth Annual Report of the Board of
Health (Jan., 1875), page 45, under the head
" Intemperance as a Cause of Pauperism," the

chairman, Dr. Bowditch, gives the result of answers received from 282 of the towns and cities to the two following questions :

" 1. What proportion of the inmates of your almshouses are there in consequence of the deleterious use of intoxicating liquors ? "

" 2. What proportion of the children in the house are there in consequence of the drunkenness of parents ? "

While it appears that in the country towns the proportion is quite variable and less than the general current of statistics would lead one to expect, which is fairly attributable in part, at least, to the extent to which both law and public opinion has restricted the use and traffic in liquors, yet we have from the city of Boston, the headquarters of the traffic, this emphatic testimony from the Superintendent of the Deer Island Almshouse and Hospital :

" I would answer the above by saying, to the best of my knowledge and belief, 90 per cent. to both questions. Our register shows that full one-third of the inmates received for the last two years are here through the direct cause of drunkenness. Very few inmates (there are exceptions) in this house but what rum brought them there. Setting aside the sentenced boys (sent here for truancy, petty theft, etc.), nine-tenths of the remainder are here through the influence of the use of intoxicating liquors by the parents. The great and almost the only cause for so much poverty and distress in the city can be traced to the use of intoxicating drink either by the husband or wife, or both."

A startling testimony as to the effect of this cause in producing the allied evil and even nuisance of vagrancy, is given in the answer from the city of Springfield :

"In addition to circular, I would say that we have lodged and fed eight thousand and fifty-two persons that we call 'tramps ;' and I can seldom find a man among them who was not reduced to that condition by intemperance. It is safe to say nine-tenths are drunkards, though we have not the exact records."

It were easy to accumulate statistics from other States and countries to the same effect ; but what is needed is rather a realization of the facts for which figures stand. Think of what pauperism is ; count its cost of annual millions to public and private charity ; and consider how much of higher culture for the masses, of refinement and social elevation this wasted treasure might secure ; see how this evil drags its victims down to the abysses of disease and crime, and reflect upon that solemn law of human solidarity expressly stated by the great Apostle, by which "if one member suffer, all the members suffer with it ;" and that other law of human descent by which after-generations suffer for the guilty parents,* and say if you can see the great cause of all this accumulated evil standing revealed before you without an irresistible impulse to seize the deadliest weapon for its destruction?

---

* The tendency of pauperism to perpetuate itself is so marked as to have attracted the attention of all observers. Every lawyer knows the carefulness and pertinacity with which " pauper cases " are contested, because the municipal authorities know that a pauper settlement once fixed upon their town is likely to be a burden for generations. An extraordinary instance of this tendency is given by Dr. E. Harris, Registrar of the Board of Health of New York. A pauper named Margaret lived in Ulster Co., some eighty-five years ago. She and two sisters have begotten generations of paupers and criminals to such an extent that the total number now known, mainly from Margaret — convicts, paupers, criminals, beggars, and vagrants, including the living and dead—is six hundred and twenty-three! This mother of criminals cost the county hundreds of thousands of dollars. [Cited in *N. A. Review*, April, 1875. Art. " Pauperism."]

CHAPTER V.

INJURY TO PUBLIC HEALTH.

" Health is the capital of the laboring man."—LATHAM.

" In as far as human life is more important than all financial interests, and even in the financial view, the creative power of human force is more valuable than all created capital, this cardinal interest of the people, individually and collectively, should take precedence of all other provisions in all legislation. Every law, grant, or privilege from the Legislature should have this invariable condition : That human health, strength, or comfort should, in no manner or degree, be impaired or vitiated thereby."—DR. EDWARD JARVIS.

THAT the use of intoxicating liquors to such an extent as to produce drunkenness is a cause of disease and death, is too obvious and universally admitted to allow of argument. Of course, if it shortens life it renders health less perfect while life lasts. But perhaps few who assent to these general propositions have an adequate idea of the aggregate loss of vitality from this cause. We have now at hand instructive observations in this matter, taken by competent persons not in the interest of any theory, but of business and to regulate the operations of Life Insurance Companies.

In the Twenty-third Registration Report of

(34)

Massachusetts (pages 61, *et seq.*) will be found instructive tables, selected and digested by Dr. Edward Jarvis, from the result of the investigations of Mr. Neison, Actuary of the Medical, Invalid, and General Life Insurance Company of London. It is necessary to premise, in order to appreciate the full force of the tables, that under the designation "General Population" are of course included both the temperate and the intemperate ; and that the latter designation includes "only such as were decidedly addicted to drinking habits, and not merely occasional drinkers or free livers."

The same general result is displayed in several ways, thus :

RATE PER CENT. OF ANNUAL MORTALITY.

Among Beer Drinkers, ...	4,597
Spirit Drinkers, ...	5,995
Mixed Drinkers, ...	6,194
General Population :	
Males, ...	2,316
Females, ...	2,143

COMPARATIVE DEATH RATE AT DIFFERENT AGES.

If the death rate of the general population be constantly represented by 10, for purposes of comparison, then the death rate among the intemperate between the ages of 15 and 20 would be represented by 18; between 20 and 30, by

51; between 30 and 40, by 42; between 40 and 50, by 41; between 50 and 60, by 29, and so on.

SURVIVAL AT SUCCESSIVE AGES.

If we take 100,000 intemperate persons and 100,000 of the general population, starting at the age of twenty years, we shall find there will be living at successive periods as follows:

AGE.	INTEMPERATE.	GENERAL POPULATION. [*]
25	81,975	95,712
30	64,114	91,577
35	50,746	86,830
40	39,671	82,082
50	21,938	70,666
60	11,568	56,355
70	5,076	35,220
80	807	13,169

These tables preach their own sermon.

AS TO "CAREFUL DRINKERS."

Beyond these, which deal with the results of acknowledged intemperance, the limited and yet valuable experience of a few English Life Insurance Companies who have a separate section for total abstainers, while they refuse all who are more than "careful drinkers," shows that any use of such liquors as a beverage tends

[*] I have given only the males. Dr. Jarvis adds the females, but the general result is substantially the same.

to shorten life. I give a single illustration. In a paper read by E. Vivian, M.A., on "Vital Statistics," before the British Association for the Advancement of Science, at its annual meeting in 1875, he exhibited the following as the result of statistics kept by the " United Kingdom and General Provident Institution " of two classes of persons insured—one total abstainers and the other not :

RATE OF MORTALITY DURING THE LAST NINE YEARS, ENDING
30TH DECEMBER, 1874.

In the Total Abstinence Section :

Expected deaths, ...	549
Actual deaths, ...	411
Difference, ...	138

Or 25 per cent. below the average.

In the General Section :

Expected deaths, ...	2,002
Actual deaths, ...	1,977
Difference, ...	25

Or one per cent. below the average.

It gives the impressive emphasis of statistical demonstration to the late weighty utterance of Sir H. Thompson, a practitioner of European reputation, in his letter to the Archbishop of Canterbury, in which he says :

" I have long had the conviction that there is no greater cause of evil, moral and physical, in this country than the use of alcoholic beverages. I do not mean by this that extreme indulgence which produces drunkenness. The habitual use of fermented liquors to an extent far short of what is necessary to produce that condition, and such as is quite common in all ranks of society, injures the body and diminishes the mental power to an extent which, I think, few people are aware of. Such, at all events, is the result of observation during more than twenty years of professional life, devoted to hospital practice, and to private practice in every rank above it. Thus I have no hesitation in attributing a very large proportion of some of the most painful and dangerous maladies which come under my notice, as well as those which every medical man has to treat, to the ordinary and daily use of fermented drink taken in the quantity which is conventionally deemed moderate."

THE NIDUS OF DISEASE.

When the census gives us the deaths by drunkenness, it not only frames its reports from the indulgent verdicts of surviving friends, but what is more necessary to observe, it leaves out of view the indirect, but vastly more important, influence of intemperance as the preparation for, and ally of almost every disease that flesh is heir to.

In considering the relation of alcohol to the public health, we are not to confine ourselves to its effect upon its immediate victims, but to look at its effect upon the sanitary condition of community and its tendency to produce a propagating *nidus* of disease. And here, first, we notice that the poverty of which drink is the principal cause, especially in our large cities, is one of the prime factors of all disease. It is this poverty, hopeless and degrading, which compels its victims to huddle together in tenement-houses, where the decencies of life are not possible, and where the malignant influences of the external situation are reinforced by the pestiferous influences within. When to all these is added the lack of clothing for the changes of our climate, the insufficient and unhealthy food, the overwork of mothers, and the premature work of children, we can see at once that in such *homes* as these is the origin and nutriment of malaria and fever; and then it finds for its ready victims the inmates with systems enfeebled and corrupted by debauch and vitiated by hereditary alcoholism.

An epidemic does not create these deadly influences, but only intensifies and so magnifies them as to render them visible to the popular eye. At such times alcohol is seen to be the forerunner of the pestilence. The following impressive facts are taken from Dr. Lees' "Condensed Argument:" "In the great fever which raged in London in 1739—the era of the gin mania — the drinkers were the first and greatest victims. Dr. Short observes:

'The like was the fate of all tipplers, dram-drinkers, and punch-merchants — scarcely any other died of this severe fever.' The Asiatic cholera, too, singles out the drinker with fatal precision, where it leaves the sober generally unscathed. So well known was this fact, that the authorities at Philadelphia closed the grog-shops as a nuisance to the public health. In Albany, the same year, while only one in 2,500 of the teetotalers were seized, one in sixty of the general population perished. The *Volks-vriend* for August, 1854, states that 'out of 900 persons who died in Rotterdam the preceding year from cholera, only three were abstainers.' It is the same at home. In New-castle, within a period of two months of the ravages of the cholera, it struck down one drinker out of fifty-six, of course a far greater proportion of drunkards; only one in 625 of the teetotalers. Throughout the country it always broke out afresh after a *festival* occasion, and increased after the Sunday, when the people consumed a little more drink than usual. Dr. Cartwright, of New Orleans, writes, in 1853, to the Boston *Medical Journal :*

" 'The yellow fever came down like a storm upon this devoted city with 1,127 dram-shops, in *one* of the *four* parts into which it has been divided. It is not the citizen proper, but the foreigners, with mistaken notions about the climate and country, who are the chief supporters of these haunts of .intemperance. *About five thousand of them died before the epidemic touched a single citizen or sober man, so far as I can get at the facts.'"*

It is upon the last clause we would pause a moment. Five thousand drunkards *first*— and then? Why, then, the disease acquiring virulence by feeding upon such material, spreads like a conflagration far and wide, and spares not the noblest and best. Another impressive lesson of the law of Human Solidarity. The same great Lawgiver who has bound us in ties of duty, has also bound us in ties of interest to the lowest of His children.

THE INTEREST OF THE STATE.

A Government that professed no interest in the health of its people would deserve neither the endurance of its subjects nor the respect of the civilized world. Whatever refinements speculative philosophers may have taught as to the sphere of the State in regard to public morals, but few have been audacious enough to question its duty to care for the public health. But as sometimes a most impressive view of the magnitude of an object is obtained from a survey of its confessedly least and lowest, and yet most measurable side, it may not be amiss

to show the economic interest which the nation
has in the vital force of its citizens.

Dr. William E. Boardman, of Boston, in a
paper on "The Value of Health to the
State," published in the Sixth Annual Report of the State Board of Health, computes
"the total average loss of *working* time
by sickness during one year" in Massachusetts as 20.914 years.   Dr. Jarvis, the
eminent statistician, in a paper in the Report
of the previous year, by another calculation,
gives the loss per year among the people of the
State between the "working ages" (20 to 70)
as 24.553 years.   Dr. Boardman, upon his
basis, states the "total annual loss to the State
by sickness alone (of the working classes), at
the lowest calculation, is $15,267,322."   He
considers two dollars per day "as the minimum
average cost of sickness," which he divides
equally between loss of wages on the one hand,
and medical attendance, medicine, care, and
incidentals on the other.   So far as relates to
loss of wages merely, we have alluded to this
in our chapter on "Waste."

But we are now to call attention to a public
loss, of no part of which have we taken previous account.   In the paper of Dr. Jarvis
above referred to, he presents a calculation
which shows that Massachusetts averages an

annual loss of children under 20 years of age whose aggregate years amount to 41,823. Now, he maintains that, "simply as a vital productive machine, a child at any age is worth the cost that has been expended on him for his support and development;" and that such cost averages not less than fifty dollars a year. He adds that both English and German political economists arrive at similar conclusions. Upon this basis he reckons that Massachusetts loses over two millions of dollars yearly from the premature death of children. But a still more impressive view is given of the loss by premature death in the "working period." He calculates that there is here an average annual loss of 276,461 years of prospective service. We shall not attempt to compute the enormous value of this in money to the State; nor shall we attempt to estimate what percentage of this loss is attributable directly and indirectly to intemperance; suffice it to have directed the attention of the thoughtful reader to a new and most important chapter in political economy.

CHAPTER VI.

THE CHIEF OCCASION OF CRIME.

The malignant action of alcohol upon the brain, and through this organ upon the mind itself, is sometimes spoken of as that of an excitant of the lower faculties or the animal passions ; and sometimes as that of a depressant of the higher and rational nature. Perhaps it is both ; but we have no occasion to enter into the discussion. Whether the animal nature is excited unduly or the spiritual deadened, the same result follows. The " moral equilibrium of character" is destroyed. It matters little whether we fire up the locomotive beyond control or pitch off the engineer. It is more to our purpose to notice, as observers, the proximate methods in which the use of intoxicants leads to crime. The subject compels brevity, and we do little more than suggest lines of thought.

First. Drunkenness itself is, by statute and by reason, a crime—a social nuisance.

Second. Drink excites the evil passions—how much or how little it takes to do it is a question of temperament and circumstance.

Third. It fortifies for crime.*

Fourth. It throws off the reins of prudence. Recklessness is one of the first fruits of drink. Reason teaches that crime is folly; alcohol clouds the reason.

Fifth. It tempts to crimes, especially of lust and robbery, by putting the victim in the power of the criminal.

Sixth. And emboldens to crime by rendering its detection difficult where the necessary witness is wholly or partially insensible.

Seventh. Idleness and poverty are prolific agencies in the production of crime ; but intemperance is the main cause of these.

Eighth. Truancy is regarded as one of the most common proximate causes of crime. But

---

* In Governor Andrew's "Errors of Prohibition," I find a curious passage. After describing a horrible murder in the County of Bristol, Mass., he says : " I suppose this murder is reckoned among the crimes chargeable to drinking. And, perhaps, the mixture of whisky and gunpowder which he drank blunted his nerves and calmed his agitation, and thus fortified his audacity to the extent of enabling him to do what would otherwise have been too much for him. . . . . . But the *purpose* of violence and robbery was formed before he drank. The crime was sufficiently complete, as a purpose of the mind, without the draught." Suppose this to be so ; has society any less interest in protecting itself against the *proximate* cause of the crime ? If, without the whisky, there would have been no murder, then is not the murder "chargeable to drinking," even though it be also chargeable, as the old indictments had it, to the " instigation of the devil ? "

Mr. Philbrick, for so many years the Superintendent of Schools in Boston, in one of his reports, tells us that "among the causes of truancy, that which so far transcends all others as to be properly considered the cause of causes, is the immoderate use of intoxicating drinks. This is the unanimous testimony of the truant officers."

Ninth. Intemperance is the efficient ally of other vices. Wine has been well styled, "The Devil's Water-Power." Without it much of the machinery of evil would stand still. It is the life of the gaming-house and the brothel, and surely these are hot-beds of crime.

From this rapid glance at the *rationale* of the relation between crime and intemperance, we are prepared to pass to a view of results. And here we are embarrassed only by the uniformity and abundance of the testimony.

As long ago as 1670, Sir Matthew Hale, Chief-Justice of England, said:

"The places of judicature I have long held in this kingdom have given me an opportunity to observe the original cause of most of the enormities that have been committed for the space of nearly twenty years; and, by due observation, I have found that if the murders and manslaughters, the burglaries and robberies, the riots and tumults, the adulteries, fornications, rapes, and other enormities that have happened in that time, were divided into *five* parts, *four* of them have been the issues and product of excessive drinking—of tavern or ale-house drinking."

And through the centuries since, the same testimony has been borne by judges of the highest and lowest courts exercising criminal jurisdiction. I need only cite from a recent letter of Lord Chief Baron Kelley to the Archdeacon of Coventry, in which he says "two-thirds of the crimes which come before the courts of law of this country, are occasioned chiefly by intemperance" (Report to Convocation of Canterbury, p. 52).

Still more impressive is the evidence of those whose official duties have brought them into close personal contact with criminals. Says Mr. Clay, the chaplain of the Preston House of Correction (England), in 1855:

" I have heard more than 15,000 prisoners declare that the enticements of the ale and beer houses had been their ruin. . . . If every prisoner's habits and history were fully inquired into, it would be placed beyond doubt that *nine-tenths* of the English crime requiring to be dealt with by the law arises from the English sin, which the same law scarcely discourages."

Frederick Hill, late Inspector of Prisons in England, and a high authority in all matters of penal science, writes :

"I am within the truth when I state, as the result of extensive and minute inquiry, that in *four cases out of five*, when an offence has been committed, intoxicating drink has been *one* of the causes. Nothing serves more to explain the good conduct of prisoners than their complete withdrawal from the excitement and temptation of intoxicating liquors. Removed from these, they become different men, and are no more deserving the epithets which are often applied to them, than a person who has ceased to be in a passion merits the name of a madman."

Similar testimony is borne by Dr. Elisha Harris, of New York, after an inspection of prisons, in a paper on " The Relations of Drunkenness to Crime" (1873). He says:

"As a physician, familiar with the morbid consequences of alcoholic indulgence in thousands of sufferers from it; as a student of physiology, interested in the remarkable phenomena and results of inebriation; and as a close observer of social and moral wants, it was easy for the writer to believe that not less than one-half of all crime and pauperism in the State depends upon alcoholic inebriety. But after two years of careful inquiry into the history and condition of the criminal population of the State, he finds that the conclusion is inevitable, that, taken in all its relations, alcoholic drinks may justly be charged with far more than half of the crimes that are brought to conviction in the State of New York; and that full *eighty-five* per cent. of all convicts give evidence of having in some larger degree been prepared or enticed to do criminal acts because of the physical and distracting effects produced upon the human organism by alcohol, and as they indulged in the use of alcoholic drinks."

So, too, the Board of Police Justices of the city of New York, whose testimony is specially valuable because of their daily observation of crime and criminals at the start, in their Annual Report for 1874, say:

" We are fully satisfied that it (intoxication) is the one great leading cause which renders the existence of our police courts necessary" (p. 17).

If figures are to any one more impressive, they could easily be accumulated to express the same result. Suffice it to give here what we happen to have at hand—an extract from the report of a committee made to the "Dominion House of Commons," at Ottawa, Canada, in May, 1875: . '

"Your committee further find, on examining the reports of the prison inspectors for the provinces of Ontario and Quebec, that out of 28,289 commitments to the gaols for the three previous years, 21,236 were committed either for drunkenness or for crimes perpetrated under the influence of drink, thus corroborating the statements of the magistrates and others above alluded to."

But why roam abroad when the proof is at

3

our doors? Three district attorneys of the County of Suffolk, embracing the city of Boston, speak to us with equal emphasis. The first in order of time, Hon. John C. Park, says:

" While district attorney, I formed the opinion (and it is not a mere matter of opinion, but is confirmed by every hour of experience since) that ninety-nine one-hundredths of the crime in the commonwealth is produced by intoxicating liquors."

Hon. Geo. P. Sanger (ex-judge of the Court of Common Pleas, and at present the United States Attorney for the District of Massachusetts), speaking from his experience as the prosecuting officer of the same District, says:

" There are very few cases into which the use of intoxicating liquor does not more or less enter."

The last attorney for the same district, J. Wilder May, writes:

" According to my official observation, drinking in some form is directly responsible for about three-fourths of the crime that is brought to the cognizance of the county, and indirectly for about three-quarters of the other crimes."

Successive Reports of the Board of State Charities of Massachusetts proclaim the same result. Thus the Secretary says in the Report for 1867 (p. 202), speaking of the aggregate returns of convicts:

"About two-thirds are set down as intemperate, ' but this number is known to be too small. Probably *more than* 80 *per cent.* come within this class, intemperance being *the chief occasion of crime*, as it is of pauperism, and (in a less degree) of insanity."

The Report of 1868 (p. 137) says:

"Of all the proximate causes or occasions of crime, none is so fruitful as intemperance. The returns show that from 60 to 80 per cent. of our criminals are intemperate, and the proportion of those whose crimes were occasioned by intemperance is probably even greater."

The Report of 1869 (p. 175) repeats the same statement:

"The proportion of crime traceable to this great vice must be set down, as heretofore, at not less than four-fifths."

The Inspectors of the Massachusetts State Prison arrive at the same conclusion in regard to the graver crimes punishable there. Thus, in their Report, Pub. Doc., 1868, (No. 13, p. 4,) they say of the convicts:

"About four-fifths of the number committed the crimes for which they were sentenced, either directly or indirectly by the use of intoxicating drinks."

And so we end with the same estimate that Sir Matthew Hale gave two hundred years ago.

The only attempt to break the force of these statistics, of which I am aware, is in the argument of Governor Andrew on the " Errors of Prohibition."

He seeks to invert the real relation between poverty, intemperance, and crime by making the former the efficient cause of both the latter.

But, in the first place, it is very doubtful whether *mere* poverty has any important tendency to produce crime.

Recorder Hill, of Birmingham, England, a high authority, both from his long experience as a criminal magistrate, and from ·the philosophic and philanthropic interest exhibited in these matters in his volume of papers on the " Repression of Crime," says :

"I could almost count upon my fingers all the cases which have fallen under my observation, either at the bar or on the bench, of crimes originating in the pressure of want."

There is more reason for regarding a sudden influx of prosperity among those not accustomed to moral control as a favorable condition for the generation of crime. Thus, the Rev. John Clay, styled by our Board of State Charities,

"A prison chaplain of great experience," in an
elaborate paper before the "British Association
for the Advancement of Science," maintains
that the laboring classes are most criminal, because most intemperate, in what are called good
times ; and he declares that "want and distress,
uncombined with dissolute habits, are rarely operative in producing crime."

In the course of pretty extensive reading of
the discussions of the problem of drunkenness,
by English statesmen and social reformers of all
shades of opinion, I have myself been struck
with their agreement, that increased wages has
been one of the causes of increased drunkenness.

That *vicious* poverty engenders crime we
have before maintained. And so far as the factor of poverty is concerned, we have already
demonstrated that it is itself mainly created,
especially in America, by the intemperance of
its victims or their natural supporters. What
else, I ask, in this country of ours, where, under
equal laws and with equal rights, labor finds it
just reward, and the hum of industry never
ceases from early morn to eventide, and where
the demand for simple, honest labor still out-
runs the supply, should reduce a man to the
ranks of poverty but vice? The providences
of life, sickness, and casualty I do not forget.
But for these the hand of Christian beneficence

is always open, and neighborly kindness rarely suffers temporary misfortune to degrade any one to the ranks of pauperism. "I have been young, and now I am old; yet have I never seen the righteous forsaken, nor his seed begging bread." The testimony of the Psalmist remaineth sure.

CHAPTER VII.

ALCOHOL VITIATES HUMAN STOCK.

WE have so far dwelt upon the effects of intoxication upon society through its effects upon the individual victim. We are now to consider it in wider relations. By the operation of the laws of solidarity and of hereditary descent, we are all interested in the physical, intellectual, and moral qualities of the human stock. " If (say the Massachusetts Board of State Charities) it could be proved that the use of any imported or manufactured article vitiates the breed of horses and cattle, farmers, at least, would look for some power to interdict it, and would not hesitate much about using that power. But the race of man is of vastly greater importance, and the purity of the human stock should be far more carefully guarded."

Sagacious observers in early times have been aware of the tendency of vicious habits or states to transmit themselves. Thus it was a saying of Aristotle that " Drunken women bring forth children like unto themselves ; " and Plutarch writes that " One drunkard begets another." But it has been reserved for men of this genera-

tion, patient in research and philosophic in
thought, to unfold the exactness, the univer-
sality, and the far-reaching extent of nature's
laws in this matter.

Dr. Ray, one of the first authorities in this
country upon the subject of insanity, says in his
" Mental Hygiene " (p. 44) :

"Another potent agency in vitiating the quality of
the brain is habitual intemperance, and the effect is
far oftener witnessed in the offspring than in the
drunkard himself. His habits may induce an attack
of insanity where the predisposition exists ; but he
generally escapes with nothing worse than the loss
of some of his natural vigor and hardihood of mind.
In the offspring, however, on whom the consequences
of the parental vice may be visited, to the third if
not the fourth generation, the cerebral disorder may
take the form of intemperance, or idiocy, or insanity,
or vicious habits, or impulses to crime, or some minor
mental obliquities."

Dr. S. G. Howe, in a report to the Massachusetts Legislature on Idiocy, made in 1848
(Senate Doc. No. 51), states that "out of 359
idiots, the condition of whose progenitors was
ascertained, 99 were the children of drunkards.
But this does not tell the whole story, by any
means. By drunkard is meant a person who is
a notorious and habitual sot. . . . . By pretty
careful inquiry as to the number of idiots of the

lowest class whose parents were known to be *temperate* persons, it is found that *not one-quarter* can be so considered." But this terrible fact is more fearfully significant in what it points to. If in so many cases *idiocy* was produced, in vastly how many more is there reason to believe that degrees of degeneracy, falling short of this recognized status, resulted. When idiocy is reached, then comes extinction ; but through how many generations, and with what wide-spread collaterals, may imbecility of the physical, mental, and moral nature, or of all combined, propagate itself.

Morel, a French author of the highest authority, and as a superintendent of large hospitals, of the widest experience, in his great work entitled, " *Des Dégénérescences de l'Espéce Humaine* " (which Dr. Jarvis well paraphrases as " the waste of constitutional force in the human family "), speaks thus of " the abuse of alcoholic liquors and of certain narcotics, such as opium. Under the influence of these poisonous agents, there have been produced perversions so great in the functions of the nervous system, that in the result, as we have demonstrated, are the true degeneracies of the present time, whether in influence direct from the poisonous agent, or by the transmission of hereditary power in the child."

3*

Magnus Huss, the eminent Swede, in his treatise on "Alcoholisms," and Carpenter, the English Physiologist, bear emphatic testimony to the same point.

In an article in the *Contemporary Review* for January, 1873, Dr. Carpenter says :

"We have a far larger experience of the results of habitual alcoholic excess than we have in regard to any other 'nervine stimulant ;' and all such experience is decidedly in favor of the *hereditary transmission* of that acquired perversion of the normal nutrition of the nervous system which it has induced. That this manifests itself sometimes in a congenital idiocy, sometimes in a predisposition to insanity, which requires but a very slight exciting cause to develop it, and sometimes in a strong craving for alcoholic drinks which the unhappy subject of it strives in vain to resist, is the concurrent testimony of all who have directed their attention to the inquiry."

Sir Henry Thompson, in his letter to the Archbishop of Canterbury, from which we have already quoted in another connection, says :

"There is no single habit in this country which so much tends to deteriorate the qualities of the race, and so much disqualifies it for endurance in that competition which, in the nature of things, must exist, and in which struggle the prize of superiority must fall to the best and to the strongest."

We will add the testimony of Mr. Darwin :

" It is remarkable that all the diseases arising from drinking spirituous or fermented liquors, are liable to become hereditary even to the third generation, increasing, if the cause be continued, till the family becomes extinct."

The Second Report of the Board of State Charities of Massachusetts, signed by Dr. S. G. Howe as chairman, and among others by Dr. Nathan Allen as one of its members, contains a paper upon " Alcohol as a cause of Vitiation of Human Stock," which treats the subject scientifically and yet most impressively. What we have further to say upon this topic can not be better said than by condensed selections from this able paper.

" A prolific cause (of this vitiation) is the common habit of taking alcohol into the system, usually as the basis of spirits, wine, or beer. The effects of alcohol upon the senses, and even upon the bodily functions, vary according to the medium in which it is conveyed; but the basis being the same in all, the *constitutional effects* are about the same.

" If its general use does materially influence the number and condition of the dependent and criminal classes, it is the special duty of those holding official relations with those classes to furnish facts and materials for public consideration.

" It is well known that alcohol acts unequally upon man's nature; that it stimulates the lower propensities and weakens the higher faculties. . . . .

"If this process is often repeated, the lower propensities are strengthened by exercise until, by and by, they come to act automatically, while the restraining powers, or the will, weakened by disuse, are practically nullified. The man is no longer under control of his voluntary powers, but has come under the dominion of automatic functions, which are almost as much beyond his control as the beating of his heart. But the habitual stimulus of the brain by alcoholized blood, in ever so small doses, must produce the same *kind* of results, only in a lesser degree." . . . .

The paper then proceeds to show that "*persistent functional disturbance at last brings about organic change.*" It also suggests, in view of the rapidity of its elimination from the system compared with other poisons, " Whether this peculiarity of alcohol does not make its constant use in small doses worse for posterity than its occasional use in large quantities; that is, whether tippling is not worse than drunkenness, as far as it affects the number and the condition of the offspring."

And, in conclusion, they say :

"The facts and considerations just named make clear the sad truth that the children of parents whose systems were tainted by alcoholic poison do start in life under great disadvantage. While they inherit strong animal propensities, and morbid appetites and tendencies, constantly craving indulgence, they have weak restraining faculties. Their temptation is greater, and their power of resistance is less than in children of purer stock. They are, therefore, more likely to fall into the pauper or criminal class." *

That this transmission of misery which alcohol effects is attracting more and more the attention of the medical fraternity, may be seen from one of the resolutions passed by the National Medical Association of the United States, at their meeting in Detroit in 1874, in these words :

" That we are of the opinion that the use of alcoholic liquors as a beverage is productive of a large amount of physical and mental disease ; that it *entails diseased appetites and enfeebled constitutions upon offspring ;* and that it is the cause of a large percentage of the crime and pauperism in our large cities and country."

We may then assume that alcohol, after its work of ruin in one generation, leaves as a heritage of evil to the next weakened and demoralized stock, which—

First. Lessens the physical and mental force, and so reduces the power of industrial production, and makes the man in every way of less worth to the State.

---

* The same subject is ably treated again in the Ninth Annual Report of the Board, pp. XXIX.–XXXIII.

Second. Entails disease and lowers the tone of the public health.

Third. By impairment of vital force, increases pauperism.

Fourth. And by animalizing the moral nature, fosters crime.

CHAPTER VIII.

THE UNIVERSAL ALLY OF EVIL—THE UNIVERSAL ANTAGONIST OF GOOD.

" Not only does this vice (intemperance) produce all kinds of wanton mischief, but it has also a *negative effect* of great importance. It is the mightiest of the forces that clog the progress of good. It is in vain that every engine is set to work that philanthropy can devise, when those whom we seek to benefit are habitually tampering with their faculties of reason and will, soaking their brains with beer or inflaming them with ardent spirits. The struggle of the school, the library, and the church, all united, against the beer-house and gin-palace, is but one development of the war between heaven and hell."— CHARLES BUXTON, M. P.

THE vices are at least as sociable as the virtues. But beyond this general affinity the drinking habit sustains peculiar relations to other social evils and crimes. We have already considered its direct influence as a stimulant of crime and its indirect as the great cause of poverty and pauperism. We have also seen how it animalizes human nature and debases human stock. But we have now to notice that it intensifies all the perils of our civilization ; and perils which affect the integrity of our national life and the stability of our government.

It is characteristic of the courage of the American mind that but few of our people seem apprehensive as to the result of our experiment ▸of universal suffrage. And yet the world has seen nothing like it, or even approximating it, before. By it all men are made sovereigns, and every man has an interest in the character of his co-ruler. Every drunken ballot imperils every sober man's interest. Every whisky-shop is a recruiting station for any party having evil designs. The dram-shop is the ally of every corrupt political ring. It is ready to capture the caucus or to stuff the ballot-box. In some of our large cities it is able to dictate nominations. In more it is able to defeat any one who incurs its ill-will. * Great cities are becoming more and more the great powers in

---

* I do not know whether it will afford any consolation to read what John Adams wrote of his own county in the "good old times" of 1761. "In most country towns in this county you will find almost every other house with a sign of entertainment before it. If you call, you will find dirt enough, very miserable accommodations of provision and lodging for yourself and your horses. Yet, if you sit the evening you will find the house full of people, drinking drams, flip, toddy, carousing, swearing; but especially plotting with the landlord to get him, at the next town meeting, an election either for selectman or representative. Thus the multiplicity of these houses, by dividing the profits, renders the landlords careless of travelers, and allures the poor country people, who are tired with labor and hanker after company, to waste their time and money, contract habits of intemperance and

politics, and the actual or threatened supremacy of the dangerous classes there can not but excite the anxiety of the most determined optimist. The State of New York, by the joint action of the Legislature and the Governor, has recently appointed an able commission, at the head of which is the Hon. William M. Evarts, to :"devise a plan for the government of cities." It is well for the State to stir ere it finds the cities, and the worst element of her cities, governing *it*. But no schemes or plans will work without the public virtue of citizens.† The dram-shop mocks the name and destroys the very substance of that virtue. Within its sphere it makes bad citizens faster than schools and churches can make good citizens.

That terrible vice of large cities—prostitution —which appalls the senses with its physical re-

---

idleness, and, by degrees, to lose the natural dignity and freedom of English minds, and confer those offices which belong by nature and the spirit of all government to probity and honesty. *on the meanest and weakest and worst of human characters."*

† Since this was written the Commission have made their Report. It deals only with *machinery*. I can not characterize it better then by using the words of H. D. Cushing: "If shipwrights, striving to make a seaworthy vessel, should look only at the shape and model, and do nothing to disturb the worms that were making honeycomb of every timber, it would scarce seem to us more absurd or ludicrous than the New York effort to make good city governments without disturbing the dram-shop or its allies."

sults, vitiates human stock more horribly than alcohol itself, shocks the moralist with the extent and depth of the ruin of the higher nature which it causes, and baffles the best efforts of the philanthropist for its eradication—derives essential support from intoxicants. The brothel requires the dram-shop to stimulate the passions and to narcotize the conscience.

So, too, the gambler's den maintains its bar, and the gamester draws his boastful courage from his cups, or drowns therein his disappointment and remorse.

Without entering upon any questions of religious controversy, he must be a shallow observer who does not see how vital to our national weal is the substantial preservation of the American Sabbath. It is emphatically what Ebenezer Eliot, the "corn-law rhymer," called it—"the poor man's day;" it is the best conservator of Home, the guardian of the public morals, and the only guaranty in this busy day and world of some due attention to the cultivation of that spiritual nature in man which gives life and force even to his work among material things. But the liquor traffic and the Sabbath are in natural enmity. It is no chance association which leads to the cry, "Down with the Sunday Laws and the Liquor Laws," in so many parts of our country. The traffic wants the day. It wants the Saturday night wages; it wants the opportunity and the temptation to drink of the day of rest; it has the day in Europe, it covets it in America. It will have it unless the political power of the traffic is broken.

With the Sabbath go our schools and churches, as three great educational agencies. We shall hereafter examine how far religious and intellectual culture can be relied on as the sole cure of intemperance; but we only desire here to note that it paralyzes the very agencies which Governor Andrew and others have proclaimed as adequate for its own extirpation. Neither the drunkard nor his children are often brought within the influence of the Church, nor are those who are habitually muddling their brains and hardening their hearts with liquor responsive to the gentle touch of more private ministrations. Even where the drinking is within a conventional standard of moderation, it quickly narcotizes the religious faculties of the soul. An alcoholized brain has but little susceptibility to the higher spiritual influences. The most impressive testimonies upon this point might be introduced, were it not too obviously true to need them. Let a single one suffice. The Convocation of Canterbury expresses it as the sentiment of the English clergy, that " no evil

more nearly affects our national life and character; *none more injuriously counteracts the
spiritual work of the Church.*" A body of
testimony from parish ministers, published in
the appendix, fully supports this deliverance.
Let no one think I am here departing from my
subject—the relation of Alcohol to the State;
for as the third article of the original Bill of
Rights of the Constitution of Massachusetts
well puts it:

" The happiness of a people, and the good order
and preservation of civil government, essentially depend upon piety, religion, and morality; and these
can not be generally diffused through a community
but by the institution of the public worship of God
and of public instructions in piety, religion, and morality."

Nor is the influence of this traffic less markedly adverse to education. Intemperance blinds
the intellect as well as deadens the heart; and
it makes truants from school as well as ab-
sentees from church. Mr. Philbrick, for many
years the Superintendent of Schools in the
city of Boston, and thoroughly competent to
judge in the matter, summed it up thus tersely
in one of his reports: " *The liquor-shops and
the schools are, in all respects, antagonistic to
each other.*"

The Commonwealth of Massachusetts alone

expended during the year 1875 five million eight hundred and ninety-one thousand six hundred and sixty-six dollars ($5,891,666) for her *public schools* only,* and gave to the work of teaching in them nine thousand two hundred and sixteen (9,216) of the best of her sons and daughters. Must she permit the liquor-shops, declared by her official authorities to be the natural and perpetual antagonists of her schools, to flourish by their side ? It is a sad thought to add that the education of the school is soon over ; the training of the liquor-shop is for life.

---

* This includes $1,533,142.54 for school-houses.

CHAPTER IX.

IS THERE A SET-OFF OF BENEFITS?

" If this agent do really for the moment cheer the weary and impart a flush of transient pleasure to the unwearied who crave for mirth, its influence (doubtful even in these modest and moderate degrees) is an infinitesimal advantage by the side of an infinity of evil for which there is no compensation and no human cure."—DR. RICHARDSON in " Cantor Lectures."

HAVING thus rapidly portrayed the evils of the liquor traffic, so far as they concern the various interests of political society, it may be well, before we proceed to discuss the problem of legislative interference, to consider whether there is a useful side to the traffic which we are bound to respect and to keep in view.

And here let me say at the outset, that I disclaim any desire to found any part of this argument upon what may be considered " extreme" views. It was a skillful movement on the part of Governor Andrew, in commencing his attack upon prohibition, in his famous plea before the Committee of the Massachusetts Legislature, to announce that its advocates " base their argument in part upon the assumption that alcohol is a poison in the sense in which strychnine or arsenic is poison, to be administer-

(70)

ed to the human system only under the restrictions applicable to the administration of fatal
drugs."* It is a great advantage in a desperate
contest to select the ground upon which your
opponent must fight the battle. If the horrors
of the traffic and the efficiency or inefficiency
of the modes resorted to for its restraint can be
kept out of sight, while a vigorous contest is
kept up over the definition of a " poison," the
test of a " food," or the elimination or trans-
formation of alcohol in the human system, a
defeat may be prevented if a victory can not be
won.

No part of the field of natural science is more
obscure than that which deals with the chemistry of animal life. In human physiology, theories
chase each other with perplexing swiftness, and
leave behind but unsatisfactory results. But
so far as relates to the use of alcohol in *disease*,
we have here nothing to say. It relates itself to
a still larger question, as to the use of all drugs,
and the nature, conditions, and limitations of

---

* According to Governor Andrew, the argument for prohibition rests wholly upon two " assumptions ; " the one being as
stated above, and the " further assumption that the use and the
sale of alcoholic beverages are essentially immoral." But this is
not so. Prohibitionists do not rest their argument on " assumptions," but on carefully-observed facts ; not on scientific or ethical
theories, but on the ascertained injury which the liquor traffic
inflicts upon every interest of the State.

their power. When alcohol is relegated to the
shelf of the apothecary, it is to be judged like
other narcotics or irritant stimulants, as you
may choose to classify it. Every actual or proposed system of legislation makes provision for
its medicinal use. To determine the mode and
amount of such use is exclusively the physician's problem ; only it may be well to remember that we are individually safer in the hands
of one who has no personal appetite to bias
him in the advocacy of this fascinating draught,
and who never forgets that one of the masters
of his profession has said that it is "a shroud
which covers more than it cures ;" even here
too often playing its old part as "a mocker."

The scientific controversy also as to the
action of alcohol in the living organism I dismiss, not because I am not interested in it; not
because I fear it ; I am tolerably familiar with
its literature. The present phase of the discussion is not unfavorable to the rigid total ab-
stainer. The last utterance of science is in the
six "Cantor Lectures," delivered before the
Society of Arts in England, by Dr. Benjamin
W. Richardson, one of the leading medical
writers of the day, professing to "stand forth
simply as an interpreter of natural fact and law,"
and whose utterances are publicly commended
and indorsed by the Nestor of our American

physicians, Dr. Willard Parker, of New York.*
Dr. Richardson finds alcohol, in all its forms and
combinations, essentially a paralyzer ; and closes
his discussion with the affirmation that it "is
neither a food nor a drink suitable for his (man's)
natural demands. Its application, as an agent
that shall enter the living organization, is properly limited by the learning and skill possessed
by the physician—a learning that itself admits
of being recast and revised in many important
details, and, perhaps, in principles."† But I

---

* It may be added that *The Lancet*, one of the very first
medical journals of England, in its issue of February 13, 1875,
speaks of the lecturer as "a member of our body, who, belonging
to no particular community of reformers, and pledged to the support of no sectarian advocacy, should be able to speak with
authority ;" and after a summary of his lectures, and a reference to certain observations detailed by him, says : "The practical deductions from these observations accord with the modern
experience that is now being gained under the new light by
which this subject is surveyed. To the professional mind the
facts have for some time past been gradually developing, and
have afforded striking evidence of the value of properly-con-
ducted experimental research."

† Or, as he expresses it in a still more recent work on "The
Diseases of Modern Life:" "The physician . . . . can find no
place for alcohol as a necessity of life. . . . In whatever direction he turns his attention to determine the value of alcohol to
man beyond the sphere of its value as a drug, which he may at
times prescribe, he sees nothing but a void ; in whatever way he
turns his attention to determine the persistent effects of alcohol,
he sees nothing but disease and death ; mental disease, mental
death ; physical disease, physical death " (pp. 209, 210).

4

desire to confine myself more narrowly to my precise subject.

The problem of legislation, as I have before said, concerns itself only with the sale of intoxicants *as ordinary beverages.* That (to put it mildly, and yet for our purpose effectively,) there is no occasion for the State to make any provision for this on sanitary grounds is the general judgment of the medical profession. Indeed, I suppose that but few thoughtful persons would dissent from the negative part of this statement in the *Quarterly Review,* of England (Oct., 1875):

"The common-sense and experience of educated minds bear witness that only a comparatively small number—the feeble and the sick—actually require stimulating drinks."

Whether the feeble and the sick *do* require these, and if at all, what and when, are questions to be settled by physicians and not by legislators; and if prescribed, they are to be procured as medicines and not as drams.

As to the general inutility of these beverages, we are not left without an impressive mass of medical testimony, and we propose to introduce it simply in masses.

Dr. Carpenter, of England, the distinguished physiologist and scientist, appends to his essay

" On the Use of Alcoholic Liquors," the following certificate, which he says had been signed by " upwards of *two thousand* physicians in all grades and degrees, from the court ·physicians and leading metropolitan surgeons to the humble country practitioner : "

" We, the undersigned, are of opinion—

" 1. That a very large proportion of human misery, including poverty, disease, and crime, is induced by the use of alcoholic or fermented liquors as beverages.

" 2. That the most perfect health is compatible with total abstinence from all such intoxicating beverages, whether in the form of ardent spirits or as wine, beer, ale, porter, cider, etc.

" 3. That persons accustomed to such drinks may, with the most perfect safety, discontinue them entirely, either at once or gradually after a short time.

" 4. That *total and universal abstinence from alcoholic beverages of all sorts would greatly contribute to the health, the prosperity, and happiness of the human race.*"

In Feb., 1873, ninety-six physicians of Montreal, Canada, twenty-four of whom were professors or demonstrators in the medical schools there situate, united in a similar declaration ; averring "that total abstinence from intoxicating liquors, whether fermented or distilled, is consistent with, and conducive to, the highest degree of physical and mental health

and vigor;" and "that abstinence from intoxicating liquors would greatly promote the health,
morality, and happiness of the people."

The National Medical Association of the
United States, at their convention at Detroit in
June, 1874, which was attended by over four
hundred physicians, resolved :

" That in view of the alarming prevalence and ill
effects of intemperance, with which none are so
familiar as members of the medical profession, and
which have called forth from English physicians the
voice of warning to the people of Great Britain concerning the use of alcoholic beverages, we, as members of the medical profession of the United States,
unite in the declaration that we believe that *alcohol
should be classed with other powerful drugs ;* that when
prescribed medicinally, it should be done with conscientious caution and a sense of great responsibility."

" That we would welcome any change in public
sentiment that would confine the use of intoxicating
liquors to the uses of *science, art, and medicine.*"

And lately, under the lead of Dr. Willard
Parker, one hundred and twenty-four physicians
of New York city and vicinity, including
among them such men as Alonzo Clark, Prof.
E. R. Peaslee, Prof. Alfred C. Post, Dr. Edward
Delafield ; John M. Cuyler, Medical Director in
the United States Army ; Stephen Smith, President, and Elisha Harris, Secretary, of the Amer-

ican Health Association, declared their views in almost the same language as above cited, closing thus :

"We would welcome any judicious and effective legislation, State and national, which should seek to confine the traffic in alcohol to the legitimate purposes of medical and other sciences, art, and mechanism."

And as the last voice of the medical profession, I give the report of the Section on Medicine in the International Medical Congress, held at Philadelphia in September last (1876), on the paper of Dr. Hunt on " Alcohol in its therapeutic relations as a food and a medicine : "

" *First.* Alcohol is not shown to have a definite food-value by any of the usual methods of chemical analysis or physiological investigation.

" *Second.* Its use as a medicine is chiefly as a cardiac stimulant, and often admits of substitution.

" *Third.* As a medicine it is not well fitted for self-prescription by the laity, and the medical profession is not accountable for such administration or for the enormous evils resulting therefrom.

"*Fourth.* The purity of alcoholic liquors is, in general, not as well-assured as that of articles used for medicine should be. The various mixtures when used as medicine should have definite and known composition, and should not be interchanged promiscuously."

CHAPTER X.

A CASE FOR INTERVENTION.

"There are some cases in which the power of injuring may be taken away by excluding what Tacitus calls *irritamenta malorum*, as the prohibition of the sale and fabrication of dies for coining, of *poisonous drugs*, of concealed arms, of dice, and other instruments of prohibited games."—BENTHAM.

HERE let us pause a moment for retrospection. We have seen that intemperance antedates the very birth of its innocent victim with curses; that it is the enemy of the human race itself by giving us humanity under enfeebled, diseased, and depraved conditions; that it follows as the most prolific source of disease and vice, culminating so frequently in insanity, and still more frequently in premature death, infecting the whole social atmosphere with physical and moral malaria; that it wastes our resources, increases our taxes, and diminishes our productive capacity; that it degrades labor and destroys home; that it fills our almshouses with paupers and our prisons with criminals; and that it is the strongest antagonist of every educating agency which tends to make good citizens, and the unfailing ally of every vice that

makes bad. And intemperance not only requires for its production the two factors of
"appetite and opportunity," but opportunity, or,
more accurately speaking, temptation, begets
appetite itself. So that the liquor traffic is the
prime factor in the production of intemperance
and all its horrible train of sequences. Can we
fail, then, to see that in this traffic the State has
its deadliest enemy, and that the strongest possible case is made for its arrest?

The relation between intemperance and the
enticements of the dram-shop, in all its forms
and disguises, is one too constant, too obvious,
too well-recognized as the basis of legislation
for centuries, and will hereafter receive too frequent statistical confirmation to allow further
urging here. Its *rationale* is, however, so
forcibly stated by Dr. Wayland in his "Moral
Philosophy," under the head of "Justice to
Character," that I can not forbear to quote it;
more especially as it suggests another ground
upon which legislation against the liquor traffic
may properly rest in addition to the protection
of society, namely, the protection of the individual victim:

"Such is the relation of the power of appetite to
that of conscience that, where no positive allurements
to vice are set before men, conscience will frequently
retain its ascendency. While, on the other hand, if

allurements be added to the power of appetite, reason and conscience prove a barrier too feeble to resist their combined and vicious tendency. Hence he who presents the allurements of vice before others, who procures and sets before them the means of vicious gratification, is, in a great degree, responsible for the · mischief he produces. Violations of this law occur in most cases of immoral traffic, as in the sale and manufacture of opium to the Chinese, etc. Under the same class is also comprehended the case of female prostitution."

And here let me add the pertinent testimony of one of the most competent of experts, Dr. Day, the Superintendent for many years of the " Washingtonian Home," in Boston :

" A mistaken idea seems to prevail that the inebriate becomes and continues a drunkard because he has no desire and makes no effort to reform. No error can be more complete. To shake off the shackles of his slavery is the dream by day and night of its unfortunate victim ; and how to accomplish it is the question he most eagerly asks, and for whose answering he waits with most intense desire."

So the same cry for deliverance from the body of this death comes from our prisons. Listen to the voice which articulates itself through the chaplain of the Massachusetts State Prison :

" Of the 534 men now here, the greater portion

would be glad to vote for the prohibitory law: for many of them feel that their safety from the perils of drunkenness depends, in a great degree, on such a law. They realize their weakness and are fearful of themselves, and desire such a law to strengthen them in their resistance to the seductions of the cup which has been their bane and curse. When about being discharged, to go out again into the world to combat its varied trials and temptations, in answer to the hope expressed that they will do well, they often say: ' I shall do well enough if I let liquor alone. If I can resist when urged to take a drink, or can go to some place where I can't get it, I shall do well enough.' " (Mass. Pub. Doc., 1868, No. 13, p. 43).

Beyond the aid which is afforded, by legislation against the liquor traffic, to these special classes who are struggling to establish their moral freedom, there can be no doubt that all laws which check the sale, diminish the consumption, and that this is desirable, to a certain extent, at least, almost every one admits. When we come to consider the extent and mode of interference, we shall find objections made to certain laws which apply logically to *all* laws, and which, if they are sound, would require that the traffic be left entirely free. With these we shall deal hereafter. For the present we close the discussion with a summary of the argument we have heretofore used, in the words of one whose utterance may carry weight

4*

as the voice not only of an earnest Christian philanthropist, but of one of the calmest thinkers, who was constitutionally averse to extending needlessly the sphere of governmental action— William Ellery Channing:

"Now if it be true that a vast proportion of the crimes which government is instituted to prevent and repress have their origin in the use of ardent spirits; if our poor-houses, work-houses, jails, and penitentiaries are tenanted in a great degree by those whose first and chief impulse to crime came from the distillery and the dram-shop; if murder and theft, the most fearful outrages on property and life, are most frequently the issues and consummation of intemperance, is not government bound to restrain by legislation the vending of the stimulus to these terrible social wrongs? Is government never to act as a parent, never to remove the causes or occasions of wrong-doing? Has it but one instrument for repressing crime, namely: public, infamous punishment, an evil only inferior to crime? Is government a usurper, does it wander beyond its sphere by imposing restraints on an article which does no imaginable good, which can plead no benefit conferred on body or mind, which unfits the citizen for the discharge of his duty to his country, and which, above all, stirs up men to the perpetration of most of the crimes from which it is the highest and most solemn office of government to protect society?" (Works, Vol. II., p. 377).

BOOK II.

THE STATE *vs.* ALCOHOL.

CHAPTER XI.

THE PROVINCE OF LAW.

"Virtue must come from *within*; to this problem religion and morality must direct themselves. But vice may come *from without*; to hinder this is the care of the statesman."—Prof. F. W. NEWMAN.

As we have thus far restricted our view of the evils of alcohol to what it does to the *State*, so we now desire in turn to limit this inquiry to what the *State* should do to alcohol. What the individual should do, in what way the good Samaritan can best act, what should be the attitude of the Christian Church, and what should be the utterance of the Christian pulpit, are all questions of momentous, yes, of *primary* importance. We put them aside here simply because they do not belong to the present discussion.

But so far from there being any antagonism between what is called "moral suasion" and political action, or the coercive action of the law, the latter is the outgrowth and the inevitable consequent of the former.

All this seems so obvious, and the relation between moral and legal effort so simple, that

(85)

it is discouraging to find such paragraphs in
the press as the following in the columns of an
intelligent, but conservative religious weekly.
After allusion to there having ·been found in
a certain assembly " two opinions as to the
policy of prohibition," it. adds immediately:
" The success of reform clubs has shown
clearly that it is possible to resume the moral
and educational methods which were so useful in the earlier days of the temperance
movement." Possible to *resume* them! When
and by whom have they been abandoned?
While these Rip Van Winkle "moral suasion-
ists" have been asleep, the friends of legal *and*
moral suasion have been ever at work. I suppose, of all the·permanent temperance organizations in this country, the Massachusetts
Temperance Alliance stands before the public
the most prominently committed to .the advocacy of law as an indispensable ally to the success of this reform. And yet it has always in-
sisted upon the importance of religious teaching and of all " educational methods " as the
very foundation of all other work. It was the
first society to employ a special agent to visit
the public schools, and in other ways to interest
the young. It has filled the Christian pulpits
with the labors of clergymen ; it has organized
reform clubs ; it has employed for years a lec-

turer upon the physiological aspects of the question, and circulated publications covering every phase of the temperance movement. Its annual report for 1875 gives as the

SUMMARY OF WORK FOR ELEVEN YEARS.

Sabbath Congregations addressed, . . . 1,337
Sabbath-schools addressed, ... 1,012
Sabbath Evening Union Temperance Meetings, 1,033
Public Schools addressed, ... 3,411
Addresses on Secular Days, ... 4,622

Total Addresses, ... 11, 415

Over Sixteen Million Pages of Tracts distributed.
More than One Hundred Thousand Children and Youth have adopted the pledge.
Thirty-four Reform Clubs organized, and many *Local Temperance Societies and Bands of Hope.*
Over Seven Hundred District Temperance Conventions held.

The quality of this work may be criticised. Undoubtedly its value is various. Let the critic furnish better. But it does not lie in his mouth to object that the support of prohibition has diminished the amount of moral effort.

Consider also the work of the National Temperance Society and Publication House. Its officers and members believe in the value and efficacy of the law—its resolutions affirm it, its publications maintain it. But "the first great work of the Society, after its organization, was to create a temperance literature." A recent circular says :

" During the last nine years over forty thousand dollars have been spent for stereotyping and literary labor and publishing to the world a sound, reliable literature upon every phase of the question. The moral, social, political, financial, scientific, and religious aspects are presented. . . . . The work among the young is carried on through the medium of the *Youth's Temperance Banner*, 150,000 copies of which are issued every month, and by means of attractive books for Sabbath-school libraries, pictorial tracts, badges, singing-books, pledges, etc."

Will the advocates of moral suasion, pure and simple, *show us their work* by the side of this ?   Until they can, will they have the modesty to be silent ?

The ludicrous confusion of ideas which leads men to talk of legal and moral suasion as antagonistic forces will at once be seen if applied to other social vices.   Imagine a sane man proposing to abolish all laws against prostitution, or to license it on the Continental plan, and in this way expect to make the moral and religious protest against it stronger ; or to have the ban of the law removed against lotteries and gaming-houses, or its execution relaxed, so as to awaken a revival of moral influences.

There are some men who *talk* moral suasion antagonistically, who deserve the rebuke administered years ago by Judge Sprague :

" If they are real friends of temperance, why don't they *use* moral suasion? And when they shall have *persuaded themselves*, they will have made an auspicious beginning." *

But it will be found that the great mass of the sincere and earnest *workers* in this field of moral effort are the last men to depreciate the aid of law. Let a man set himself *to work* to reclaim the fallen and I will risk the result of his ultimate opinion.

The historical development of a temperance movement is this : Individuals are deeply moved by a consideration of the evils of intemperance, and they become abstainers ; then they are led by philanthropy to seek out and save the lost ; in this work they soon encounter the temptation of the dram-shop and the tempter in the bar-tender. Indignantly they turn to their fellow-men and ask the protection of the Commonwealth against this conspiracy to ruin the saved. Turn where you will, you shall find the result of every reform movement a new demand for protective legislation. Such, notably, was the experience in our country at first, and after the " Washingtonian " movement; and the reform movement of the present hour is unmistakably developing the same history.

* Argument before Committee of Massachusetts Legislature against the repeal of " The Fifteen-Gallon Law " (1839).

And the hardest workers in this field of philanthropy come to the clearest vision and the
deepest conviction as to the province of the law.
No weak sophistry can induce them to antagonize the Law and the Gospel. If the law is
impotent to lift their brother from the gutter, it
can, at least, prevent the liquor-seller from
pushing him back. Such a use of the law they
believe to be in the spirit of the Gospel, and a
sure outgrowth of wise Christian love.

The chief apostle of moral suasion (Father
Mathew) left on record this testimony:

" The principle of prohibition seems to me to be
the only safe and certain remedy for the evils of intemperance. This opinion has been strengthened and
confirmed by the hard labor of more than twenty
years in the temperance cause."

I do not quote this here except as bearing
upon the general value of *law;* nor do I wish
to press the language used to its full force. I
disclaim all intention to advocate *any* law as a
panacea for intemperance. It is only as *one*
of the remedies. It is only as a supplement
and bulwark to educational, moral, and religious
effort, but as such, *indispensable* and *necessary*,
that I invoke the aid of law. And my call is
reinforced by the more powerful one of all
engaged practically in the reformation of the

fallen. As Cardinal Manning recently put it in a speech at Bolton, England :

" It is mere mockery to ask us to put down drunkenness by moral and religious means, when the Legislature facilitates the multiplication of the incitements to intemperance on every side. You might as well call upon me as a captain of a ship and say : ' Why don't you pump the water out when it is sinking, when you are scuttling the ship in every direction.' If you will cut off the supply of temptation, I will be bound by the help of God to convert drunkards ; but until you have taken off this perpetual supply of intoxicating drink, we never can cultivate the fields. You have submerged them, and if ever we reclaim one portion, you immediately begin to build upon it a gin-palace or some temptation to drink. The other day, where a benevolent man had established a sailor's home, I was told there were two hundred places of drink round about it. How, then, can we contend against these legalized and multiplied facilities and temptations to intoxication? This is my answer to the bland objurgation of those who tell us the ministers of religion are not doing their part. Let the Legislature do its part and we will answer for the rest."

The law does not propose to deal directly with the personal habits of men. It lays its hand on a traffic. Sales are public acts, and always within the domain of law. The law, for sufficient reasons of policy, prescribes the

manner and mode of sales of real and personal
property, makes void what it chooses, regulates
what it deems dangerous, forbids, under penalties, what it thinks mischievous. If it lays
either a regulating, a restraining, or a prohibiting hand upon the traffic in intoxicants, it does
no differently from what it does in regard to
adulterated milk, unwholesome meat, dangerous explosives, fireworks, obscene publications,
lottery tickets, and numerous other subjects of
sale. The only questions society asks, are :
Is the trade injurious ? Is it sufficiently so to
call for the interference ? If these questions are
answered affirmatively, then, if the evils are
incidental and remediable, the trade is regulated ; if essential and inherent, it is prohibited.
But this topic we shall treat more at large in
another connection.

It can not be necessary to resort to any elaborate proof of the general utility of law in this
sphere. It would seem well-nigh self-evident
that (as expressed by that eminent magistrate,
Recorder Hill, in his volume on " The Repression of Crime," p. 379,) " the traffic in alcoholic
drinks obeys that great law of political economy,
which regulates all other commerce, viz. : *that
any interference with the free action of manufacturer, importer, vender, or purchaser, diminishes consumption.*"

This proposition does not, however, rest alone upon its reasonableness, but is abundantly fortified by history and experience. Such proof will hereafter appear in the discussion of special phases of our general problem ; and we pause here for only a few items.

The same high authority from whom I last quoted, after alluding to restrictive legislation in England, says :

"We need no statistics to prove to us that the state of the country in 1830 was much better in regard to temperance than it was a century before that period—an improvement which none will attribute to education who are acquainted with the slow progress which it made during that interval, however it may have aided us since. At the latter date, a great change was effected."

He then alludes to the "Beer Bill," the results of which, and of subsequent legislation, we give in the words of the executive of the United Kingdom Alliance :

"In 1830 our Legislature passed the Beer-house Act. The result was that the consumption of malt in England and Wales rose from 26,900,902 bushels in 1830 to 36,078,856 bushels in 1835, whilst the consumption of spirits increased in about the same proportion.

"From 1840 to 1860 there was not much change in the laws affecting the sale of intoxicating liquors ;

what changes took place were in the direction of restriction ; hence, there was not much increase in the
value of intoxicating liquor consumed, the amount
for the year 1841 being £78,797,000, while in 1860 it
was £86,897,683—an increase about on a par with
the increase of population.

" In 1860 the Legislature again stepped in, and increased the facilities of the liquor traffic by passing
the Wine Licensing Bill ; and in 1862 the sale of
single bottles, by the wholesale trade to private
houses, was licensed ; provision was also made for
special licenses for fairs, races, exhibitions, balls, etc.

" In 1870 there were 186,096 persons who were
engaged in selling intoxicating liquors, or one to about
every thirty-five houses. These liquor-shops, if put
end to end, would form a street upwards of 700 miles
long.

" As a consequence of this vast machinery of temptation, the apprehensions for drunkenness, which in
1863 were 94,745, in 1872 had reached 151,084—an
increase of 59 per cent.

" In 1860 the money spent upon intoxicating
liquors was £86,897,683 ; in 1872 it amounted to
£131,601,490, being an increase of 51 per cent."

Scotland has not an enviable reputation for
sobriety, but there, as elsewhere, drinking is
proportioned to the facilities allowed. Thus
in the year 1849, the Church of Scotland appointed a committee to make investigations as
to the causes of intemperance, and report.
They sent out circulars, and received reports

from 478 parishes; from these returns they drafted a report, in which they say:

" The returns made to your committee's inquiries clearly prove that the intemperance of any neighborhood *is uniformly proportioned to the number of its spirit licenses.* So that, wherever there are no public-houses, nor any shops for selling spirits, there ceases to be any intoxication."

The working of what is known as the " Forbes-Mackenzie Act" in this country supplies an interesting illustration of the general law we are considering.

In a recent debate in the British Parliament upon the Sunday Closing Bill for Ireland, Mr. Gladstone said:

"A law substantially in conformity with this bill has been in operation in Scotland for twenty years; and, I would observe, that the only question with respect to this law is not whether it has done evil, but whether the amount of good it has done is great or small. That, I think, is a fair statement of the case with regard to the Forbes-Mackenzie Act in Scotland."

An elaborate paper upon the working of this Act, read in 1874, before the Social Science Congress of Great Britain, seems conclusively to demonstrate that the operation of the Act was one of very marked beneficence for some

years. The leading features of the law were,
the inhibition to grocers to sell to be drank on
the premises, the shortening of the hours of
sale, and the abolition of all Sunday sales,
except by inn-holders to "*bona fide* guests."
These features were not entirely new; but now
made a matter of imperial legislation, they seem
to have been for the first time well enforced.
The Act took effect in 1854. It should be added that, contemporaneously with this Act, and
co-operating with it, there was an increase of
the tax upon spirits. The author of the paper
I have alluded to shows that while for the five·
years preceding (1849–1853) the aggregate
consumption of spirits, as shown from the Government returns, was 30,039,712 gallons; the
total in the five years succeeding fell to
29,079,188 gallons, and during the next period
of five years (1859–1863) to only 25,089,168,
and this, it is to be remembered, with a very
considerable increase of population. From the
Reports of the Prisons of Scotland, it appears
that in the five years previous to the Act, the
average daily number of criminals therein was
14,676, and for the succeeding five years 11,507,
showing a daily decrease of 3,169. So also a
marked decrease is shown in the arrests for
drunkenness in the Kingdom, and especially in
the cities of Edinburgh and Glasgow. But the

paper well says : "The crucial test of the Act is the effect it has had in diminishing the cases of drunkenness on the Lord's day." I quote the statistics as to Edinburgh :

"The number of persons apprehended in Edinburgh for drunkenness, between eight o'clock on the Sunday mornings and eight o'clock on the Monday mornings, is as follows: In 1852 there were 401, in 1853, 333 cases, while in 1855 and 1856 there were 82 and 119 respectively—a decrease in the latter years of 533, and during the last seven years there have been fewer cases than in any of the previous years. There is an important point brought out in the annual report of the Superintendent of Police for Edinburgh, which clearly shows that while there is an increase within the last few years in the number of persons apprehended for crimes, who were drunk when they committed them, the number of persons apprehended for drunkenness on Sundays within these years has not increased. In 1852 there were 3,400 cases in which drunkenness and crime were combined. In 1873 there were 3,741, an increase of 341. The apprehensions of persons for drunkenness on the Lord's day, were, in 1852, 729, while in 1873 there were only 153. An equally gratifying result is seen in the number of apprehensions for drunkenness between eight o'clock on the Sunday mornings and eight o'clock on the Monday mornings. In 1852 there were 401, in 1873 only 52."

I also cite the closing paragraph, as it suggests an explanation of the somewhat varying

estimates of the amount of good proceeding
from this Act to which Mr. Gladstone alludes:

" In conclusion, if all the results which were obtained by the earlier closing of public-houses on week
days by the Forbes-Mackenzie Act are not now maintained, it is simply because the hours at the disposal
of the working classes do not now bear the same proportion to the hours at which the public-houses are open.
To secure the same benefits under the altered circumstances, the public-houses would require to be closed
as much earlier as the workshops are now generally
closed, and experience has shown, in the few cases
where this has been done, that the result was what
might have been expected — namely, diminished
drunkenness and crime."

To multiply illustrations would be needless
and wearisome.   But it may be well to refer to
the fact that the instinct of "the trade" always
scents danger and loss in restrictive legislation.
And at the Brewers' Congress held in Cincin-
nati in 1875, Mr. Louis Schade, their special
agent, in an address before the convention bore
this emphatic testimony:

" Very severe is the injury which the brewers have
received in the so-called temperance States.   The
local option law of Pennsylvania reduced the number of breweries in that State from 500 in 1873, to
346 in 1874; thus destroying 154 breweries in one
year.   In Michigan it is even worse; for of 202 brew-

eries in 1873, only 68 remained in 1874. In Ohio the Crusaders destroyed 68 out of 296. In Indiana the Baxter law stopped 66 out of 158. In Maryland the breweries were reduced from 74 to 15, some few of those stopped lying in those counties where they have a local option law."

After referring to the increase of the trade in certain States, but to the general reduction, notwithstanding, in the country at large, he says: " There is no doubt that the temperance agitation and prohibitory laws are the chief causes of the decrease compared to the preceding year."

CHAPTER XII.

In England no question has ever arisen as to the extent of legislative *power* over the liquor traffic, for it is a fundamental maxim there, that Parliament is politically omnipotent, or as Blackstone puts it, "it can, in short, do everything that is not naturally impossible" (Com. Book I., p. 161). But in governments like those of the United States, deriving all their powers from, and expressly limited by, the provisions of written constitutions, it was inevitable that all legislation affecting the interests of so powerful a traffic should receive jealous examination to determine whether it could be set aside as unconstitutional. "There is no law," says Tarbell, J.,* "which is as resolutely resisted by the utmost ingenuity of the human mind and by the ablest talent, as the statutes regulating the traffic in intoxicating liquor."

"The question of the constitutionality of such statutes," says Mr. Bishop (Statutory Crimes, sec. 989), "has been more frequently agitated

---

* Riley *vs*. The State, 43 Missis., 420.

than any other constitutional question presented to our tribunals." And yet it will be found that both the principles and essential features of the varying laws upon this subject have been uniformly upheld by the highest courts in every part of the land.

To give even a bare array of the names of the multitudinous cases would here savor of pedantry, and I prefer to present a summary of the well-settled doctrines as given in a work of standard authority by Judge Cooley, of Michigan, on " Constitutional Limitations ":

" That legislation of this character was void, so far as it affected imported liquors, or such as might be introduced from one State into another, because in conflict with the power of Congress over commerce, was strongly urged in the License Cases before the Supreme Court of the United States; but that view did not obtain the assent of the Court. The majority of the Court expressed the opinion—which, however, was *obiter* in those cases—that the introduction of imported liquors into a State and their sale in the original packages as imported could not be forbidden, because to do so would be to forbid what Congress, in its regulation of commerce and in the levy of imports, had permitted. But it was conceded by all that when the original package was broken up for use or for retail by the importer, and also when the commodity had passed from his hands into the hands of a purchaser, it ceased to be an import or a part of foreign commerce." . . . .

"It would seem from the views expressed by the several members of the Court in these cases, that the State laws known as Prohibitory Liquor Laws, the purpose of which is to prevent altogether the manufacture and sale of intoxicating drinks as a beverage, so far as legislation can accomplish that object, can not be held void as in conflict with the power of Congress to regulate commerce and to levy imports and duties."

(The reader who cares to see the array of cases which sustain these propositions may find them well collected in the United States digest (First series), Vol. VII., p. 806, *et seq.*)

"The same laws have also been sustained when the question of conflict with State Constitutions or with general fundamental principles has been raised. They are looked upon as police regulations, established by the Legislature for the prevention of intemperance, pauperism, and crime, and for the abatement of nuisances." . . . .

"And it is only where, in framing such legislation, care has not been taken to observe those principles of protection which surround the persons and dwellings of individuals, securing them against unreasonable searchers and seizures, and giving them a right to trial before condemnation that the courts have felt at liberty to declare that it exceeded the proper province of police regulation " (p. 581, *et seq.*)

And it has been since decided by the same Court, that neither the provisions of the Internal Revenue Act which required payment of a license fee by dealers in liquors, nor the tax affixed to sales, interfered with the operation of the State laws. (McGuire *vs.* Commonwealth, 3 Wallace, 387; Purvear *vs.* Commonwealth, 5 Wallace, 475).

Mr. Bishop, the well-known writer on Criminal Law, sums up the matter thus :

" The State, in the enactment of its laws, must exercise its judgment concerning what acts tend to corrupt the public morals, impoverish the community, disturb the public repose, injure the other public interests, or even impair the comfort of individual members over whom its protecting watch and care are required. And the power to judge of this question is necessarily reposed alone in the Legislature, from whose decision no appeal can be taken, directly or indirectly, to any other department of the Government. When, therefore, the Legislature, with this exclusive authority, has exercised its right of judging concerning this legislative question, by the enactment of prohibitions like those discussed in this chapter, all other departments of the Government are bound by the decision which no court has a jurisdiction to review " (Statutory Crimes, sec. 995).

Any attempt to distinguish between the power to regulate and the power to prohibit finds no judicial support.

In the celebrated " License Cases " (5 Howard, 504) above referred to, Mr. Webster had argued that as the County Commissioners in

Massachusetts had authority from the Legislature to refuse licenses, and had in fact refused to license, that the law was substantially one of prohibition. Several of the judges do not hesitate to meet this suggestion.

Thus Chief Justice Taney says :

"And if any State deems the retail and internal traffic in ardent spirits injurious to its citizens, and calculated to produce idleness, vice, or debauchery, I see nothing in the Constitution of the United States to prevent it from regulating or restraining the traffic, or from *prohibiting it altogether*, if it thinks proper."

Justice McLean :

" The necessity of a license presupposes a prohibition of the right to sell as to those who have no license. . . . . If the foreign article be injurious to the health or morals of the community, a State may, in the exercise of that great and conservative police power which lies at the foundation of its prosperity, *prohibit* the sale of it. No one doubts this in relation to infected goods or licentious publications. . . . . Any diminution of the revenue arising from this exercise of local power would be more than repaid by the beneficial results. By preserving, as far as possible, the health, the safety, and the moral energies of society, its prosperity is advanced."

Justice Catron :

" I admit as inevitable that, if the State has the power of restraint by licenses to any extent, she has the discretionary power to judge of its limit, and may go to the length of *prohibiting* sales altogether."

Woodbury, J. :

" It is the undoubted and reserved power of every State here, as a political body, to decide, independent of any provisions made by Congress, though subject not to conflict with any of them when rightful, who shall compose its population, who become its residents, who its citizens, who enjoy the privileges of its laws, and be entitled to their protection and favor, and *what kind of property and business it will tolerate* and protect. . . . . The power to forbid the sale of things is surely as extensive and rests on as broad principles of public security and sound morals as that to exclude persons."

Justice Grier :

" It is not necessary to array the appalling statistics of misery, pauperism, and crime which have their origin in the use and abuse of ardent spirits. The police power, which is exclusively in the State, is competent to the correction of these great evils, and all measures of restraint or prohibition necessary to effect that purpose are within the scope of that authority; . . . . and if a loss of revenue should accrue to the United States from a diminished consumption of ardent spirits, she will be a gainer a thousand-fold in the health, wealth, and happiness of the people."

It may seem to some superfluous to cite these

5*

opinions of eminent judges upon a matter so
well settled; but they are valuable not merely
as authorities, but because they are based upon
principles, a familiar recurrence to which is useful to protect the popular mind from the loose
sophistries of the hour.

The reader who cares to examine the adjudi-
cated cases further (to which I have referred
him), will find them to justify and fortify the
language of Chief Justice Harrington, of Delaware:

" We have seen no adjudged case which denies the
power of a State in the exercise of its sovereignty, to
regulate the traffic in liquor for restraint as well as
for revenue; and, as a police measure, to restrict or
prohibit the sale of liquor as injurious to public morals
or dangerous to public peace. The subjection of
private property, in the mode of its enjoyment, to the
public good and its subordination to general rights
liable to be injured by its unrestricted use, is a principle lying at the foundations of government. It is a
condition of the social state; the price of its enjoyment; entering into the very structure of organized
society; existing by necessity for its preservation, and
recognized by the Constitution in the terms of its
reservation as the 'right of acquiring and protecting
reputation and property, and of attaining objects suitable to their condition without injury one to another.'"
(The State *vs.* Allmond, 2 Houst. R., 612).

The only new legal *principle* involved in

what is called the prohibitory law, is the procedure *in rem.* against liquor unlawfully kept
to obtain its judicial confiscation.

But, as Mr. Bishop shows, "the earliest of
the old English enactments on this exact subject (12 Edw. 2, c. 6, A.D. 1318,) provides for
this forfeiture." So that, as he adds, it "is one
of the modes of fine known in that fountain of
laws from which our jurisprudence is drawn."
(Statutory Crimes, sec. 993).

And some of the analogies of the law and the
reason thereof are clearly stated by Chief
Justice Shaw, in the leading case of Fisher *vs.*
McGirr, 1 Gray, p. 1 (Mass.) :

"We have no doubt that it is competent for the
Legislature to declare the possession of certain articles
of property, either absolutely or when held in particular places, and under particular circumstances, to
be unlawful, because they would be injurious, dangerous, or noxious ; and by due process of law, by proceedings *in rem.*, to provide both for the abatement
of the nuisance and the punishment of the offender
by the seizure and confiscation of the property, by
the removal, sale, or destruction of the noxious
articles. Putrefying merchandise may be stored in a
warehouse, where, if it remain, it would spread con-
tagious disease and death through a community.
Gunpowder, an article quite harmless in a magazine,
may be kept in a warehouse always exposed to fire,
especially in the night; however secreted, a fire in

the building would be sure to find it, and the lives and limbs of courageous and public-spirited firemen and citizens, engaged in subduing the flames, would be endangered by a sudden and terrible explosion. It is of the highest importance that such persons should receive the amplest encouragement to their duty, by giving them the strongest assurance that the law can give them that they shall not be exposed to such danger. This can be done only by a rigorous law against so keeping gunpowder, to be rigorously enforced by seizure, removal, and forfeiture. The cases of goods smuggled, in violation of the revenue laws, and the confiscation of vessels, boats, and other vehicles subservient to such unlawful acts, are instances of the application of law to proceedings *in rem.*

" The theory of this branch of the law seems to be this: That the property of which injurious or dangerous use is made, shall be seized and confiscated, because either it is so unlawfully used by the owner or person having the power of disposal, or by some person with whom he has placed and entrusted it, or at least, that he has so carelessly and negligently used his power and control over it, that by his default it has fallen into the hands of those who have made, and intend to make, the injurious or dangerous use of it, of which the public have a right to complain, and from which they have a right to be relieved. Therefore, as well to abate the nuisance as to punish the offending or careless owner, the property may be justly declared forfeited, and either sold for the public benefit or destroyed, as the circumstances of the case may require and the wisdom of the Legislature direct. Besides, the actual seizure of the property intended to be offensively used may be effected, when it would not be practicable to detect and punish the offender personally."

The common liquor traffic and its instruments is thus remanded to the sole jurisdiction of the Legislature for license, regulation, restriction or prohibition, and destruction.

Assuming, then, the right of the State to control the traffic so as most effectively to suppress intemperance, we come to consider how this can best be done.

CHAPTER XIII.

LIBERTY AND GOVERNMENT.

" It is a common fault of enthusiasts for Liberty that they do not clearly define what it is they would make free. . . . There are some things which can not be liberated too much ; and there are some things which devour all rational and enriching liberty, if they are not effectually tied up ; and partisans of liberty who are so blindly its partisans that they will not discriminate, will not organize a means to liberate what is really liberal, and bind what makes a vicious and destructive bondage, are its partisans without being its promoters."—D. A. WASSON.

CERTAIN notions as to individual liberty and the functions of government which obtain among a recent school of writers, are frequently made to play an important part in the argument against certain forms of restrictive legislation against the liquor traffic. It is obvious, however, that if valid at all, they are equally valid against all forms of such legislation.

At the head of this school stands Herbert Spencer, who, in the reckless audacity of his intellect, and with his omniscient style, announces in his " Social Statics " that " as civilization advances, does government decay ; " " We call government a necessary evil " (p. 25).

" Government is essentially immoral " (p. 230),
and defines the State to be a body of men
" voluntarily associated " " for mutual protection " (p. 303).

The doctrine that the only true function of
government (if an essentially immoral institution can have any *true* function) is " mutual
protection," is one that is opposed to the practical judgment of all statesmen, as well as the
general theoretical judgment of past philosophers, and is so subversive (as we shall see) of
what appear, at least, to be among the fairest
results of our political institutions, that it ought
to be supported by a great weight of reason to
win our acceptance. And to what does it make
its appeal ? Why, it is said, to our sense of justice. Society being formed only upon the " voluntary association " of individuals, and for purposes of " mutual protection," the presumed
assent of each member is limited to that object,
and it is a species of tyranny to compel him,
either by taxation or coerced obedience, to contribute to any other end. But if it be granted
that each member of society desires " protection," and so may justly, as an abstract principle,
be compelled to contribute money and obedience
therefor, yet, when you come to *apply* this
principle, you at once meet with difficulty.
Protection against what ? One man is satisfied

with protection to his life and property; another man thinks protection against injuries to reputation should be included, and still another, that injury to the character of his children by the evil excitement of passions and appetites, calls loudly for protection; and that the man who seduces the affections of his wife is not only a villain, but a criminal, against whom society, if it calls itself civilized, is bound to protect him. Or, if you reduce protection to its lowest terms and include therein only defense from bodily injury, still you do not escape the difficulty that you must coerce some one against his convictions. The non-resistant believes that love is better than bars; perhaps some student of Spencer believes that if government is an "essentially immoral" institution, we had better hold to the absolute right and let it go.* What, then, shall we do with such men? If we are to have anarchy, we must let them alone; if we value government more than the Spencerian philosophy, we must make them submit to the will of the majority. The result is inevitable;

---

* It is, perhaps, just to Spencer to say that in the preface to his "Social Statics," from which our quotations are made, he expresses regret that he has no time to re-write some chapters, and remarks: "In re-stating them, he would bring into greater prominence the transitional nature of all political institutions, and the consequent *relative* goodness of some arrangements which have no claims to absolute goodness."

if men live in a civil society and enjoy its advantages, they must pay therefor, by a surrender
in some matters to the will of the majority.
We are, in fact, all under a sort of betterment
law; and whenever society determines that any
policy improves the value of property and the
comfort of life, the individual, even though he
dissents, must contribute his share. It is one
of the necessary conditions of government, and
one on which, in the long run, the happiness of
every one depends.

Mr. Spencer follows out with stern consistency
to the end, his theory of mutual protection, and
that interpreted in the baldest sense, as the sole
function of government. Thus, in his " Social
Statics," he not only opposes all State provision
for the poor, but he says, "the State has no
right to educate" (p. 361); and he even opposes all sanitary inspection by the State as " a
violation of rights" (p. 406). To state such
propositions is to refute them, so far as the
common-sense and the common judgment of
mankind is the arbiter. But if we try them by
the test of reason, what is the strength of the
argument for thus reducing the functions of
government to what Huxley calls " Administrative Nihilism?"

To the believer in human government, as in
its essence, though not in its special forms, a

divine institution, ordained, like the family, as a means, not merely of protection, but of culture and development of the individual, this theory is as baseless as the supposition of a mutual compact, as the origin of government on which it rests. But even those who are not prepared to recognize any divine authority in government, must see that it is illusory to rest it upon the voluntary assent of its subjects. The bad, who on the Spencerian theory have the only need of government, can not certainly be presumed to assent to the laws which antagonize them; while, as a matter of fact, we know that no one has come under the domain of law by any process of voluntary assent. The simple fact is, that men are born under government as they are born into society. They have the power of withdrawal from either; but if they remain and accept the advantages, they must pay the price. The vast majority of the people of New England, for instance, believe that the material prosperity and the highest good of the whole community are promoted by universal education; they also believe that this can be secured in no other way than by a system of State schools. Must they abandon the system and forego all its blessings, because a few crotchety individuals dissent from this view? If so, where shall we stop? The very high-

ways are not built for "protection," but for convenience. Is it not *reasonable* to say to the
dissentient members of society, To government you owe not only the security of life and
property, but its enhanced value? You can not
have at once all the added wealth of civilization,
with the wild freedom of the forest.

Various attempts have been made to define
the sphere of government. The definitions do
not stand the test of criticism. As practical
limits, no one will ever accept them.* The
truth is, no definition which deals in much limitation is practicable. We may safely say with
the Bill of Rights in the Constitution of Massachusetts (Art. VII.), that "Government is instituted for the common good; for the protection, safety, prosperity, and happiness of the
people; and not for the profit, honor, or private
interest of any one man, family, or class of men."
But what government may properly do for "the
prosperity and happiness of the people" varies

---

* Arthur Helps, in his "Thoughts on Government," well says:
"There are persons who theoretically declare that they desire the
least possible of governmental interference in all their affairs;
but when any calamity occurs, or when any great evil, socially
speaking, comes to the surface, and is much talked about, these
same persons will be found joining in the cry that government
ought to have foreseen this—ought to look to that, and, in short,
all of a sudden (often when it is too late) they are willing greatly
to extend their views with regard to the proper functions of government."

greatly with time and place. In one country it may even be inexpedient to establish a system of common schools; in another, it may be well to supplement the best schools (common only in the sense of universal) with free public libraries, with national galleries of art, with civic parks and gardens. At times it may be well for the State to assume the control of postal and telegraphic service; at other times, to leave it to private enterprise. I know it is said that it is dangerous to allow this broad scope to government. To this I can not give a better answer than in the common-sense words of Huxley:

" It was urged, that if the right of the State to step beyond assigned limits were admitted, there was no stop, and the principle which allowed the State to enforce vaccination or education would allow it to prescribe his religious belief, or the number of courses he had for dinner, or the pattern of his waistcoat. The answer to that was surely obvious, for on similar grounds the right of a man to eat when he was hungry went, for if they allowed a man to eat at all there was nothing to stop him from gorging. In practice, a man left off when he had sufficient. So the co-operative reason of the community would soon find out when State interference had been carried far enough."

JOHN STUART MILL.*

The speculative views of Spencer upon government have been less familiar to the public
than the essay of Mill upon " Liberty." Certain
high-sounding sentences from this book have
served to garnish attacks upon restrictive legislation upon the liquor traffic, and the very name
of Mill has lent a sort of respectability to the
advocacy of free trade in intoxicants.

It can not be denied that John Stuart Mill
has exercised a considerable degree of fascina-
tion over a class of generous-minded young
people. Some degree of that personal magnet-
ism which availed in his lifetime, as sturdy John
Bright recently confesses, to make him for the
time against his judgment a supporter of female
suffrage, seems transfused into the written page.
And as our steadfast friend, during the dark

---

* If I seem, to the general reader, to devote too much attention to the speculations of Mill, I beg to quote an incident related by Rev. Mr. Vibbert in a paper read before the National
Temperance Convention at Chicago in 1875: "Several years
ago I wrote to a judge of the Supreme Court of Massachusetts,
to the United States District Attorney, to a candidate for Secretary of State, now a member of Congress, all men of high worth
and ability, asking them for the strongest objections to prohibition. Each gentleman in his reply referred me to ex-Governor
Andrews' argument, and to the fourth chapter of John Stuart
Mill's 'Essay on Liberty.'" I may add that Andrew himself
placed great stress upon the opinion of Mill.

days of the Rebellion, when English friends seemed few, he seemed to have an additional claim to a favorable reception on this side of the Atlantic.   And if we add to these considerations a recognition of his pellucid, clear-cut style, it will not be difficult to understand his popularity.   I should be ashamed to invoke against Mr. Mill the *theologicum odium*, but it seems fair to say that since the publication of his Autobiography, the reader will find his admiration so mingled with commiseration, that he will be indisposed to lean upon Mill as an *authority*, or to trust him as an intellectual guide any further than the light of his reason shows the path.   Fitz James Stephen, in his able critique on · Mill (entitled " Liberty, Equality, and Fraternity "), points out the fact, which no careful reader of Mill's Essay could fail to notice, that he uses a great deal of assertion and very little argument.   And this is the more remarkable as he is a decided opponent of the intuitional school.   We are, therefore, rather to examine statements than to discuss proofs.

HIS ·DOCTRINE OF LIBERTY.

We desire to give Mr. Mill's idea of personal liberty and the sphere of government in his own words.

In the introduction to his Essay he says:

"The object of this Essay is to assert one very simple principle, as entitled to govern absolutely the dealings of society with the individual in the way of compulsion and control, whether the means used be physical force in the form of legal penalties, or the moral coercion of public opinion. That principle is, that the sole end for which mankind are warranted, individually or collectively, in interfering with the liberty of action of any of their number, is self-protection. That the only purpose for which power can be rightfully exercised over any member of a civilized community against his will, is to prevent harm to others" (p. 23).

Here we come again upon the Spencerian theory of government, which we have already examined. But in protesting against a limitation of the powers of government, which would deprive it of all right to promote the common welfare by public improvement; to satisfy the common-sense of humanity by public provision for the poor, the sick, and the class of "defectives;" to educate beyond such elementary instruction as may tend to prevent such gross ignorance as threatens the safety of the State; to care in any way for the higher development of society—yet it is to be observed, that the *principle* which Mr. Mill lays down, instead of overturning, directly recognizes the *central* basis upon which the advocate of the suppression of the liquor traffic rests his case. If we have proved anything in the course of this discussion, we have proved exactly this: that the liquor dealer is doing "*harm to others.*" That is the exact and foreknown result of his business. Nor does it constitute any shield to him that in order to effect this harm, he has to entice or to enslave the will of the drinker. The State suffers no less, and is no less clearly bound to interfere "to prevent harm to others," which is the inevitable sequence to the traffic and disappears with its suppression. This would be so if the drinker himself were the only victim; the case is still stronger because of the fact that the innocent wife and children, and society itself in its every interest, feel the "harm."

APPLICATIONS.

But the "applications" which Mill makes are far more shocking than the principle he lays down. "Fornication, for example, must be tolerated, and so must gambling" (p. 191).

As to the marriage relation, after quoting the opinion of Wilhelm von Humboldt, to the effect that it "should require nothing more than the declared will of either party to dissolve it," he calls attention to the fact that in many cases "the relation between two contracting parties has been followed by consequences to others," giving rise to obligations, and he adds, "even if as von Humboldt maintains, they ought to make no difference in the *legal* freedom of the parties to release themselves from the engagement (and I also hold that they ought not to make *much* difference); they necessarily make a great difference in the *moral* freedom" (p. 201).

Of course he regards "Sabbatarian legislation" as an "important example of illegitimate interference with the rightful liberty of the individual, not simply threatened, but long since carried into triumphant effect" (p. 174).

Of these evil things he is sure. Of some others even his great mind is left in doubt. Thus, after stating that fornication and gambling must be tolerated, he puts the question: "But should a person be free to be a pimp or to keep a gambling-house? The case is one of those which lie on the exact boundary-line between two principles, and it is not at once apparent to which of the two it properly belongs. There are arguments on both sides" (p. 191). And after stating them, he naively says: "I will not venture to decide" (p. 193).

In such a state of mind, it is, perhaps, not strange that he deprecates all interference with the liquor traffic. He is too clear-sighted not to see that restriction must rest upon the same

6

ground as prohibition ; and he declares for free trade in the commodity.   He says:

" To tax stimulants for the sole purpose of making them more difficult to be obtained, is a measure differing only in degree from their entire prohibition ; and would be justifiable only if that were justifiable."

And after approving certain police regulations of the traffic, he adds :

" Any further restriction I do not conceive to be, in principle, justifiable.   The limitation in number, for instance, of beer and spirit houses for the express purpose of rendering them more difficult of access, and diminishing the occasions of temptation, not only exposes all to an inconvenience because there are some by whom the facility would be abused, but is suited only to a state of society in which the laboring classes are avowedly treated as children or savages, and placed under an education of restraint, to fit them for future admission to the privileges of freedom " (p. 196).

Mr. Mill thus explicitly holds that society has no right to protect itself or its members against the conceded evils which flow from the liquor traffic, either by diminishing facilities or temptation.   And he thus stands opposed, not merely to the prohibitionist, but to the wellnigh unanimous considerate, practical judgment of those who in all ages and in all countries have been called upon to face and to deal with this liquor problem. And yet it may be that he is more logically consistent than the advocates of "half-way measures."

Mr. Mill's cardinal objection is to all laws "where the object of the interference is to make it impossible or difficult to obtain a particular commodity. These interferences are objectionable, not as infringements on the liberty of the producer or seller, but on that of the buyer" (p. 185). But if the sale is admitted or proved to be, not in every individual case, but in the aggregate, the cause of vast injury to the public welfare, upon what ground is the liberty of the buyer to be preferred to the safety of the State? When the Government has the undisputed right to deprive the subject temporarily of all liberty, and even to impair the security of his life by compulsory military service in time of danger, has it no right to curtail his freedom to buy liquor, if thereby it can render its streets more safe, depopulate its almshouses, and thin out its prisons? The moment any business or pursuit becomes dangerous to the State, that moment the State acquires jurisdiction over it, and it has only to consider in determining either its regulation or suppression the degree of inconvenience to the individual caused by such interference as compared with the degree of danger to the State.

CONCESSIONS.

If duly weighed, the concessions in this Essay itself destroy the application which Mr. Mill makes of his doctrines to the liquor traffic.

Thus, on page 94, he says :

> " The interest, however, of these dealers in promoting intemperance is a real evil, and justifies the State in imposing restrictions and requiring guarantees, which but for that justification would be infringements of legitimate liberty."

But why should people who have an interest in promoting intemperance be allowed to ply their vocation at all? And what if it so happens that long experience of many years and places has proved these " restrictions " and " guarantees " to be futile? Common-sense would seem to say that in such case, unless the drink-shops do some good equivalent to the evil of promoting intemperance, it were the part of wisdom to suppress them. And the cursory reader would suppose that Mr. Mill would assent to this when he reads on page 183 :

> " Trade is a social act. Whoever undertakes to sell any description of goods to the public does what affects the interest of other persons, and of society in general ; and thus his conduct, in principle, comes within the jurisdiction of society."

The leading principle of his chapter on the " Limits to the Authority of Society over the Individual " is stated thus :

"Whenever, in short, there is a definite damage, or a definite risk of damage, either to an individual or to the public, the case is taken out of the province of liberty and placed in that of morality or law."

If the term " definite " is used here as synonymous with clear or positive, the rule is broad enough to support legislation against the liquor traffic. I do not see how the word " definite " can have any other reasonable meaning in this connection. For surely, it is the evident *quantum*, and not the exactness with which the estimate of damage can be made, that gives society occasion to interfere. *"De minimis non curat lex"* is no doubt a wholesome maxim to be applied to the making as to the administration of laws ; but when it is *de maximis*, if the evil is so vast and varied as to be incapable of computation, and is in that sense indefinite, it surely furnishes no reason for forbearance. It is a truism to say that no business or pursuit known to civilized life inflicts greater damage or exposes society to greater risks than the traffic in question. It is not " definite " simply because it is too great to be calculable ; it is fearfully indefinite, but it is a fixed fact in the past and morally certain in the future.

We might well rest the argument here. We have shown that even upon the necessary concessions of Mill, society has a right in a case of such actual damage and such constant peril to itself as the liquor traffic causes, to interfere with the "liberty" of the seller; and if this be so, it is immaterial that the liberty of the buyer is incidentally affected. But if there were occasion, the argument might be pushed much further. Such interference seems maintainable upon principle; leaving its extent to be determined by considerations of practicability and expediency. Let us not be misled by favorite words. "Liberty," says Dr. Arnold, "is a means, and not an end;" and that true liberty which secures the free development of man's higher nature frequently depends upon the restraint of the lower appetites. So

" —Wholesome laws *preserve us free*
By stinting of our liberty." *

Every one recognizes the authority of society to interfere by outward restraint in case of individuals of unsound or immature mind, and

---

* Or, as Thomas Carlyle, in his rough prose, sets forth the converse: "No man oppresses thee, O free and independent franchiser! but does not this stupid pewter pot oppress thee? No son of Adam can bid thee come or go, but this absurd pot of heavy-wet can and does! Thou art the thrall not of Cedric the Saxon, but of thy own brutal appetites, and this accursed dish of liquor. And thou pratest of thy 'liberty,' thou entire blockhead!".

recognizes the further fact that such interference, though nominally as one of restraint, is really in the interest of normal development. Now, where society sees that individuals, even where they fall short of that actual state of drunkenness which the Greeks expressively designated as "brief madness," are yet exposed to that overpowering temptation which the liquor dealer presents, by which their inner will is mastered, may not society take off the external force, and so leave the man to be his own master? To this extent, at least, it seems to us that Government not only may, but *ought* to go. And no prohibitory laws yet enacted have attempted to go further. They have not prohibited buying; they have not made it impracticable for any man whose sober judgment approves the drinking habit to procure by forethought such a supply of "pure" imported liquors as will allow him the inestimable privilege of such a diet or such a stimulant. As this treatise has a practical object, it is unnecessary here to consider how much farther the right of society may extend.*

---

* The reader who wishes to follow a suggestive discussion of the *rationale* of Government interference with outward freedom in the interest of a higher, as applied to English "Factory Legislation," will read with interest the chapter on "Law in Politics," page 324, of a book entitled "The Reign of Law," by the Duke of Argyll.

THE OPPOSITE DRIFTS.

It is a striking fact that while Spencer and his school have largely led the speculative mind of the present generation in the direction of " nihilism " in government, the practical and legislative mind has been going exactly in the contrary.

Spencer says, as we have before quoted: " Thus as civilization advances does government decay."

Arthur Helps, in his " Thoughts on Government," directly antagonizes him thus:

"It is the opinion of some people, but, as I contend, a wrong and delusive opinion, that, as civilization advances there will be less and less need for government. I maintain that, on the contrary, there will be more and more need."

So far, the practical victory remains most markedly with Mr. Helps. And the causes for this are not difficult to understand. In the first place, as one of the results of modern civilization, men are brought closer together in every way, and their relations multiplied in number and complexity; so that, as Prof. Huxley observes, the action of one man has more influence over another, and it becomes " less possible for one to do a wrong thing without interfering more or less with the freedom of his fellows."

Then, again, a closer study of the laws of human solidarity has shown how the well-being of all depends on the well-being and well-doing of each ; while a better acquaintance with the moral and physical laws of the universe has revealed kinds of injury and damage unnoticed by former generations. At the same time, the intense pursuit of wealth, and the creation of vast moneyed corporations, as a necessary means for carrying on the great enterprises of the day, has made labor, while nominally free, quite at the mercy of capital at vital points, without legislative protection. Simultaneously with this, there has grown up under the educating influence of Christianity, a tenderer sympathy for the weak, a stronger sense of human brotherhood. And when to these causes we add the historic fact, that in all civilized countries the *people* have been steadily, if slowly, " coming to power," it is not strange that legislation has been growing more philanthropic, and government more paternal.

· 6*

CHAPTER XIV.

LAW A NECESSITY.

"DRUNKENNESS," says Gov. Andrew, in his famous plea for license, "will disappear as the light shines in on the darkened intellect, as opportunity develops manhood, as hope visits and encourages the heart." This is an eloquent way of saying what he attempts to maintain in detail, that prosperity, education, and religion will take care of intemperance without the aid of law.

Facts, stubborn facts, teach the contrary. Let us see, first, how drunkenness has been affected by

PROSPERITY.

A recent Parliamentary return shows that the consumption of foreign spirits has increased as follows, from 1871 to 1875:

England,	2,163,430 gals., or	30 per cent.	
Scotland,	641,250 "	" 100	"
Ireland,	122,075 "	" 29	"

The consumption of British spirits has increased in the same time thus:

England,	3,868,036 gals., or	30 per cent.	
Scotland,	1,200,993 "	" 21	"
Ireland,	873,434 "	" 16	"

This is exclusive of a moderate increase in wines. "Is this," remarks the English journal from which I take these figures, "any indication of the progressive sobriety which was to follow commercial prosperity and educational advantages? Had all this arisen with a permissive bill on the statute-book, what a cry would have been raised! But it has arisen under license administered by magistrates and guarded by the police (with the publicans to help), and what a commentary it is on the predictions of the journalists and legislators who could see no need of 'extreme measures,' but trusted to 'moral influences' for a diminished use of intoxicating liquors." But there is still more direct proof that drunkenness is still on the increase in England.

The "judicial statistics" of England and Wales show the following aggregate of cases proceeded against for drunkenness and "drunkenness with disorder," for several years past, with the percentage these form of the whole number of "summary cases" of different offenses:

1867	. .	100,357	. .	21 per cent.	
1868	. .	111,405	. .	23	"
1869	. .	122,310	. .	24	"
1870	. .	131,870	. .	25	"
1871	. .	142,343	. .	26	"
1872	. .	153,084	. .	27	"

1873	. .	182,941	. .	31 per cent.
1874	. .	185,730	. .	40 "
1875	. .	203,980	. .	

Lord Aberdare has been shown to have taken too rose-colored a view of the diminution of English crime; but even he bears emphatic testimony upon this point in an address delivered before the Social Science Congress of 1875. Alluding to the experience of Glamorganshire during the period of the strikes, he says :

"There was a large decrease in the number of committals to the county gaols. But although during this period there was ample leisure, no money could be earned, and strict economy was imperatively necessary. Hence the public-houses were deserted, and the police courts almost as empty as the public-houses. I most heartily rejoice in that general and gradual increase of wages, which of late years has brought comfort into so many homes, and given occasional respite from their labor to so many industrious workmen. But this satisfaction, which I am convinced is shared in by all those now present, is sadly marred by the reflection forced upon me of the misuse of these advantages by so many of our countrymen, and by the fact that, whereas periods of adversity empty our gaols and almost make police magistrates superfluous, a return to prosperity restores those instruments of order and justice to their full use and activity."

So the Archbishop of York, in a special service at Westminster Abbey, on a Sunday evening of the past year, felt compelled to make what he felt to be "a miserable and shameful confession" of national weakness. Alluding to the great increase of the expenditure for drink, as shown by official returns, he said :

"If the question were asked, what was the cause of this fearful increase, he could conceive of no answer but this: that the nation had lately been growing richer, and that it drank in proportion as it could pay for drink."

After the memorable report of the Convocation of the Province of Canterbury on intemperance was made, a committee was appointed by the Convocation in the Province of York for a similar purpose, whose report was published in 1874. The committee say that "every assertion made" in the report, is "founded upon the direct testimony of numerous witnesses moving in various ranks of life, filling various offices, and all of them, for some reason or other, peculiarly fitted to pronounce an opinion." Among the conclusions which they emphasize are that intemperance "*is always in proportion to the rate of wages and the amount of facilities provided for obtaining strong drink;*" and that the large increase of intemperance during the last decade "exists principally in the great centers of manufacturing and

ˋ commercial industry, and invariably where a high
rate of wages prevails." The reader who cares
to turn to the appendix of testimony will be surprised at the unanimity on this point. As the
Northern Echo (February 22, 1874) sums it up :
" When wages are lowest, drunkenness is at a
minimum ; when wages are highest, drunkenness is at a maximum." Well may the editor
call this " a most saddening, disheartening docu-
ment."

To this observed relation, judges as well as
clergymen and statesmen have borne frequent
testimony. Thus in his charge to the grand
jury at Cavan (Ireland), August 10, 1872, Mr.
Justice Lawson said :

" He had only to regret, in conclusion, that drunkenness appeared, from the returns of the county inspector, to be on the increase in the county. He
feared it was within all their experience, that particularly in this part of the country drunkenness seemed
to increase in direct ratio to the prosperity of the
people. When wages were high and employment
abundant, the surplus earnings were too often expended in the gratification of a propensity which, it
was his experience, led to almost all the crime appear-
ing at the assizes in this country."

EDUCATION.

To make education a panacea for intemperance, is to fly in the face of both philosophy and

experience. Education is the cure of ignorance; but ignorance is not the cause of intemperance. Men who drink, generally know better than others that the practice is foolish and hurtful. They drink because appetite, when stimulated by temptation, is stronger than reason. The double cure needed for intemperance is to strengthen the power of resistance by arousing the moral nature, and to diminish the force of temptation by the removal of the outward solicitation. It is not mere clearness of mental vision; alas! that is needed for moral victory. It does not need that a man should know the language, to utter the sentiment of the Latin poet:

"Video meliora proboque;
Deteriora sequor."

Ah, Governor Andrew! It is not "the darkened intellect" alone that this monster has chained. The catalogue of his victims in this and the old world alike is starred with names brilliant in the ranks of literature and statesmanship, and happy is he who has reached middle life (if such a one there be) who can not recall among those he has counted his friends many who have sunk forever out of sight in the dark waters of intemperance, carrying with them the richest argosies of culture and of hope.

It is not the most earnest and intelligent

workers in the sphere of public education that make this overestimate of it as a specific for intemperance. While they are fully sensible of that measure of indirect aid which intellectual culture brings to all moral reforms, by strengthening the mind and purifying the tastes, they feel how weak is this agency alone to measure its strength against the powerful appetite for drink when stimulated by the dram-shop. Education looks with horror at the foe she can not conquer, and implores philanthropy and statesmanship to remove the greatest obstacle to her progress into those dark regions where she is needed most.

No statesman of England has thought more of public education than Lord Brougham. Yet, in 1839, he spoke in the House of Lords these disheartened words :

" To what good is it that the Legislature should pass laws to punish crime, or that their lordships should occupy themselves in trying to improve the morals of the people by giving them education ? What could be the use of sowing a little seed here, and plucking up a weed there, if these beer-shops are to be continued to sow the seeds of immorality broadcast over the land, germinating the most frightful produce that ever has been allowed to grow up in a civilized country, and, he was ashamed to add, under the fostering care of Parliament."

And Horace Mann, the very apostle of common school education in our country, exclaimed at the outset of his career : "If temperance prevails, then education can prevail; if temperance fails, then education must fail."

But here again, as in every stage of our discussion, our main reliance is upon massive facts ; and as in our every-day observation we have seen that individual culture is no security against the seductions of drink, so upon a larger scale we shall see that intemperance does not rise or fall with national education. But, as expressed in the Canterbury Convocation Report: "Even in highly civilized communities intemperance has been found commensurate with temptations to drink."

And, first, we note the general fact already substantiated, that while in England there has been no special cause in immigration or war to deteriorate the national life, and while the schoolmaster has been abroad as never before, yet the publican and the brewer have been more than a match for him.

We note again that Scotland, "the most educated and religiously-instructed portion of the British Empire, and her people naturally the thriftiest," presents an appalling picture of the results of the liquor traffic. Unfortunately, Scotland is as notorious for whisky-drinking as for religious and educational institutions, and from the Parliamentary returns we have given above, it will be seen that the drinking more than keeps pace with the population. The reader will notice the increase in the consumption of all kinds of liquors is very much larger in Scotland than in Ireland. In the correspondence of the State Board of Health of Massachusetts (Report 1871, p. 297), I find in a letter from the Consul at Manchester extracts from a table of Professor Levi, giving the consumption per head of proof spirit* in 1866 in the different countries of the United Kingdom. Scotland and Ireland stands thus:

	Scotland.	*Ireland.*
Gin and Whisky, . . .	1.659 gals.,	0.800
Brandy, Rum, etc., . .	0.188 "	0.057
Beer and Ale, ...	1.050 "	0.710
Wine, ...	0.087 "	0.064
Total, . . .	2.984	1.631

Or nearly three gallons in one, and a little more than a gallon and a half in the other. The superior prosperity and education of Scotland, it will be seen, is unable to keep down the drinking to the Irish standard.

In regard to Ireland itself, some curious and instructive statistics may be found in a paper

---

* "English proof spirit is about one-half alcohol and one-half water, or exactly (by volume), alcohol .57, water .43."

read before the British Association at Dublin, in 1857, by James Moncrieff Wilson, the Actuary. Dr. Lees, in his " Condensed Argument," summarizes and classes together the statistical elements for several provinces, of (1) education, (2) occupation, (3) house accommodation, (4) drunkeries, (5) drunkenness, and (6) crime. The " clear deductions," from the table exhibited, I give in his own words :

" I. That education combined with occupation tends powerfully towards the diminution of crime, more especially towards the decrease of offences against property without violence.

" II. That low-class dwelling-house accommodation tends towards the increase of crime.

" III. That the sale of intoxicating liquor has, perhaps, as powerful an effect upon crime in increasing it, as education and occupation combined have in lessening it. ' Thus Connaught is by far the worst educated Province in Ireland, with the largest unoccupied population, yet the tendency to crime is less than in any other Province except Ulster. This can only be accounted for by the considerations, that in Connaught there are forty-two drink-houses fewer to every 100,000 of the population than in any other Province ; and that the percentage of committals for drunkenness does not amount in Connaught to one-half the like percentage for the average of Ireland.'

" IV. That were intoxicating drinks less freely used, education, as a means of reducing crime, would become most powerful."

But in no country has the experiment of universal education, conjoined with free trade in liquors, been more amply tried than in Sweden. The results are striking. Without taking time to go into details of their public educational system, it is sufficient to notice the actual condition, in this respect, of her people. And the testimony as to this is concurrent and emphatic. Thus Mr. Laing, who wrote in 1838 his "Tour in Sweden," and with a special eye to "the moral, political, and economical state of the inhabitants," tells us that "in the province of Wexio-lan, in 40,000 people, only one person was found unable to read" (p. 187), and that "of the whole population, including even Laplanders, it is reckoned that the proportion of grown persons in Sweden unable to read is less than one in a thousand" (p. 186). "Elementary education is universal in Sweden," says Appleton's American Cyclopedia; and a curious illustration of it is given in the letter from Mr. Andrews, the resident Minister of the United States at Stockholm, on crime in Sweden, which may be found in the "Foreign Relations of the United States—1875" (No. 272). Of those convicted of the more serious offenses in 1872, all but three per cent. could read. Yet such a country in 1854, through the report of a special committee of its Diet, had to confess

that "seldom, if ever, has a conviction so generally and unequivocally been pronounced as in
later years in Sweden, with regard to the necessity of rigorous measures against the physical, economical, and moral ruin with which the
immoderate use of strong liquors threatens the
nation. .... The comfort of the Swedish people—even their existence as an enlightened,
industrious, and royal people—is at stake unless
means can be found to check the evil." And
Appleton's American Cyclopedia summed up
the common judgment when it said: "Drunkenness from immoderate potations of their
fiery corn brandy has been more common than
in any other country in Europe." There is
now an improved state of things in this kingdom, but which it is only here important to
note, is not due to education.

It may be added, that there is reason to fear
that in our own country we have placed too
much reliance upon *mere* education as a preventive of crime. The Report of the Bureau
of Statistics of Labor in Mass. for 1877 (p. 220),
states that only *eleven* per cent. of all convicts
in that State are illiterates—*i. e.*, not able to
read and write; and that of the 220 sent to
the State Prison in 1876, only 21 were such
illiterates.

RELIGION.

When religion is spoken of as a cure for intemperance, a fallacy lurks in the ambiguity in the phrase. True religion is a normal cure for intemperance as for every other sin; for, unlike education, its dominion is over the heart, out of which "are the issues of life," and not over the head alone. In this sense we assent to the proposition. But the problem is, how are those prone to intemperance to be got and kept under the influence of this power? As Horace Mann asks, "What can Bible or Christianizing societies do with the intemperate? At best they can only address moral and religious sentiments whose animation is suspended." The ear of the spirit must be opened before the heart can be touched; and we have already seen how intemperance not only closes the spiritual senses, but keeps the victim and the whole family of which he is the center, away from the very presence of the sanctuary.

If, therefore, it is meant that religious institutions and the ordinary methods of religious education can be relied on as the sole and sufficient preventive or cure of this evil, I deny the proposition. All experience is against it. This very country of Sweden supplies the refutation.

Mr. Laing, in the work from which we have quoted, says:

"In no country are the exterior forms and decencies of public worship better attended to. The churches are substantial, and not merely well kept up, but even decorated inside and outside; the clergy fairly endowed, well lodged, and, in general, on good terms with their flocks; they are also well-educated men, and form a body of great power in the State. Yet, with all these exterior signs of a religious state of the public mind, and with all the means of a powerful Church establishment, unopposed by sect or schism to make it religious, it is evident, from the official returns of crime, that in no Christian community has religion less influence on the public morals" (p. 125).

A curious fact is stated in the letter of Mr. Andrews, the American Minister before alluded to. He does not give the whole number of convicts in all the prisons during the year 1873, · but only the average number, which he states as 4,906. He says:

"During the year, seventy-one convicts partook of the sacrament for the first time, all of the others, as it would seem, having previously done so, that religious rite being in this country a matter of course."

The experience of Sweden is well summed up by Mr. Balfour in his recent letter to Mr. Gladstone, where he says:

" Neither the spread of education nor the influence of religious observances, which are so much relied upon in England as the cure for intemperance, were found to have that effect in Sweden, and that, while these were, doubtless, important and indispensable, yet other means were absolutely essential for bringing about the reformation that has occurred in Sweden since Mr. Laing visited it " (p. 27).

A phrase in Mr. Balfour's letter suggests the query, But who is it that relies upon education and religion to extirpate drunkenness ? We fear it will be found that they are mainly the friends of the traffic, who want it extirpated very mildly and slowly, if at all, or *doctrinaires* who have a dislike to all laws in aid of public morals. Certainly it is not the men who are most awake to the need of public education ; it is not the clergy ; it is not the evangelists ; it is not the missionary who threads the lanes of poverty and disease in our large cities. All these cry aloud to us for the help of law. Thus the very able Committee of the Convocation of Canterbury, in their report which was adopted by the conservative clergy of the Establishment after careful consideration and suitable recommendation of " non-legislative remedies," place on record their emphatic testimony in these words :

" Meanwhile, your committee are convinced that

without an improved and stringent system of legislation, and its strict enforcement, no effectual and permanent remedy for intemperance can be looked for."

The same conclusion had long ago been reached by individuals whose position and life-work gave them the best opportunity to measure and watch the antagonistic forces of society. In his testimony before the Committee of the House of Lords in 1850, Rev. John Clay, the experienced chaplain of the Preston House of Correction, speaking of the passage of the " Beer Bill," exclaimed :

" Instantly 40,000 dens were opened, each of which breeds more immorality and sin in a week than can be counteracted by the minister of religion in a year."

Archdeacon Garbitt said :

" A large experience tells me that when a neighborhood is visited by this scourge (beer-shops), no organization, no zeal, no piety, however devoted, no personal labors, however apostolic, will avail to effect any solid amelioration."

Only a few months since, a memorial was presented to the Archbishop of Canterbury and the other Bishops, members of the House of Lords, asking their attention to legislative aids for the suppression of intemperance, which was

7

signed by over thirteen thousand clergymen of the Church of England, of all orders, in which occurs this emphatic utterance :

" We are convinced, most of us from an intimate acquaintance with the people, extending over many years, that their condition can never be greatly improved, whether intellectually, physically, or religiously, so long as intemperance extensively prevails amongst them, and that intemperance will prevail so long as temptations to it abound on every side."

Whose judgment can we imagine as entitled to more weight upon this precise point?

And if we turn from such impressive declarations to look at actual experiments, ex-Bailie Lewis gives us a most instructive chapter from the annals of Edinburgh. He first shows us that, in 1871, in that city the number of drunken commitments was 5,400; in 1875, 6,824, an increase of twenty-six per cent. during an increase of only seven per cent. of population; and in 1876 the number had risen to 7,114. For " the accuracy and impartiality of these returns," he gives his personal voucher, and then adds :

" It would appear as if, in the Providence of God, Edinburgh had been selected as the field for a great social experiment as to whether drunkenness can be eradicated while the drink traffic remains. It would appear as if during the last few years human ingenuity had exhausted itself in Edinburgh towards that end. Let us look at what has been done. By the administrators of the poor-law during the last five years £265,000 have been expended in support of pauperism, four-fifths of which were the direct result of the public-house. Sanitary reformers expended half a million sterling in erecting improved dwellings and promoting sanitary reform. Educationists also occupied the field. During the last five years one institution alone has expended £40,000 in free education among the children of the citizens, and there was the Education Act, with its compulsory clause and expensive machinery. The Christians, too, had been active in the divine work of seeking the reclamation of the lost, and a tide of revival had flowed upon the city without a parallel in modern times. Most churches have been galvanized into spiritual activity, and much good had been accomplished ; but I am free to say that the revival movement never penetrated the heart of drink—the cursed slums. Temperance reformers had also been specially active. Templar lodges had been formed by the score, and temperance societies in the Church and out of the Church had been established throughout the city. In promoting bands of hope, one gentleman had, during the last five years, expended £11,000. The magistrates had been aiming at the reduction of licenses, and during the reign of the present Lord Provost the licensed houses had been considerably reduced, notwithstanding an increase in population of nearly 9,000 during that period. We have thus seen somewhat of the combined efforts of moral, social, religious, and temperance reformers, and the question arises, What has

been the effect of all these in suppressing drinking
and drunkenness? Mark, I do not say those move-
ments have not accomplished much. God only knows
what would have been the state of the city had not
those agencies been at work. What I affirm is, that
they have not been able to check or keep abreast of
the tide of drink demoralization. . . . . The conclusion of the whole matter is this—until there is sufficient Christian patriotism among the leaders of the
people to demand the statutory prohibition of this
licensed enormity, society must make up its mind to
bear all the accumulated horrors of the drink curse."

We close this chapter with a word of repeti-
tion, rather than to leave any chance of being
misunderstood. We, too, believe in the ame-
liorating influence of popular education,—in the
all-conquering power of practical religion. But,
on the way to their triumph, they must abolish
the dram-shop. The traffic blocks their way.
It is an enemy they can not safely leave behind.

CHAPTER XV.

LICENSE LAWS.

THE first attempt of Government to deal with the traffic was as a matter of excise and of regulation. It was perceived that liquor afforded an easy object of taxation, and no one felt any scruple in subjecting it to such as would yield large revenue, while at the same time the most heedless saw that it was an exceptional traffic, liable to frightful results, and inviting the strictest surveillance.

The reader who desires to see an instructive sketch of the legislation of England on this subject from the earliest times, will find it in Dr. Lees' "Condensed Argument" (pp. 59 to 78). The *resumé* justifies his conclusion: "Britain has tried, other nations have tried, restriction and regulation. The experiment has failed—miserably failed." And he quotes from the *London Times* (of May 13, 1857). as the organ of public sentiment, this confession: "The licensing system has the double vice of not answering a public end, but a private one. *It has been tried, and has been found wanting.*" The old country is still experimenting.

If such is the result across the water, we might anticipate that such laws would avail still less in a country like ours, where the machinery for the enforcement of all laws is generally less complete and less energetically put in motion.

It is impracticable, of course, to attempt a history of License, or an outline of the various statutes in the several States of the Union. But as they all have a family likeness, and their results are not widely variant, I shall do the system no injustice by confining my attention to its working in a single State. And I select Massachusetts, because no State commenced the experiment of license earlier, has tried it under more variety of conditions, or has brought more ability and earnestness to the solution of the problem. And yet, throughout the course of legislation, there is the constant struggle after stringency, and the confession of prior inefficiency.

THE HISTORY OF LICENSE IN MASSACHUSETTS.

The first law I find in the Old Colony provides :

"That none be suffered to retail wine, strong water, or beer, * either within doors or without, except

---

* It is quite evident that our forefathers early learned *what* were intoxicating liquors, if they did not find out how to manage them.

in inns or victualling houses allowed "(1636; Plymouth
Colony Records, Vol. I., p. 13).

In 1646, the Massachusetts Colony declared:

" Forasmuch as drunkenness is a vice to be abhorred
of all nations, especially of those who hold out and
profess the Gospel of Christ Jesus, and seeing *any
strict law will not prevail unless the cause be taken
away*, it is therefore ordered by this Court,—1st. That
no merchant, cooper, or any other person whatever,
shall, after the first day of the first month, sell any
wine under one-quarter cask, neither by quart, gallon,
or any other measure, but only such taverners as are
licensed to sell by the gallon; and whosoever shall
transgress this order shall pay ten pounds."

" Any taverners or other persons that shall inform
against any transgressor shall have one-half of the
fines for his *encouragement*."

Section 4 forbids drinking or tippling after 9 P.M.

Section 7 forbids

" Any person licensed to sell strong waters, or any
private housekeeper, to permit any person to sit drinking or tippling strong waters, wine, or *strong beer*, in
their houses " (Mass. Colony Records, Vol. II., p. 171).

The law of 1661 prefaces its enactment thus:

" Upon complaint of the great abuses that are daily
committed by the retailers of strong waters this Court
doth order, etc."

In 1665, *cider* takes its place among the inhibited liquors; as it appears to have done in Plymouth Colony in 1667 (Records, Vol. XI., p. 218).

In 1670, keepers of public-houses are warned not to allow "noted" drunkards on their premises. In 1680, it is provided that licenses shall first be approved by the Selectmen of the town before they are granted by the Court, and that they shall not be granted "till after the Grand Jury present their indictments."

The statute of 1692 prefaces certain stringent provisions as to public-houses with this preamble:

"And, forasmuch as the ancient, true, and principal use of inns, taverns, ale-houses, victualling-houses, and other houses for common entertainment is for receipt, relief, and lodging of travelers and strangers, and the refreshment of persons upon lawful business, or for the necessary supply of the wants of such poor persons as are not able by greater quantities to make their provision of victuals, and are not intended for entertainment and harboring of lewd or idle people to spend or consume their time or money there; therefore, *to prevent the mischiefs and great disorders happening daily by the abuse of such houses*, It is further enacted," etc. (Province Laws, Vol. I., p. 57).

The following year witnessed another advance, the law requiring—

"That every master or head of a family shall be accountable for the transgression of the law relating to retailing without license, whether it be by his wife, children, servants, or any other employed by him" (*Id.*, p. 119).

Two years later we find another statute forbidding retailers to sell other drinks than those which they are licensed to sell, or to suffer drinking on their premises when not so licensed, with provisions for inspection by officers, and penalties for the receipt of bribes, and threats of forfeiture of license for violation of terms, prefaced with the complaining preamble:

"Whereas, divers persons that obtain license for the retailing of wine and strong liquors out of doors only, and not to be spent or drunk in their houses, do notwithstanding take upon them to give entertainment to persons to sit drinking and tippling there, and others who have no license at all are yet so hardy as to run upon the law, in adventuring to sell without tending to the great increase of drunkenness and other debaucheries" (*Id.*, p. 190).

The statute of 1695, after reciting that "divers ill-disposed and indigent persons, the pains and penalties in the laws already made not regarding, are so hardy as to presume to sell and retail strong beer, ale, cider, sherry wine, rum, or other strong liquors or mixed drinks, and to keep common tippling-houses, thereby harbor-

7*

ing and entertaining apprentices, Indians, negroes, and other idle and dissolute persons,
tending to the ruin and impoverishment of
families, and to all impiety and debaucheries,
and if detected, are unable to pay their fine,"
goes on to sentence such to the whipping-post.

The second section of the same statute provides for the seizure by officers of the law of
liquors in the house of any person "suspected
of selling strong drink without license, having
once been convicted thereof," and for the taking
of the same before the Court; "and if the
quantity of drink so seized shall be judged by
said court or justices to be more than for the
necessary use of the family, and what their condition may reasonably allow them to expend, or
otherwise to have in their custody, it shall and
may be lawful to and for such court or justices
to declare all such drink to be forfeited"
(Province Laws, Vol. I., p. 224).

In 1698, we find an elaborate "Act for the
Inspecting and Suppressing of Disorders in
Licensed Houses." There are provisions
against selling to servants or negroes; against
suffering tipplers; against harboring any but
travelers on the Lord's day; against allowing
drinking on any day after 9 P.M.; for bonds
with sureties to observe the law; "for tything-
men" to inspect and inform; and, finally, "*the*

*better to prevent nurseries of vice and debauch-
ery,"* it is further declared:

"That the justices of the General Sessions of the
peace in each county respectively be and hereby are
directed, *not to license more persons* in any town or
precinct to keep houses for common entertainment,
or to retail ale, beer, cider, wine, or strong liquors,
within or out of doors, than the said justices shall
judge necessary for the receiving and refreshment of
travelers and strangers, and to serve the public occasions of such town or precinct; having regard to the
law for the qualification and approbation of the persons so to be licensed. And all public-houses shall
be on or near the high streets, roads, and places of
great resort" (*Id.*, pp. 327–330).

In the statute of 1710 appears a provision
that no person shall be licensed without a "certificate from the Selectmen of the town where
they dwell, of their recommendation of them to
be persons of sober conversation, suitably qualified and provided for such an employment."
And it was further provided that "no town, except the maritime towns, shall have more than
one inn-holder and *one* retailer at one and the
same time, unless the Selectmen of the town
shall judge there is *need* of more for the better
accommodations of *travelers*" (*Id.*, p. 662).
And the next year there appears in "An Act

against Intemperance, Immorality, and Profaneness, and for Reformation of Manners," with a
collection of directions, provisions, prohibitions,
and penalties, the same dreary preamble :

" For reclaiming the over great number of licensed
houses, many of which are chiefly used for revelling
and tippling, and become nurseries of intemperance
and debauchery, indulged by the masters or keepers
of the same for the sake of gain " (*Id.*, p. 679).

But even this partial enumeration of acts is
becoming tedious, and perhaps can serve no
useful purpose. The frequent renewal of old
provisions is partly due, it is proper to state, to
the fact that some of them were incorporated
into excise acts. The general features of the
license policy remained unchanged during the
provincial government.

In the Diary of John Adams, under date
February 29, 1760 (Works, Vol. II., p. 84),
there may be found this graphic picture :

" Few things, I believe, have deviated so far from
the first design of their institution, are so fruitful of
destructive evils, or so needful of a speedy regulation, as licensed houses. . . . . At the present day,
such houses are become the eternal haunt of loose,
disorderly people of the same town, which renders
them offensive, and unfit for the entertainment of a
traveler of the least delicacy; and it seems that

poverty and distressed circumstances are become the strongest arguments to procure an approbation ; and for these assigned reasons, such multitudes have been lately licensed that none can afford to make provisions for any but the tippling, nasty, vicious crew that most frequent them. The consequences of these abuses are obvious. Young people are tempted to waste their time and money, and to acquire habits of intemperance and idleness, that we often see reduce many to beggary and vice, and lead some of them, at last, to prison and the gallows. The reputation of our county is ruined among strangers, who are apt to infer the character of a place from that of the taverns and the people they see there. But the worst effect of all, and which ought to make every man who has the least sense of his privileges tremble, these houses are become, in many places, the nurseries of our legislators. An artful man, who has neither sense nor sentiment, may, by gaining a little sway among the rabble of a town, multiply taverns and dram-shops, and thereby secure the votes of taverner, and retailer, and of all ; and the multiplication of taverns will make many, who may be induced by flip and rum, to vote for any man whatever. I dare not presume to point out any method to suppress or restrain these increasing evils, but I think, for these reasons, it would be well worth the attention of our Legislature to confine the number of, and retrieve the character of, licensed houses, lest that impiety and profaneness, that abandoned intemperance and prodigality, that impudence and brawling temper, which these abominable nurseries daily propagate, should arise at length to a degree of strength that even the Legislature will not be able to control." *

In 1787, after the adoption of the State Constitution, a codification of all provisions of existing laws which were deemed useful, with some additional provisions, were embraced in the Act of February 28 (Laws of Mass., Vol. I., p. 374). As this remained in substance the law for fifty years, it may be well to note its provisions somewhat in detail.

First. There is a general prohibition of sales of " wine, beer, ale, cider, brandy, rum, or any strong liquors, in a less quantity than twenty-eight gallons, except under a license." Half of the fines were given to the informer.

Second. Licenses are to be given for only

---

* Under date August 28, 1811, Mr. Adams writes to Mr. Rush: " Fifty-three years ago I was fired with a zeal, amounting to enthusiasm, against ardent spirits, the multiplication of taverns, retailers, dram-shops, and tippling-houses. Grieved to the heart to see the number of idlers, thieves, sots, and consumptive patients made for the physicians in these infamous seminaries, I applied to the Court of Sessions, procured a Committee of Inspection and Inquiry, reduced the number of licensed houses, etc.; but I only acquired the reputation of a hypocrite and an ambitious demagogue by it. The number of licensed houses was soon reinstated ; drams, grog, and sotting were not diminished, and remain to this day as deplorable as ever. . . . . Sermons, moral discourses, philanthropic dissertations, are all lost upon this subject. Nothing but making the commodity scarce and dear wil have any effect." And he speaks afterward of " prohibitory taxes " as " the only remedy." (Works, Vol. IX., p. 657)

one year at a time; to be granted by the County Court of General Sessions, but only upon the recommendation of the Selectmen of the applicant's town. If the license is a new one, the Selectmen are to certify that they approve and recommend the applicant "as a person of sober life and conversation, suitably qualified and provided for the exercise of such an employment, and firmly attached to the Constitution and laws of this Commonwealth." If it is a renewal, the certificate must be that the party had, during the last year, "to the best of our knowledge, maintained good rule and order in the house or shop, and conformed to the laws and regulations respecting licensed persons."

The Selectmen are, in addition, "to certify to the Court, at the beginning of their term for granting licenses, what number of inn-holders and retailers in their respective towns they judge to be *necessary for the public good.*" And thereupon the Court are enjoined "not to license more persons in any town or district" than they shall "judge necessary for the receiving and refreshment of travelers and strangers, and to serve the public occasions of such town or district, as are necessary for the public good: and all public-houses shall be on or near the high streets, roads, and places of great resort."

Third. Licensees are forbidden to supply minors or servants with drink without permission of parents or masters.

Fourth. The Selectmen of each town are to post in licensed houses and shops, "the names of all persons reputed to be common drunkards," and also to give notice of any person who by excessive drinking should expose himself or family to want, or "greatly injure his health;" and until such persons "have reformed," it is made penal to sell to them.

Fifth. No credit above 10 shillings to be given.

Sixth. Various provisions are made as to recognizances with sureties to be entered into by licensees to observe the laws.

Seventh. Tything-men are specially charged with the duties of inspection and complaint.

The ingenuity or the hopefulness of the friends of sobriety seems at this time to have exhausted itself, for no attempt at greater stringency, or more effective execution of license laws, was attempted for more than forty years. During this long period drunkenness fearfully multiplied, and the presumed "moral character" of the venders of liquors was seen to have no effect in checking the poisonous influences of their beverages upon body or soul.

But in 1816, an important step downwards

was taken. By the Act of Dec. 14th, at first
limited in its operation to the city of Boston,
but afterward extended throughout the State,
licenses were authorized to be issued to common victuallers "who shall not be required to
furnish accommodations" for travelers, and to
"confectioners," on the same terms as to inn-
holders, that is, to sell to be drunk on the
premises. Of this law, Judge Aldrich, in 1867
(House Doc. No. 415, p. 47), spoke in these
strong terms:

"Contemporary history will satisfy any honest
student that it was one of the most fruitful sources
of crime and vice that ever existed in this Commonwealth."

Perhaps this is attaching too much importance
to a *single* act.

In the Report of the Board of Counsel of
the Massachusetts Society for the Suppression
of Intemperance, written by Nathan Dane* in
1820, it is said: "There can be no doubt but
that the evils of intemperance are far greater
now in our country than they were in the times
of the Colony and Province." From returns
from four large counties of the number of li-

---

* Who will be remembered as the framer of the famous
"Northwest Ordinance," and the founder of the professorship
in Harvard Law School so long filled by Judge Story.

censed persons, the estimate is made that "there constantly must be near 6,000 in the State." Upon the basis of population, this would be equivalent to about 19,000 in 1875. As one of the evils resulting "from the very great number of persons in the State licensed to sell ardent spirits," attention is called to the "very great facility in buying them in any quantities; also in obtaining them often in exchange for the bread and scanty necessaries of a poor family. And the more numerous these licensed places are, the more easily are they resorted to in all hours and in all kinds of weather, and the more probable it is that such a wretched barter trade will be carried on."

The County Commissioners in after years took the place of the Court of Sessions; but what has been styled "the double imposition of hands, to set apart a person for the business of liquor selling," continued to be required. And as it was found that the hands of the Selectmen, at least, were often laid on suddenly and irregularly, it was required by the Act of March 19, 1831, that they should first be sworn "faithfully and impartially, without fear, favor, or hope of reward, to discharge the duties of their office respecting all licenses, and respecting all recommendations;" and that the certificate, when granted, should, in addition, set forth that, "After mature consideration, we are of opinion that the *public good requires* that the petition be granted."

The next year (1832, Ch. 166, sec. 9), it was further provided that the certificate should state that it was granted by the Selectmen, "at a meeting held for that purpose, at which we were each of us present." The law of 1832, which was a revision of the precedent statutes, was substantially that which was inserted in the Revised Statutes of 1836, as Ch. 47. The next year (1837, Ch. 242), it was enacted that not even licensed inn-holders should sell any intoxicating liquor on Sunday. This was the last attempt to patch up the law.

FAILURE CONFESSED.

Another generation was to grow up in Massachusetts before we should hear again of the merits of a stringent license law. It was all failure—sad, disheartening, *confessed* failure.

Miserable in principle, license laws were found no less inefficient in practice. The conclusions of intelligent observers were well summed up by Linus Child on behalf of a Committee of the Legislature, in 1838:

"Laws professing to regulate the sale of spirituous liquors have, it is believed, existed in every State of the Union. But has their effect been to check the

progress of intemperance? Have they so far restrained the manufacture and sale of intoxicating
liquors as to prevent the formation of those intemperate habits and appetites which have been the
cause of ruin to millions of our race? *It may well
be doubted whether intemperance would have increased
with more rapid strides, if no legislative regulation of
the sale of intoxicating liquors had ever been made."*

LOCAL PROHIBITION.

Meantime the battle against the liquor traffic
had been fighting in detail. In 1835, the office
of County Commissioner (the licensing authority), theretofore an appointive, was made an
elective office, and the people of the counties
began to make their wishes felt at the ballot-
box. That very year the Old Colony counties
of Plymouth and Bristol elected boards committed to the policy of no license. The battle
went on in other counties. To save all question of the right to refuse every license, the
power was expressly conferred by law of 1837.
Of the results of this action the Judiciary
Committee of the House in 1837, after a
thorough investigation, reported that,—

" The evidence was perfectly incontrovertible that
the good order, the physical and moral welfare of the
community had been promoted by refusing to license
the sale of ardent spirits, and that the consumption
of spirits has been very greatly diminished in all in-

stances by the refusal to grant licenses ; and that, although the laws have been and are violated to some
extent in different places, the practice soon becomes
disreputable, and hides itself from the public eye, by
shrinking away into obscure and dark places; that
noisy and tumultuous assemblies in the street, and
public quarrels cease, where licenses are refused ; and
that pauperism has very rapidly diminished from the
same cause."

THE "FIFTEEN-GALLON" LAW.

In 1838 (Ch. 157), appears what was so well
known as "the Fifteen-Gallon Law." It was
the first attempt at entire prohibition of the retail liquor traffic, and forbade all sales of spirituous liquors "in less quantity than fifteen gallons, and that delivered and carried away all at
one time," except that apothecaries and practic-
ing physicians might be licensed to sell for
"use in the arts or for medicinal purposes
only."

This law took effect in July of that year. At
the next Legislature, a strenuous effort was
made for its repeal. Harrison Gray Otis and
a long array of the "solid men" of Boston
petitioned therefor ; but the conscience of the
State spoke through such men as William Ellery
Channing, Dr. John C. Warren, Jonathan Phillips, and Joseph Tuckerman in remonstrance,
and for the time the attempt failed. But in the

fall of the same year there was a political revolution, which placed a Democrat by one majority
in the Governor's chair, and it was thought to
be due to the clamor against this law. Then,
as now, the friends of temperance were ready
with arguments, but the friends of the traffic
were ready with votes; and the latter command
the respect and obedience of the politician. The
new Legislature hastened to repeal the statute
after it had been in operation only a year and
a half. No reasons were given; none were
needed; *voluntas pro ratione.*

NO LICENSE.

But the State, while the memory of license
was fresh, was not to fall again under its sway.
The struggle for local prohibition was at once
renewed, and, in a few years, licenses had
ceased throughout the Commonwealth. The
statement may surprise many, but I have the
authority of the City Clerk of Boston for saying, that "no licenses for the sale of intoxicating liquors were granted in Boston between
1841 and 1852." * The causes of this disuse
of the license law in Boston, where, of late, it
has been maintained that such laws were espe-

---

* Licenses issued in 1852 were just before the prohibitory law
took effect, and for the purpose of evading it; but this action
was subsequently decided to be inoperative.

cially needed, were various. The friends of temperance, when there were 700 licenses issued in 1833 to a population less than a quarter of the present, saw little encouragement in prosecuting the unlicensed, and the whole system fell under that moral contempt expressed by Dr. Tuckerman in his " Tenth Semi-Annual Report," as Minister at Large in that city:

" Is it (legislative power) limited to acts which do not, and which it is known can not, and will not, impose the smallest possible restraint upon the sale of these spirits? Why, then, waste time and money in laboriously framing and modifying legislative enactments, which not only go for nothing in the cause, either of private virtue or of public security, but which themselves virtually sanction debasement and crime, and indirectly call up any sentiments in the public mind respecting other legal restraints than that of respect, and a sense of the importance of regarding them? "

And, on the other hand, why should the licensee take the trouble to seek renewal of a license which he held in common with so many others, and which gave him no practical advantage over his unlicensed neighbor? And surely there was some gain in saving the strain of conscience it must cost intelligent men at that day to declare that " the public good " required the establishment of " respectable " dram-shops.

THE VERDICT.

And so the chapter of license was apparently closed. It had not only its " day," but its centuries in court ; and the well-nigh unanimous verdict was : " *disgrace—failure.*"

Down to 1861, at least, that judgment stood as the general judgment of the people of Massachusetts. So moderate a man as Governor Bullock, then acting as the Chairman of the Judiciary Committee on the part of the House, in that capacity bore this emphatic testimony:

"It may be taken to be the solemnly-declared judgment of the people of the Commonwealth, that the principle of licensing the traffic in intoxicating drinks as a beverage, and thus giving legal sanction to that which is regarded in itself an evil, is no longer admissible in morals or in legislation. The license system, formerly in operation, was the source of insoluble embarrassments among casuists, legislators, courts, and juries. A return to it would re-open an agitation long since happily put to rest ; it would invade the moral convictions of great numbers of our people ; it would revive the opprobrium which public sentiment always adjudges to a monopoly established by law, rendered all the more intense by the offensive nature of the business thus supported by the sanction and protection of the Legislature."

THE EXPERIMENT OF 1868.

The history of prohibition, both in Massachusetts and other States, is the subject of another chapter. Suffice it here to say that the prohibition of the traffic began in 1852 and continued until 1875, with the exception of the period from the session of 1868, when a license law was enacted, to that of 1869, when it was repealed—in fact, less than a single year. I am not aware that any one considered *that* experiment a success; and the "Report of the Secretary of the Board of State Charities" ("Fifth Annual Report," p. 35) says:

" The law (the License of 1868) was enacted through the influence of those who (without regard to the consequences of their action on the poor and weak) wished to drink more and those who hoped to sell more. And it is undoubtedly the case, that more is actually drunk and sold. The result at once began to exhibit itself in our jails and houses of correction; and, as usual, now begins to make its record directly and indirectly on the registers of our various State pauper establishments, lunatic hospitals, and reformatories. . . . . If it is desired to secure, in the best manner, the repression of crime and pauperism, the increase of production, the decrease of taxation, and a general prosperity of the community, so far as this question of intemperance is concerned, it is clearly my judgment that Massachusetts should return to the policy which

8

prohibits the sale of intoxicating drinks except for mechanical or medical purposes. When most carefully enforced, such a policy amounts, in practice, only to a restriction on such sales, for every law on this subject will be more or less evaded. But to the poor, and the wives and children of the poor, it makes a wide difference whether we take our departure from the point of prohibition or from that of license. In the latter case, as has been seen the past year, the current sets in favor of more selling and more drinking; and this means, to the poor laboring man or woman, and to the children growing up amid bad influences, more poison of the blood, more delirium of the brain, more idleness, more waste, more theft, more debauchery, more disease, more insanity, more assault, more rape, more murder, more of everything that is low and devilish, less of everything that is pure and heavenly. Poverty and vice are what the poor man buys with his poisoned liquor—sickness, beastliness, laziness, and pollution are what the State gives in return for the license-money which the dram-seller filches from the lean purse of the day-laborer and the half-grown lad, and hands over, sullied with shame, to the high-salaried official who receives it. But the treasury reaps little from this revolting tribute; for, along with the licensed shops and bars, twice as many that are unlicensed ply their trade and debauch the poor, without enriching anybody but the dram-seller. These are the practical results of a license system in Massachusetts now."

Such was the indignant indictment of the legalized liquor traffic of 1868—not by a temperance reformer, but by a State official appointed by Governor Andrew, and well and widely known as a close observer and student of social science.

THE LAST EXPERIMENT.

But again, in 1874, the forces of evil triumphed, and the result was the enactment of another license law on the 5th of April, 1875. The two laws of 1868 and 1875 are alike in their general features. There is an appearance of stringency, to be sure, in the provision in the latter law requiring licensees to furnish a bond to abide by the provisions of the law in the penal sum of one thousand dollars with sufficient sureties; but until we have information that the treasury of some city or town has been enriched to the extent of a dollar therefrom, or that any bond has even been put in suit, we need not trouble ourselves to consider the value of this section of the law. The clerk of the Superior Court for the transaction of criminal business for the County of Suffolk, reports that up to September 1, 1876, not one of such bonds had, to his knowledge, even been put in suit; and I have not heard of one so prosecuted since, either in that or any other part of the State. There is also a provision that persons licensed to sell, to be drunk on the premises, shall not keep a public bar; but we are not aware that this provision is anywhere enforced; and, indeed, in the city of Boston, the License Commissioners have publicly stated that the inhibition is an impracticable one, which they can neither define nor enforce.

The law also contains a provision that licenses to sell liquor, "to be drunk on the premises," *shall* only be issued to "innholders and common victuallers." A detailed statement before me shows that, in a single year, the number of these, in the cities alone, rose from 660 to 2,914! Of many of such places, James Henderson, the English Factory Inspector, who recently visited Boston, truthfully says (*Contemporary Review*, May, 1877):

"The Act was complied with so far that a cooking-stove was provided, and on the shop-counter and in the windows there was a display of stale biscuits, buns, and tinned meats, which were evidently placed there to be looked at, not consumed. In many of the licensed houses at Boston it would have been as difficult to get anything eatable as in a London gin-palace."

The methods of enforcement seem to have been as loose as the construction of its provisions.

From returns collected from ten of the principal cities (Boston excluded), it appeared that during the first six months only 264 cases were brought in their municipal courts, and the most of these ultimately disappeared. By the report of a committee of the Legislature, made March 22, 1877, it appears that the Boston police were active enough to bring 2,200 cases before their municipal courts prior to September 1, 1876; but only in twenty-two were fines paid there; the vast majority being appealed to the Superior Court. And the Clerk of that Court, in a statement appended to the report, shows that from May 1, 1875, to March 1, 1877, there were 1,605 cases laid on file, or *nol pros'd*, and only 427 reached sentence, which was generally a moderate fine. (See " House Doc.," 1877, No. 227).

The visible results of the new law soon appeared throughout the State. Thus, in September, 1875, the City Marshal of Lynn wrote: " We have neither more nor less than free rum." The City Missionary of Lowell said in the same year: " In its *ostensible* aim, it (the License Law) is a sad failure; in its real aim, a perfect success." So of Worcester, the Mayor writes: " More selling goes unpunished, and thereby a greater injury is done to the community." And the Springfield *Republican* notes that "employers of labor find that their hands are more demoralized by drink on Mondays than they were under the prohibitory law."

I might multiply opinions of magistrates, police officers, city missionaries, and other experts as to the operation of this law upon drunkenness and crime, but, in the absence of reliable and digested returns, I select only a single city, that of New Bedford, of which I know most. In 1874, under enforced prohibition, there was a total of 748 arrests, 707 of whom were brought before the Court. In 1875, under license, there were 1,085 arrests, 847 of whom were brought before the Court (the 238 "let off" were probably first offenses of drunkenness).

In 1874 there were 242 cases of drunkenness. In 1875, the number was 445 (besides those "let off"), an increase of over 83 per cent. in a single year of license.

"Lodgers" likewise increased, from 1,124 in 1874 to 1,691 in 1875. Well might the City Marshal, though the appointee of a license administration, say in his report:

"During the year, the day-police have been kept generally busy, in consequence of the repeal of the prohibitory law, and the lack of employment through the country, making their duties more arduous than any previous year."

Bad as has been the operation of the License Law throughout the State, its immediate and visible effects have been somewhat checked by several causes. In the first place, under the power reserved in the law, all licenses have been refused in nearly three-quarters of the towns of the Commonwealth ; in the second place, the long-continued and severe depression of business, and the lessening of wages, has diminished the number of dram-shops and the consumption of liquors ; and, in the last place, the tidal wave of the great "Reform" movement has reached the State during this period. The full operation of a license law can not be seen at once ; bitter as are its fruits to-day, the bitterest remains for the morrow, when the enthusiasm of the new movement shall have spent its force, and when a new generation of drinkers, "according to law," shall have taken their place in the army of drunkards.

A bold attempt has been made to show an exceptional success in the city of Boston. The Chief of Police reports that the arrests for drunkenness in 1874 were 11,880, and in 1876 were only 8,564, showing, in two years, an aggregate decrease of 3,316. He also reports, that on the 1st of January, 1876, there were 2,411 places where liquor was sold, and on the 31st of December, only 1,971 (divided thus—

licensed, 1,103 ; unlicensed, 868), showing a reduction of 440 for that year.

On the strength of these statements, a claim has been put forth that the law in Boston is a measurable success.* Let us examine this claim.

And first, as to the validity of the statistics. No criminal statistics are so flexible. In the year 1864 the Police Report showed the arrests for drunkenness for the preceding year to number 17,967. Much public comment was made, and the very next year, with no change of law or police, the reported arrests for the same offense dropped to 2,561, while the " lodgers " rose from 9,897 the previous year, to the enormous number of 23,638. It appeared plain that the change was of names and not of things. The cases of drunkenness were reported at more than double for 1865 ; and thenceforward there was a steady increase, until the arrests for. the year ending December 31, 1874, were reported as 11,892. In 1875 the city authorities undertook the enforcement of the new License Law, and the number of arrests for

---

* Governor Rice, in his Message of May 15, 1877, quotes from the Chief's Report, that the " number of places abandoned " during the year was 619 ; but he omits to add that the same Report shows 179 new places opened, and explicitly states the whole "number of places reduced during the year " to be 440, as given above.

drunkenness during that year was reported as 10,325, a decrease of 1,567 ; and for the year 1876, a further decrease of 1,761. During all these years the increase in that class of tramps called "lodgers" continued to be enormous. In 1874 the number reported was 58,449 ; in 1875, 62,740 ; and in 1876, 63,720. I have no disposition to assail the fairness of the present excellent Chief of Police, but; of course, his report merely shows the doings of his subordinates ; nor is it necessary to say of any of them more than this, that with the consciousness that the City Hall desired to make out a case for the License Law, it would show an impartiality beyond the average lot of humanity, if, in a matter so vague as that of arrestable drunkenness, where the officer is accustomed to exercise so wide a discretion, many should not be aided home, classed among lodgers, or winked at, who might, with at least equal propriety, have appeared in the column of arrests, and who, under other circumstances, would have so appeared.*

---

* The present Chief of Police (then Deputy) testified thus before the Legislative Committee in 1867 : "In 1864, you will remember that the Chief testified it was ordered that those parties who were arrested, and were but partially drunk, and whom it was thought proper and humane to discharge, should be classed amongst 'lodgers.' These are therefore here put down as lodgers, although under the influenct of liquor. From an ex-

I suppose few persons who have not given the matter attention, are aware of the small ratio which the arrests for drunkenness bear to the whole number of persons who, in common parlance, might be called drunk. I call the reader's attention to an interesting investigation recently made, the result of which appears in a note below.*

As to the number of liquor-shops reported, I believe that these also were underrated. While the number of licensed places is given

---

amination of the books, and from my own knowledge, I believe that *at least one-half* of those designated as lodgers in the reports of the captains and lieutenants, were more or less under the influence of intoxicating drinks." (" License Law Report," House Doc. No. 415, p. 237).

* Joseph Chamberlain, M.P., in a speech in the House of Commons, March 13, 1877, made the startling statement, that "while on a certain Saturday the whole number of persons arrested and brought before the magistrates of Birmingham was only 29, that by actual count **838** persons came out drunk in the course of three hours of the same day from only **35** of the liquor establishments." A correspondent of the *Alliance News* more than confirms this by a minute tabular statement of the *products* of each of 51 of these places, " representing a fair average of the whole," which " were watched on an average three hours and five minutes each on a Saturday night. The number of drunken persons seen coming out of these houses during the three hours was 1,067 males, 369 females ; total, 1,436." " Strict instructions· were given that no person seen coming out was to be considered drunk unless unmistakably so." This would give a fearful aggregate for the 675 public-houses, exclusive of beer-shops, in Birmingham.

as 1,103, the number " supposed to be selling
without license" is estimated at only 868. If
the reader will recur to what is shown above,
as to the inefficient punishment of unlawful liquor
dealers, can he readily believe that sufficient coercion had been applied to effect a reduction to
that extent, especially in view of what the License Commissioners say in their last Report:

" Nothing is more common among the dealers than
the saying that they are better off without than with
a license; and, as a matter of fact, few of the whole
number of persons holding licenses are in good faith
keeping the conditions of them; and the enforcement of the law against those who sell liquor *without*
licenses seems to have but little effect, either on the
parties prosecuted or their neighbors in the trade."

With such a report of the estimate liquor
dealers have of the value of a license, and of
the effect of prosecutions, from those who are
fully competent witnesses, can we easily believe
that the result was so different from the universal experience heretofore and elsewhere, and
that the unlicensed dealers were only 44 per
cent. of the whole number? *

If it should seem to the candid reader that,

---

* A striking illustration of the importance of the *animus nu-
merandi* is given in the count in Boston of liquor-shops in January, 1867, by the State Police as 690, and by the City Police as
1,951.

after all, it is possible that there was some
temporary reduction, he may still think with
the License Commissioners themselves (Report, Feb. 1, 1877), that "it may be question-
able how much of the result is due to the law,
and how much to the general depression in
trade, and the so-called hard times, from which
all are more or less suffering." Beyond this
he may deem it doubtful how much is gained
by a slight reduction in the number of dram-
shops, if the supply remains so abundant that
there is no substantial diminution either of in-
citement or of facility for drinking. And when
he finds in the same report the Commissioners
say:

"It must be admitted that the business of liquor-
selling in the city is, to a very large extent, in the
hands of irresponsible men and women, whose idea
of a license law ends with the simple matter of paying a certain sum, the amount making but little difference to them, provided they are left to do as they
please after the payment. Besides the saloons and
bar-rooms, which are open publicly, the traffic in
small grocery stores, in cellars, and in dwelling-
houses, in some parts of the city, is almost astound-
ing. The Sunday trade is enormous, and it seems as
if there were not hours enough in the whole round
of twenty-four, or days enough in the entire week, to
satisfy the dealers. The Commissioners consider the
three greatest abuses of the traffic to be sales of

impure liquors, sales on Sunday, and sales at late hours."

If such are the facts, it is not strange to find the Commissioners in this report saying in so many words, " *The law can not be called a success* ; " although it is a little-difficult to discover upon what ground they add that " it is a step in the right direction ! "

But this temporary show of triumph, which was but a *show*, has already passed away. If the estimate of December last be taken as correct, a rapid increase has taken place. From an official report recently made by the same Police Department, the number of places where liquor is sold is given, from a count made by the captains of the districts on the 31st of May, 1877, as 2,341 — an increase of 370 in five months.

But more than this. The whole number of licenses issued for the present year since the 1st of May up to this date (August 8, 1877) is 2,349 ; making a deduction for double licenses (which were 128 the first year, and only 86 the second), it will be within the mark to say that there are 2,200 *licensed places* of sale to-day in Boston. If we estimate the unlicensed at only 800, we have an aggregate of 3,000. Probably a low estimate ; and with the subsidence of the reform movement, and the return of "good times," threatening an indefinite increase.

As a final consideration, it is to be borne in mind that the city of Boston, as a municipality, had from the start contemned and thwarted the prohibitory law, and that this state of things ultimately led to the establishment of the State Police ; that, on the other hand, they had pledged themselves in the strongest way beforehand to enforce a license law, and that during this last experiment the Mayoralty had been filled by a man of ability and determined will, who was elected in spite of the lower liquor class, and who set out with courage and faith to do all that could be done to vindicate the policy of license.* The State Police, to whom (not by statute, but in fact) the sole execution of the prohibitory law was entrusted, had in Boston, when the force was at its maximum, not over 40, while the force of the City Police is now 700. The candid reader will observe that we have seen here license working with every advantage, while in the chapter on Prohibition he will see the latter, *so far as Boston is concerned*, working at disadvantage. Nevertheless, we invite attention to the two pictures.

---

* The present year has witnessed the advent of a more "liberal' administration, and a new Board of Commissioners. The least offensive chapter of license, we think, is closed.

CHAPTER XVI.

THE NECESSARY FAILURE OF LICENSE.

LICENSE laws have not only failed in the past, but it is certain that they can not succeed in the future, because of inherent weaknesses. If the history of license in the old world has been one of such long continued failure in any large results as to justify the London *Times*, in a recent leader, in saying, " What is to be done? is the wild, despairing cry heard on every side," still more clearly is the failure of license inevitable in the United States. It must fail in its immediate results ; and even if it could succeed in these, it would fail in its ultimate object, if that object be assumed to be the protection of the State against the evils of the traffic. It will fail of enforcement, and when partially enforced it will fail in effectiveness. Its failure in enforcement is the kind of failure that we refer to as most inevitable in our own country. In the first place, the administrative part of our Government is the weakest, and the enforcement of our criminal laws generally is less uniform and thorough than in England ; and it is notorious that liquor laws do not belong to the

self-executing class. There is no individual
personal interest behind them. If a man's
house is entered or his horse stolen, he is the
person who is eager to apprehend and convict
the burglar or the thief, and he stimulates the
policeman and every other servant of the law.
Not so with offenses against the public. Their
punishment must, in the first instance, depend
solely on the activity and fidelity of the policeman, and in America it is the voting power that
controls his action, because it makes or unmakes
him. Now, any enforcement of a license law,
such as its "respectable" friends sometimes
talk of and rarely attempt, which would crush
out the bar-rooms and the "small dealers,"
would turn many a recruiting-station of "the
party" into a hostile camp, and the dram-shop
interest united to that of the wholesale dealer,
whose sales would be diminished, would work
a political revolution. A successfully enforced
prohibitory law has to meet with the opposition
of the liquor interest, it is true; but a successfully enforced license law would not only encounter the opposition of the bulk of the same
interest, but for obvious reasons fully developed
hereafter, would fail to secure the counteracting
support of the active temperance sentiment.
Such laws are, therefore, in this dilemma. To
be retained in any community where the

temperance reform has made any considerable progress, against the moral sentiment of those sympathizing with this reform, they must have the united support of the liquor interest. If the law is enforced, the latter is lost; if the law is unenforced, it sinks into contempt.

In addition to the peculiar embarrassments to the execution of the law from political considerations, the license law encounters in America a wide-spread odium as sustaining a monopoly. So long as it is a dead-letter this is not strongly felt; but when any resolute enforcement is attempted, this feeling is at once aroused. No principle is more firmly implanted in the American mind than that which John Adams placed in the Bill of Rights prefixed to the frame of Government established by the Constitution of Massachusetts :

" No man, nor corporation or association of men, have any other title to obtain advantages or particular and exclusive privileges, distinct from those of the community, than what arises from the consideration of services rendered to the public."

Be it observed that I am not attacking the constitutionality of license laws which have been established by uniform judicial decisions, and no doubt correctly, for the court must accept such laws as a legislative determination (to borrow the language of earlier statutes) that "the public good requires" that a sufficient number of "suitable persons" should be selected by certain public authority to sell intoxicants as beverages. But even those who accept the theory smile at the application ; and the general public hardly appreciate the "services rendered to the public" by the concrete dram-seller A, which entitles him to the exclusive privilege over B, who is refused, or to any privileges "distinct from those of the community." On what principle shall we grant or withhold licenses ? Shall we give to every one for a nominal fee? Then it is equivalent to no law. Shall we fix a high rate? Then it is simply a revenue measure, and, besides, awakens both the prejudice against monopolies and against distinctions in favor of the rich against the poor. Or shall we fix a moderate fee and limit the number according to some supposed public convenience? But how, then, are we to select the favored ones? How justify to the rejected debarring them from participancy in a profitable monopoly? Shall we attempt to discriminate on the ground of qualifications? Alas! what moralist has limned the features of the Good Rum-seller? What writer of fiction even has portrayed him? Where shall the licensing board turn for the record of his needed virtues?

Such a task as the moral classification of the trade may well be given up in despair, as sooner or later it has been by every licensing board.

But to return to the peculiar difference between the American and the English mind in the view it takes of special privileges. Abhorrent to the former, it seems to the latter, who accepts his sovereign by birth, who calls his "lords" those made so by inheritance or special gift, as in the normal order of society. Not only does it not offend his sense of justice that one man should receive from the State a "privilege" denied to another, but a privilege conferred ripens in his view into a right owned, and with all other complexities of the liquor problem on hand, the British press and public are discussing the question of compensation to the unlucky publican or beer-houseman whose annual license may fall in from some change of legal policy. In such a country it is *comparatively* easy to enforce a license law to such an extent as to become some protection of the "sacred right of property," while it excludes others from the gains of the traffic.

We have so far dealt with the problem as if there were an intention to enforce license laws when made. Such was the intention in the past, when our ancestors used them as the best means of restraint of the traffic which they knew—with what kind of success we have seen. Undoubtedly, among the makers and supporters of the license laws of to-day, there are those who have a similar. desire. But the license laws enacted *over prohibitory laws* have had in the main another *animus.* What the Secretary of the Massachusetts Board of State Charities (5th Report, p. 35) said of a single law will apply to others:

> "The law was enacted through the influence of those who (without regard to the consequences of their action on the poor and the weak) wished to drink more, and those who hoped to sell more." *

I am not aware that the friends of license, *as a party*, have ever troubled themselves about the machinery of enforcement. They have always deprecated, even as against unlicensed dealers, the "harsh measures" of the prohibitory *régime.* They declined to allow, in the Massachusetts Licence Laws of 1868 and of 1875, the use of that most effective weapon against an unlawful traffic, the search and seizure provisions. They have just been in-

---

* It was of this law that Dr. Miner, at the hearing for its repeal before the Committee of the Legislature the next year, said: "Some people say the License Law is a failure. I think that is a mistake. It is a complete success. It has accomplished exactly what its framers expected. It has made selling easy and drinking plentiful."

serted in the Massachusetts Law, to be sure (1876, chap. 162), but as crafted and urged by prohibitionists, backed by only a comparatively small minority of the license men, and against the votes of the mass. I do not doubt the good faith of individuals ; but the trouble is, that the strongest and most active section of the license party is in the liquor interest, and I do not see that it can be otherwise in the future.

For whatever view any one may himself take of the matter, it is an undeniable *fact*, and entitled to weight *as such*, that a vast majority, approaching to unanimity of the *active* friends of Temperance, in every organization and in every sphere of effort, are opposed by sentiment, by education, and by conviction, to any law sanctioning the sale of intoxicants as a common beverage. And I see no indications that the views of this class of men are undergoing, or are likely to undergo, any modification. We have, then, the problem presented to us of a proposal to deal, in the way of limitation and restraint, with a vast moneyed interest, and with a measure of monopoly odious to the popular mind, and yet without the support of that active moral sentiment which is the only force ultimately stronger than apparent self-interest. Is there reason to expect success ? But let us suppose all superficial obstacles

surmounted. Let us start with a law made and
meant to work, and with a sufficiently powerful
force of opinion behind it. Imagine that we
have reached the first stage of apparent success. The unlicensed dealers are suppressed;
the low groggeries are out of sight; the liquors
dispensed are pure alcoholic poisons, without
even the adulteration of water; the bartenders
are all "respectable" men or comely maidens.
What then? Here is the "moderate drinker's"
paradise. What fruits shall it bear? In the
first place, an inevitable percentage of drunkards; and this class will in time create a demand
which will insure a supply of the old groggeries.
For these latter are as necessary a complement
of the dram-shop system as the dens of vice
are of that system of prostitution which takes
its first steps in the elegant mansion. No system of legislation can do much for the suppression of a sensual vice which does not aim to
eradicate the appetite for it by removal of the
temptation and the facilities for its constant indulgence. These remaining substantially the
same, whatever other changes in accessories
may be made, about the same percentage of
physical and moral wrecks will be found.

But this is not the worst. When the State
sets up its primary schools for drinking, it not
only prepares the way, by a necessary law of

succession, for its most loathsome underground universities of intemperance, from which graduate the most disgusting of the human species, but the terrible truth is, that it makes this primary school attractive to the innocent and young with all the glamour and fashion which wealth and reputation can throw about it. It is not the low bar-rooms that *make* drunkards; they only *finish* them. And the drinking in reputable places is the sadder when it is indulged in by the rich and the educated, who add to their own personal danger the evil of influential example. Thus, to the thoughtful observer, it is the high and not the low drinking-places of our great cities which chiefly attract his attention as pests and perils. I remember to have heard one who has adorned the highest judicial station, and who was not friendly to prohibitory legislation, yet pronounce the most fashionable establishment in Boston, especially attractive as is reputed to Harvard students, a veritable *nuisance.* What wise parent would not fear such a seductive place for his children, more than the dens of North Street?

And when to the fascinating influences of an enticing traffic, carefully pruned of repulsive surroundings, we add the educational influence of a bad law, we have rather interposed a formidable barrier to the progress of the temperance reform than aided it by all our measures of restriction and regulation.

License laws rest upon the implied assumption that there is such a legitimate demand for the sale of intoxicating liquors as a common beverage as, notwithstanding the admitted perils of the traffic, to call upon the State to make convenient provision therefor. And the State assumes to hold out the licensee as a suitable person to supply this public want. The State thus endorses the traffic and selects the trafficker.

With the State as the tempter to the indulgence, the patron and the educator of an evil appetite, how can that appetite be eradicated? Our fathers essayed the problem; shall not their sad experience suffice their children?

CHAPTER XVII.

HALF-WAY MEASURES.

" Never believe, then, that we oppose restrictive measures. We hail them, and will do our best to make them efficient; but, convinced as we are that no amount of regulation can ever be satisfactory, we are bound in conscience, even though, Cassandra-like, we prophecy to unbelieving ears, still to insist that nothing but the suppression of the traffic can deliver our country from the grievous woes and burdens under which she groans."— EDWARD PEARSON.

" All past legislation has been ineffectual to restrain the habit of excess. Acts of Parliament intended to lessen have notoriously augmented the evil; and we must seek a remedy in some new direction, if we are not prepared to abandon the contest or contentedly to watch with folded arms the gradual deterioration of the people.

" Restriction, in the forms which it has hitherto assumed, of shorter hours, more stringent regulations of licensed houses, and magisterial control of licenses, has been a conspicuous failure. For a short time after the passing of Lord Aberdare's Act, hopes were entertained of great results from the provisions for early closing, and many chief constables testified to the improved order of the streets under their charge; but it soon appeared that the limitation, while it lessened the labors of the police and advanced their duties an hour or so in the night, was not sufficient to reduce materially the quantity of liquor consumed or the consequent amount of drunkenness."—*Fortnightly Review*, May, 1876.

ALL restrictive laws in relation to the liquor traffic have our support, except in so far as they may stand in the way of more efficient measures, or may be so framed as to carry with them the moral sanction of the Legislature for a regulated traffic. The worst of license laws have probably, as compared with free trade, done *something* to diminish the immediate sale and consumption of alcoholic liquors, but indirectly they have in some communities done vastly more harm, as we have elsewhere indicated, in the downward education of public sentiment as to selling and drinking. But it is a sad and discouraging experience to find the value of the purely restrictive clauses in license laws, as confessed in the extract from the *Fortnightly*, so much less than was anticipated in their enactment.

But let us now proceed to consider the value and measure of success of certain special measures.

SUNDAY CLOSING.

It is not strange that special attention should be aroused to the horrors of the Sunday liquor traffic. The special evils are both dramatically and intrinsically great. The general quiet of the day forms an effective background for such scenes of noise and disorder as the tavern and the ale-house, the grog-shop and the lager-bier saloon naturally generate. The real antagonism between the dram-shop and the church, always existing, is here made conspicuous and emphatic. And the climax in the indictment of the traffic seems to be reached, when it is charged not only with imbruting its victim for the six days of the week, but with the withdrawal of him on the day of rest from all holy influences, and the shutting of his ear to all suggestions of that higher life which was his birthright as a child of God.

It is very noticeable that where the open shop invites to drink, there is unusual temptation to the poorer of the laboring classes to indulge, and especially in social drinking, both because of the fact that the Saturday night wages gives them a feeling of abundance, and the leisure of the day invites them to carousal.

In some places the extra Sunday drinking is enormous. Thus in the Convocation Report, one clergyman (No. 1685) says: " The public-house *does more business on Sundays than all the week put together."*

Yet, notwithstanding the obvious and intrusive nuisance of the Sunday dram-shop, it has not only been found difficult to eradicate it practically, but it has been found hitherto impossible to procure the withdrawal of the legislative sanction for it in a nominally Christian Government like that of the United Kingdom of Great

Britain. It is only in Scotland that the law requires an entire closing on Sunday. Ireland has sought for years this privilege of a quiet Sunday at the hands of the Imperial Government, and sought in vain. Although a very large majority of the Irish members of Parliament have supported bills for Sunday closing, the liquor interest among the English members has been too strong for them, and it was only in June, 1876, that the Government have so far abandoned their opposition to it, as to allow a bill for this object to go to its second reading; and since that they have allowed a resolute minority in the House of Commons to stave it off by parliamentary devices, so that it is still doubtful when a measure for entire closing will be carried. The English and the Catholic Church, with the dissenters thrown in, are hardly yet a match for the publican and the brewer in the halls of legislation.

I have alluded to the favorable results of Sunday closing in Scotland, under the Forbes-Mackenzie Act, in another connection. I will not repeat the statistics there given, but will content myself here simply with giving the impressive testimony of a thoroughly competent witness, ex-Baillie Lewis, of Edinburgh :

"Prior to the passing of that law, the social condition of many of our centers of population had, by the public-houses being open on Sunday, become truly scandalous. Street brawls and crowds of dissipated persons in the principal streets so shocked the sense of propriety among church-going people, that legislative interference was loudly called for. In Edinburgh the grievance had assumed all the proportions of a dreadful social nuisance. On a Sabbath in December, 1853, I personally counted nearly 1,000 persons enter one public-house, and it was found that on that same day no fewer than 41,796 persons had entered the various public-houses open throughout the city. The act came into operation in May, 1854, and it was at once found to produce order and decorum in the streets in a marvellous degree, and largely to lighten the labors of the police."

And yet, after all, obvious as are the advantages of Sunday closing, the full benefit can not be secured without week-day prohibition. In the recent debate upon the Irish Closing Bill, a member of Parliament who supported it, declared that he agreed with another Irish member, "that the greatest amount of drinking took place on Saturday evenings, and that he should certainly prefer to see a bill brought in to close at seven o'clock on Saturday evenings, than that the public-houses should be closed all of Sunday afternoons. Others deprecated the "illict sales," and the "home drinking" that would ensue. And these considerations, though not of force enough to outweigh the many reasons for abolishing the Sunday traffic by law, have still some foundation in facts.

The experience of America, where the laws prohibit all Sunday sales, shows that if you keep alive by legalized temptations and facilities for indulgence the appetite among the lower classes for alcoholics during the whole week, it is difficult to suddenly repress it on Saturday night; while it is also made more difficult to convict the seller, because of the clandestine way in which the traffic may be carried on, and because the possession of the paraphernalia and the material for the traffic avails nothing in proof if the vender has a general license to sell. It will be found, therefore, we think, that only under a prohibitory *régime* has there been a close approximation to the total suppression of the Sunday traffic.

But let the friends of the total suppression of the traffic be always among the foremost in every earnest effort for Sunday closing, even under the license *régime*, for the rest of the time. The benefits of such closing are great, and the logic of the movement points to entire prohibition. I have before me a recent circular of the Howard Association of Great Britain, issued under the special endorsement of the Archbishop of Canterbury, the Bishop of London, and the Dean of Westminster. While praising the marvelous energy of the " United Kingdom Alliance," it calls public attention to what it deems more immediately practicable modes of diminishing intemperance. Among these it places—

" VI. To prevent intemperance on Sunday, the sale of drink on that day should be prohibited."

The question at once arises, Is it not desirable to prevent intemperance on *Monday* also ? If so, why should not the sale of drink on *that* day be prohibited ?

CIVIL DAMAGE LAWS.

Great reliance has sometimes been expressed by those whose acquaintance with the matter is purely theoretical, upon what are called the " civil damage " provisions in legislation upon the liquor traffic. I have not thought it worth while to make the requisite examination to give a list of the States in which the experiment has been tried, or the varying details of the legislation. I recall Ohio, Illinois, and Indiana as prominent among these States. The Illinois law, which I have before me, in the first section requires that every person who sells intoxicating liquor, to be drunk on the premises, shall first obtain a license therefor, and, as a condition precedent, shall give bond, with sureties,

in the sum of $3,000, conditioned "that they
will pay all damages to any person or persons
which may be inflicted upon them, either in
person or property, or means of support, by
reason of the person so obtaining a license,
selling or giving away intoxicating liquors; and
such bond may be sued and recovered upon
for the use of any person or persons who may
be injured by reason of the selling intoxicating
liquors by the person or his agent so obtaining
the license."

Section 5 enacts that—

"Every husband, wife, child, parent, guardian,
employee, or other person who shall be injured in
person or property, or means of support, by any intoxicated person, or in consequence of the intoxication, habitual or otherwise, of any person, shall have
a right of action in his or her own name, severally or
jointly, against any person or persons who shall, by
selling or giving intoxicating liquors, have caused the
intoxication, in whole or in part, of such person or
persons."

Section 6 declares that all fines, costs, and
damages recovered shall be a lien on all the real
estate of the defendant not exempt from levy
on execution; and further, that in case any
owner of a building shall rent the same, or permit the same to be used for the sale of intoxicating liquors, the premises "shall be held

liable for, and may be sold to pay, all sums so recovered."

These provisions seem stringent, but I have doubts whether they will be continuously and extensively effective in restraining the abuses of the liquor traffic. There are difficulties in the way which would be obvious, at least to every legal practitioner, and if they should prove in practice surmountable, the only result under the Illinois law would be that dealers would thenceforward carry on the traffic without a license rather than under one, as the licensees alone are obliged to furnish the security of bonds.

I have no doubt of the right of the Legislature to affix any conditions it may see fit to permission to carry on the liquor trade, and it may therefore go to the extent of making the seller responsible for consequences ; but it must be admitted that this is an anomaly in legislation. As a general principle of law, it is only a wrong-doer—*i. e.*, one who does an unlawful act or a lawful act negligently—who is responsible for the consequences of the act. If it is unlawful to sell, then the seller may, with reason, be held liable for the results ; but if the State sanctions the selling, it would seem, upon general principles, that it should charge the seller with some wrongful or negligent act under its own

9*

theory before affixing to him pecuniary liability therefor. Accordingly, the "Adair Liquor Law of Ohio" has been so amended as to require that before the liability arises notice shall have been given by the persons liable to be injured not to sell or give liquor to the person for whose acts, when intoxicated, the seller is to be charged.

While these civil damage laws are most consistent with the theory of prohibitory legislation, it will, perhaps, surprise many readers to know that they are not a late invention, but were originally incorporated in prohibitory laws. Thus, in the Mass. Law of 1855, it was provided that "the husband, wife, parent, child, guardian, or employer of any person who has the habit of drinking spirituous or intoxicating liquor to excess, may give notice in writing, signed by him or her, to any person not to deliver spirituous or intoxicating liquor to the person who has such habit. If the person so notified, at any time within twelve months after such notice, delivers any such liquor to the person who has such habit, the person giving the notice may, in an action of tort, recover of the person notified any sum not less than $21 nor more than $500, as may be assessed by the jury as damages." And then follow provisions as to coverture and death. And in 1861 (chap. 136) the requiren ent of notice was stricken out.

It would be too much to venture to affirm that no case ever ripened to judgment under this section in the courts of Massachusetts; but this I can affirm, that I never heard of any, although I have been in stations where, if frequent, the fact would have come under my eye; and the published reports of the State contain no trace of any such case.

If this law of liability has anywhere brought any *solatium* to a ruined home or a desolate wife, or restrained *in terrorem* any reckless rum-seller, let it steadily be upheld for what it is worth; but it is evident that it may be dismissed as a means for general control of the traffic.

TAXATION.

We have already had occasion to notice that in accordance with the general law, that whatever imposes restraints upon the freedom of sale diminishes consumption, taxation for revenue has some beneficial effect in checking the liquor trade. This is, perhaps, more noticeable in the old world than in the United States, where the higher wages and more assured employment affords the mere day-laborer too ample means to gratify continuously his appetite for drink.

Taxation in various forms, imposed for purposes of national revenue upon the manufacturer and the dealer, is familiar to the legislation of the United States; but so far as I am aware, the State of Michigan is the first to propose a tax upon the dealer as a measure of State revenue and of regulation. The Constitution of Michigan provides that " the Legislature shall not pass any act authorizing the grant of licenses for the sale of ardent spirits or other intoxicating liquors." The prohibitory law of the State having been repealed, the Legislature being inhibited by the Constitution from granting licenses, resorted to a system of taxation as affording some slight extent of regulation and some public revenue. The act imposes a uniform tax of $40 upon retail dealers in malt liquors, and $150 upon retail dealers in spirituous liquors. If the liquor traffic is to be tolerated, either expressly or impliedly, I am inclined to think taxation is better than license.

In the administration of license laws, the traffic is practically thrown open to almost every dealer who would be able to pay a considerable tax; while this system avoids the scandal of pretending to license such a business for the " public good," and the evil example of a legislative sanction. It is, however, open to the fatal objection that it is a dis-

heartening abandonment of even a hope for
the present suppression, or strict regulation, of
the dram-shop, while it shares, with the license
system, the infamy and the evil of deriving a
portion of the public revenue from such a
source. It recalls to mind the rebuke of Lord
Chesterfield in the House of Lords in 1743 :

" Luxury, my lords, is to be taxed, but *vice prohibited*, let the difficulty in the law be what it will.
Would you lay a tax upon a breach of the Ten Com-
mandments? Would not such a tax be wicked and
scandalous? Would it not imply an indulgence to
all those who could pay the tax? . . . . It appears
to me that, since the spirit which the distillers produce is allowed to enfeeble the limbs, vitiate the
blood, pervert the heart, and obscure the intellect,
the number of distillers should be no argument in
their favor, for I never heard that a law against
theft was repealed or delayed because thieves were
numerous."

LOCAL OPTION.

This well-known American phrase is used to
describe laws essentially prohibitory of the
liquor traffic in their nature, but confined in
their authority to such local subdivisions of the
general sovereignty as may by some form of
popular vote adopt them.

Many of the States of our Union have, in
late years, tried the experiment of such a sys-

tem. Among them have been the States of Pennsylvania, Indiana, Kentucky, North Carolina, and California. Mississippi enacted a peculiar statute, which, in any community with which we are acquainted, would ensure prohi-bition, viz. : " That no license shall be granted or renewed unless signed by a majority of the male citizens over twenty - one years of age, *and a majority of female citizens over eighteen* years of age resident in the supervisor's district, incorporated city, or town." What progress has been made in the enforcement of this law we know not; probably but little, in the disturbed condition of affairs there existing ever since the time it was passed. Some other States have granted enabling acts to particular counties or districts. Notably among these are New Jersey, Maryland, Georgia, and Alabama.

It has been claimed that local option laws are unconstitutional as an attempted delegation of the legislative power to local authority. And some respectable decisions may be cited to sustain this doctrine. But the weight of opinion seems to be in favor of sustaining their validity. The question came before the Supreme Court of Massachusetts under the " Beer Law," so called (St. 1870, c. 389), which allowed the sale of malt liquors unless the municipality

should vote otherwise, " in which case the sale
of such liquors in such city or town is prohibited." The Court say :

"It has been argued .... that these statutes are
unconstitutional, because they delegate to cities and
towns a part of the legislative power. But we can
see no ground for such a position. Many successive
statutes of the Commonwealth have made the law-
fulness of sales of intoxicating liquors to depend upon
licenses from the selectmen of towns or commissioners
of counties ; and such statutes have been held to be
constitutional. (7 Dane Ab., 43, 44 ; Commonwealth
vs. Blakington, 24 Pick., 352). It is equally within
the power of the Legislature to authorize a town, by
vote of the inhabitants, or a city, by vote of the city
council, to determine whether the sale of particular
kinds of liquors, within its limits, shall be permitted
or prohibited. This subject, although not embraced
within the ordinary power to make by-laws and ordi-
nances, falls within the class of police regulations,
which may be intrusted by the Legislature by express
enactment to municipal authority. (Commonwealth
vs. Turner, 1 Cush., 493, 495 ; State *vs.* Noyes, 10
Foster, 279 : Bancroft *vs.* Dumas, 21 Verm., 456 ;
Tanner *vs.* Trustees of Albion, 5 Hill, 121 ; State *vs.*
Simonds, 3 Missouri, 414.)"

Commonwealth vs. *Bennett*, 108 *Mass.*, 27.

I have not thought it worth while to examine
the details of these laws in the different States.
The general scheme is to engraft upon a license

system a provision that the people of a specified locality, either of a county, or in some cases of a town or city, may vote that no licenses shall be granted, in which case the sale is prohibited.

The law is thus, when operating to prevent licensing, only "prohibitory" in the general meaning of that term, and lacks the peculiar machinery which gives special efficiency to the law popularly known as "the Maine Law." * Yet these local option acts, partial in operation and incomplete in detail, have yet proved benefi- cent in operation. As their success is the suc- cess of prohibition, I have given some of the facts in the chapter under that head. In some of the States these laws have been *too* success- ful, and have followed the fate of prohibitory laws, in being *repealed for that reason.* This is notably the case in Pennsylvania and Indiana. Confessed by "the trade" to be a check, and more expressively shown to be so by their clamorous activity for the repeal, thoughtful men need no further demonstration of their utility, and can only ponder the problem, how long it must be that the powers of evil continue

---

* Massachusetts is now (1876) trying the experiment of a local option, depending on the action of the municipal authorities (1875, ch. 99, sec. 5), and with the search and seizure provisions of the prohibitory law in case of all unlicensed keeping (1876, ch. 162).

practically stronger in the body politic than the powers of good, by reason of their unity and energy.

But notwithstanding the good obtainable by these laws, in addition to the obvious consideration that this is a matter in which the reverse of the old maxim, that "the half is better than the whole," applies, this legislation is open to three serious objections :

First. The State is the normal unit of sovereignty, and it is opposed to sound theories of government to transfer to local fractions the decision of a question of such general and far-reaching importance as the policy to be pursued toward the liquor traffic. Names do not alter things, and calling the power of licensing or prohibiting a "police power," can blind no thinking man to the tremendous issue involved. And if the doctrine I have sought to maintain in previous chapters is established, and the drink traffic is indeed the destroyer of national wealth, the clog that drags down labor, the poisoner of the public health, the enemy of the home, the feeder of pauperism, the stimulant of crime, the foe of Christian civilization, and the degenerator of the race, then the State clearly owes to each community of its citizens its best wisdom and its most persistent energy in the repression of such a traffic, and it may not rightfully or even prudently abandon the virtuous, or, for that matter, the vicious, citizen anywhere to the rule of a debased locality. It is as if the famous Five Points of New York city were allowed to establish their own code of criminal laws.

Second. Legislation of this kind breaks the educational force of law. What can be voted up or down by the people of a village or a county, what is right in one district and wrong in another, loses all moral significance.

Third. Unless prohibition is the uniform law of the State, its best results can not be obtained even in the communities which elect it. The force of this objection varies, of course, somewhat according to localities. There are isolated rural communities where local prohibition may be made quite effectual. But our railroad system has practically compacted the greater part of our people, and our cities where the liquor interest is strongest, are, if uncontrolled by law, centers of demoralization, with far-reaching circumferences. Even as long ago as 1839, Jonathan Phillips and 2,222 other memorialists addressed the Legislature of Massachusetts in these words:

" While the capital continues to be the headquarters of the trade, no effectual benefit can be realized in those parts of the State where licenses are refused.

Such is now the intercourse between Boston and the interior, that no man's family is safe. The youth who has been kept from the temptation to intemperance in the country, no sooner enters the city than he is beset by the enticements which a legalized body of spirit dealers hold out before him."

This, however, points out but one of the many relations in which the capital stands to the country. ·

While thus pointing out the shortcomings and weaknesses of local option laws, we are prepared to admit their utility under the conditions and limitations heretofore suggested. And besides their temporary utility, they may sometimes serve the purpose of "stepping-stones" to a higher and safer plane of legislation.

THE ENGLISH PERMISSIVE BILL.

This, known also as Sir Wilfrid Lawson's bill, from the baronet who introduced it and has so persistently pressed it to a division, year by year, in the English House of Commons, is essentially a local option measure. But it exhibits that peculiar caution so characteristic of the English mind. Sir Wilfrid is brave and radical enough, but he knows too well the conservative instincts of even the "popular" branch of the English Government. When remitted to local decision, it is only the "rate-payers" who are

to have a voice ; and so privileged a class are
the publicans and beer-house keepers, that they
are not to be ruled by a mere majority of their
tax-paying fellow-citizens ; but the liquor traffic
is only to be suppressed where a vote of *two-
thirds* so decrees.   And yet this looks to "the
trade" as "tyrannical" and "outrageous," as
the Maine Law itself to an American dram-
seller.   And although Sir Wilfrid does not

> "bate a jot
> Of heart or hope ; but still bears up and steers
> Right onward ;"

he is not yet able to gain largely in Parliamentary support for his moderate proposition.
The last division was on the 14th of June, 1876,
when (including pairs and tellers) 101 members of the House of Commons supported, and
319 opposed the bill.   The gain, however, in
the accession of influential adherents outside of
Parliament has recently been more marked.   It
is also noticeable that on the above division, Ireland, Scotland, and Wales each gave a majority
for the bill.

   This measure is actively supported by the
" United Kingdom Alliance," one of the most
powerful and best organized societies for re-
formatory agitation which the world has seen.
Its officers and executive are men as remarkable for ability and wisdom as for broad phi-

8

lanthropy. A few years ago a subscription fund of half a million dollars (£100,000) was raised to carry on its work for five years; and its expenditures for the year ending Sept. 30, 1875, amounted to over one hundred and fifteen thousand dollars.

Yet, although this organization earnestly and unanimously supports and presses the Permissive Bill as the best attainable measure, it still has placed in the forefront, from the first hour of its organization (1853), as its object, "to procure the total and immediate legislative suppression of the traffic in intoxicating liquors as beverages."

May I not rightly sum up the duty of those who believe the liquor traffic to be a curse, as this: *Wherever license prevails, wrest every inch of territory you can for prohibition; where prohibition prevails, never surrender an inch to license, except from dire necessity.*

CHAPTER XVIII.

THE GOTHENBURG SYSTEM.

IN a paper contributed by Judge Aldrich to the Fourth Annual Report of the Massachusetts State Board of Health, he alludes to Sweden as a country "somewhat isolated in position, and whose internal or domestic policy is less liable to be affected by foreign influences than that of most European countries; and the force and effect of whose legislation and domestic policy can therefore be the more surely determined." After alluding briefly to its history in previous centuries, he closes thus:

"But there is not space here further to trace this very instructive branch of the history of one of the most remarkable nations of Europe, illustrating as it does nearly every phase of the 'Liquor Question' which has arisen in this country, or is likely to arise, and the careful study of which could hardly fail to furnish our legislators and statesmen with invaluable information to guide them in dealing with a subject second in importance to no other within the range of American legislation."

But we must not permit ourselves to stray

beyond such a brief survey of Swedish affairs as may enable the reader to understand the special topic of this chapter, and to determine its relative success or failure.

The Gothenburg system has heretofore incidentally received the favorable notice of Mr. Gladstone, and of Mr. Bruce, the Home Secretary under his ministry, and has excited considerable interest in England and Scotland; and in our country has been set forth in that pretentious treatise of Mr. Weeden, on "the Morality of Prohibitory Laws" with this unqualified eulogy:

"We can offer a system of regulated traffic which is based on justice, respects the individual, and is worked in every detail for the benefit of the whole community, so far as this appetite can be controlled by any mechanism. It has the further advantages of success after more than eight years of trial" (p. 164).

As we in Massachusetts are doing what is called, in sad irony, giving the license law "a fair and full trial," which is merely living over the dreary experience of our forefathers, let us turn and examine this *novelty* in a spirit of candor.

SWEDEN.

Sweden, although by its position and the occupation of its inhabitants, free from the pres-

ence of many debasing factors which enter into
European civilization, and unusually well supplied with facilities for religious and educational
culture, has yet been for ages, as we have
heretofore had occasion to notice, wonderfully
cursed by intemperance.

For over a century, after a few brief efforts
at restriction, there had been pursued a national
policy of free trade in intoxicating liquors.
And so it had come to pass, as reported by Mr.
Laing in his " Tour in Sweden " in 1838, that
" the best informed individuals impute the extraordinary state of the criminal returns of the
country to the excessive drunkenness of the
lowest class. The evil, they say, goes beyond
the excess of all other nations, is the cause of
three-fourths of all the crimes committed, and
is destroying the very race, physically as well
as morally." At last the public sentiment of
the kingdom became aroused, and found expression in the report of a special committee
of the Diet of Sweden made in 1854, in which
it is said that " the researches of the philoso-
pher and the honest feelings of the illiterate man
have led them to the same conclusion ; and that
is, that the comfort of the Swedish people—
even their existence as an enlightened, industrious, and loyal people—is at stake, unless
means can be found to check the evil. . . . . It

might be said a cry of agony has burst forth
from the hearts of the people, and an appeal
and prayer made to all having influence in the
fate of the country for deliverance from a scourge
which previous legislators have planted and
nourished." As the result there was passed
what is known as the " Swedish Licensing Act
of 1855." The principal features of this are as
follows :

First. The Act abolishes domestic stills.

Second. It takes away the right theretofore
existing of all persons to sell spirits in quantities
of one kan (three-fifths of a gallon) and upwards. No sale can be made of less than eight
and three-fifths gallons without license.

Third. The parochial authorities or the town
councils fix, annually, the number of retail spirit-
shops and public-houses, subject to approval by
the Governor of the Province.

Fourth. There are only two classes of licenses: one for shops to sell in quantities not
less than half a kan (three-tenths of a gallon),
not to be drunk on the premises ; and the other
to public-houses (including restaurants) for
quantities however small, and with liberty to be
drunk on the premises.

Fifth. The license tax to be paid by the
store retailers is equivalent to 6d., and that by
the publicans to 9d. a gallon.

10

Sixth. There being no *minimum* fixed for the number of licenses, it is, in effect, a "local option" act.

Seventh. The licenses granted are to be sold by auction, for a term of three years, to those who undertake to pay the prescribed tax on the greatest number of kans of spirits, irrespective of their actual sales. There is also a provision that, with certain guarantees, and subject to the approval of the Governor of the Province, in case a company is formed to take the whole number of public-house licenses, the town authorities may dispose of the same to them without an auction.

"One result of the passing of this Act was the reduction of the number of distilleries from 44,000 in 1850 to 4,500, and, with the aid of auxiliary legislation, to 457 in 1869, and a reduction of the annual product from 26,000,000 to 6,900,000 gallons. All testimony concurs, also, that the effect on intemperance in the country districts was immediate and most remarkable." *

As already stated, the Act allowed of local prohibition; and under it the traffic in spirits was not licensed at all in certain parishes, and greatly restricted in others.

---

* Balfour's Letter to Gladstone, p. 12.

Mr. Balfour, in his recent letter to Mr. Gladstone, tells us that " so vigorously have the people outside of towns used their permission to limit and prohibit, that among three and a half millions of people (more than twice the population of Massachusetts) there are only 450 places for the sale of spirits.

Bailie Lewis gives us this bright picture of a parish in which he spent several days, the area of which was twenty-four by twelve miles :

" In the clergyman of the Lutheran Church we found a man of great intellect and large sympathies, and who wielded immense influence among his parishioners in the commune. In his parish—where we found sobriety, morality, and social order prevailing in a high degree—there was only one bran-vin (spirit) shop. The clergyman told us that there was a population of 7,000 persons, and with the exception of one man (somewhat weak in intellect) every adult, he said, could read and write. I took a walk of several miles through this model parish in the twilight of a Sunday evening, and the quiet and order that prevailed were most refreshing, while the voice of praise which ascended from the family altar of the peasant recalled to my recollection the early memories of a Scottish Sabbath. In the parish immediately adjoining, there resided one of the largest distillers in Sweden, who possessed an immense amount of political influence in the district and in the commune. Here the licensed grog-shops were at a maximum, and here we found drunkenness, demoralization and poverty obtruding themselves in a most offensive form."

And he well adds :

" *The social condition of Sweden, as in Scotland, England, and Ireland, and indeed everywhere else, proves that just in proportion as you limit the number of houses for the sale of intoxicating liquors, you improve the morality and social well-being of the district ;* and, in like manner, as you multiply the facilities for drinking, you increase drunkenness, with its never-failing attendants of crime, beggary, and irreligion."

GOTHENBURG.

While the application of permissive prohibition . produced remarkable results in the country districts where it was tried, and while even the substitution of restricted license for free trade in other districts and in the towns produced a very sensible amelioration, the condition of things remained deplorable in the city of Gothenburg. The second city in Sweden, with a population in 1864 of 42,433 (in 1874 of 58,307), a seaport, and largely a commercial town, with many Scotch and English merchants, it was largely under the blight and curse of the drink traffic. Mr. Balfour, in the letter to which we have referred, after alluding to some details of its wretchedness, and to the " dead

letter " of the license law as there administered,
sums it up in a single sentence :

" Competent persons testify that at that time, in
almost no community were brutish coarseness or
deep poverty more common than in Gothenburg."

In 1864, a committee of its Town Council
was appointed to inquire into the causes of its
increasing pauperism and degradation.   And
here let it be noted that if education were the
panacea for social misery which some philosophers maintain, Gothenburg should have been
a Paradise.   With a system of compulsory
education by the State, of children between the
ages of seven and fourteen, with supplemental
schools for the children of the poor under seven,
supported by private philanthropy, with excellent private schools for the prosperous classes,
all taught with the thoroughness of European
drill, and with technical schools for the practical
training of lads in the various branches of
skilled industry ; so that the total attendance
upon her various schools is more than a sixth
of her whole population ;—the verdict of an
intelligent observer is justified, that " Gothenburg is one of the best educated towns in the
world."

Such, also, is the testimony of Mr. Balfour,
who, after alluding to " the universal education

of its people, and the excellent system of religious teaching," says :

" Neither the spread of education, nor the influence of religious observances, which are so much relied upon in England for the cure of our intemperance, were found to have that effect in Sweden, and that, while these were, doubtless, important and indispensable, yet other means were absolutely essential for bringing about this reformation."

But to return. The Town Council easily found that intemperance was the chief factor in the production of their debasing pauperism. No *town* in Sweden had ever adopted prohibition ; and the Council of Gothenburg dreamed not of attempting such heroic treatment of their great evil. But their convictions culminated in this proposition :

" That public-houses should no longer be conducted by individuals for the sake of profit, but by an association, which should neither bring individual profit to the persons so associated, nor to the persons who should manage the different establishments."

This may be considered the germinal principle of the Gothenburg system, and we are now prepared to look at its methods, its machinery, and its results.

HISTORY OF THE SYSTEM.

Gothenburg, perhaps owing to the large admixture of English and Scotch blood in its business life, has never wanted for public-spirited, enterprising, and intelligent philanthropists. And when the conviction had entered the public mind that the drink traffic was so abnormal in its nature that it must be treated in a manner exactly contrary to all other traffic, and the stimulus of personal gain from its extension carefully eliminated, there were not wanting some of the most trusted men of influence and of high commercial standing to undertake the new management. A company (Swedish — Bolag) of such men was accordingly soon formed, with the following avowed as leading objects :

First. To reduce the number of public-houses.

Second. To improve their condition as to light, ventilation, cleanliness, etc.

Third. To make public-houses eating-houses, where warm, cooked food should be procurable at moderate prices.

Fourth. To refuse sale of spirits on credit or pledge.

Fifth. To employ as managers respectable persons who should derive no profit from the sale of spirits, but should be entitled to profits from sale of food and other refreshments, including malt liquors.

Sixth. To secure strict supervision of all
public-houses by inspectors of their own in addition to the police.

Seventh. To pay to the town treasury all the
net profits of sales of spirits.

The better to enable them to effect these objects, a charter was granted them by the Government, and they commenced operations in
1865. It is but fair to say here that the company seem, in the main, thus far to have steadily
pursued the objects marked out at their formation.

It will be recollected, that by the last provision stated above in the summary of the License
Act of 1855, the Town Council were empowered
to dispose of all the licenses they intended to
grant for the sale of spirits to be consumed on
the premises to su h a company. In 1865,
when this company began to operate, there
were in existence sixty-one of such licenses at the
ultimate disposal of the Town Council, besides
seven licenses held under certain vested ri h s,
over which the authorities had no control. But
of these sixty-one disposable licenses only forty-
three were in the immediate disposition of the
Council, the remainder not expiring until the
end of two years. The forty-three licenses
were immediately transferred to the Bolag,
as the company was called. Of these, seven-

teen were extinguished, so there was at once
a diminution of more than a third.* Ultimately the Bolag came into possession of
the whole sixty-one; and their report, 1st
March, 1875, shows that of these, twenty-five
were used for public-houses; nine were transferred to restaurants, for which the company
receive yearly payments; seven were used for
retail shops for sale not to be drunk on the
premises; and twenty were extinguished. It
is explained that the seven shops were opened
to "draw off customers from badly-conducted
retail shops of private individuals;" but it is
admitted that the competition proved a failure.

As has been observed, the Grocer's Licenses
continued to be held by private individuals.
These were regarded as "stumbling-blocks" in
the way of further progress; and in October,
1874, such further legislation was had as permitted the acquisition of these by the Bolag.
As the result thereof, on the 1st of January,
1875, the Town Council transferred to them the
Grocer's Retail Licenses, 20 in number (gradually
reduced by the action of the Council from 58,
the number in 1865). They thus acquired a

---

*I here follow the authority of Mr. Balfour. Both Bailie
Lewis and *McMillan's Magazine* (February, 1872) give the
number of licenses then acquired as only *forty*, which gives a
larger per cent. of reduction.

10*

pretty complete monopoly of the retail spirit
trade. Of these 20, they suppressed seven
altogether, and transferred the remaining 13,
for annual payments, to private wine merchants *as is said*, "exclusively for the sale of
the higher class of spirits and liqueurs not in
ordinary use by the working classes."

It will not be overlooked that we have been
dealing entirely with the trade in distilled spirits.
The common Swedish liquor is called " Bran-
vin," and is obtained by distillation from potatoes
and grains; resembling whisky. The distinction
between the habits of the common people and
the wealthier class, of whom a considerable
portion are foreigners, seems more marked than
can easily be appreciated by an American ; and
it has been supposed that the consumption of
malt liquors was too insignificant in amount,
and too harmless in result, to require that such
liquors should be included amongst those
against which legislation has been invoked. It
is *claimed* that the beer actually sold is milder
than its English prototype. But it is clear that
with the increasing consumption of beer, and
with closer observation of its effects and of its
disguises, it must soon take its place under the
law and in the general judgment with other intoxicants. In 1873, Bailie Lewis tells us that
he "found almost all the advocates of the

Gothenburg system of the opinion that ale, beer, and porter were unintoxicating," although he found from personal observation incontestable proof to the contrary; and he dismisses the subject by saying :

" Forty years ago, such assertions might have been listened to with becoming gravity; but in view of the parliamentary evidence on the beer bill, and the daily experience of every beer-shop in England, the discussion of such a proposition, however needful in Gothenburg, is altogether superfluous and out of place in the columns of our Scotch or English newspapers."

But let us on this point rather quote from pronounced friends of the Gothenburg system. Mr. David Carnegie, of Scotland, the author of a paper on " The Licensing Laws of Sweden," read before the Philosophical Society of Glasgow in 1872, seems to have been earliest and most earnest in pressing this scheme upon the attention of the British public. Mr. Carnegie is one of the proprietors of the Gothenburg brewery; and the porter sold therefrom bears his name as its brand. In the course of a reply to Bailie Lewis, delivered in Queen Street Hall, Edinburgh, July 14, 1873, he says:

" No traveler could land in Sweden without Gothenburg porter being brought under his notice ; but he could safely assert that the Swedes did not get drunk on that beverage. It was there the general belief

that porter rather promoted temperance by diminishing the consumption of spirits."

This was received with derisive laughter by
his Scotch audience ; but notice the significant
statement which immediately follows :

"Bailie Lewis said there were 400 beer-shops in
Gothenburg ; but he omitted to mention that 300 *of
these would probably be closed next year, in consequence
of a change in the law, placing malt liquors under the
same regulations as wine.*"

So it seems that way of "promoting temperance" has been a little overdone in the opinion
of the Gothenburgers themselves ! I will do
Mr. Carnegie the justice to add the next paragraph :

"Should the time ever come when the habits of
the Swedes are so changed that it could fairly be
maintained that the Gothenburg brewery promoted
drunkenness, he, for one, would have nothing more to
do with it."

The change in the law foretold by Mr. Carnegie seems to have been effected ; for Mr.
Balfour, in the letter before alluded to, describing the state of things in the autumn of 1875,
says there are only " 115 beer licenses held by
private persons "in Gothenburg ; and friendly
as he is to the "system," he confesses "that it
may be an omission that the Swedish law does

not deal with strong beer and porter in the same manner that it does with spirits. It is plain that beer and porter may be made to contain a larger quantity of alcohol, and thus be powerful intoxicants; and if they were so manufactured, the Gothenburg system would fail to embrace *all* alcoholic liquors, which it ought to do." And he adds in a foot note :

" The beer commonly sold in public-houses in Liverpool to workingmen, contains about 8 per cent. of alcohol. That is to say, a tumblerful of this beer contains nearly as much alcohol as an ordinary wine-glassful of brandy."

Turning back again to the Bolag, we observe that the active management of the company is in the hands of a Board of ten Directors, half of whom are elected by the shareholders at their annual meeting, and these then proceed to choose five persons to fill up their body. Any inhabitant is eligible, whether a shareholder or not; and some time ago it was said that there had been no instance of a person elected refusing to serve. The Directors determine the number of places to be kept open and their localities, and select the superintendents. These agree to furnish eatables and cooked food when called for; to sell spirits and wines for cash only; to keep and render an exact account weekly of such sales; to derive no profit therefrom; to procure such spirits from the company alone; to sell at their prices, and to derive their own profit only from the sale of malt liquors, refreshments, and food; and they furnish security for the performance of these obligations. It is stated that the profits derived by a majority of the employees of the company are so insufficient that they are induced to remain by annual subsidies, varying in amount, paid by the company out of their receipts. These superintendents, to whom the trade is farmed out, are men; but women are largely employed as the tenders of the establishments.

Some criticism has been expended upon certain details in the operations of the Bolag, such as the large allowance of 3½ per cent. for breakage and wastage made to the superintendents; but I pass over all such matters as not pertaining to the essentials of the system, and as mere errors of administration, which experience may correct; and I do not doubt the honest intention of the company to carry out its system according to its own judgment and convictions.

We may perhaps get a more vivid idea of this system by looking at it in actual operation.

PICTURES AT SIGHT.

We therefore give two pen - photographs. The first from a friendly hand in *Macmillan's Magazine* for February, 1872.

"It is a market-day; so we may count upon finding a brisk trade going on at Värdhus, No. 9, which abuts upon the market-place, and is the favorite rendezvous of the market folk. Pushing through a swinging door a few steps above the level of the street, we come at once into a large and tolerably lofty L shaped room. The sanded floor is scrupulously clean, and dotted here and there with small wooden tables. Across one end runs the bar, behind which stands the manager in snowy shirt-sleeves and apron, backed by a row of glittering wine bottles, labelled port, sherry, champagne, and punch, ranged on shelves that climb almost to the ceiling. The first glance at the bar is enough to remind us that we are not in London. Instead of the familiar row of upright handles, the center of the counter is occupied by a small army of what may be called large-sized liquor glasses, all brimming full of pure, colorless brän-vin. The flanks of this fiery army are covered by two plates, piled with broken pieces of hard rye biscuit-bread, and a powerful reserve force of spirit decanters is massed in the rear. Not without good reason, too, these preparations; for the army of glasses is being constantly attacked. One moment it is a young, smooth-cheeked wagoner, with a whip in hand; another, a sailor from the port; now a mechanic, with his tool-bag; and now a probable

tradesman, in black cloth, marches up to the bar,
tosses off one of the glasses of whisky, puts a morsel
of bread into his mouth, and a very few small bronze
coins upon the counter, and is gone again in a twink-
ling without a word to anybody. How much is that
stuff in the glass? The tariff posted on the wall
there will tell us. Three farthings! Well, at any rate
an occasional dram of the company's ordinary brän-
vin will not be ruinous to the purse ; and, to judge
from the taste, it is well-rectified, unflavored spirit,
containing about 50 per cent. of alcohol. . . . .

" But it is high time to take a look at what is going
on in the other parts of the room, away from the
bar. . . . . All the little tables are occupied by men
or women sitting in twos or threes at their morning
meal, ... served by brisk, quietly - dressed wai-
tresses, under the direction and eye of the manager's
wife, who superintends the serving out of the eatables and the cups that cheer, while her husband
watchfully dispenses the glasses that tend to inebriate. There is a low hum of conversation in the
room, but no boisterous talking or swearing or horse-
play. . . . . Still, just as it is a matter of common
experience that the quiet man at table often has the
knack of playing a highly effective knife and fork, so
the orderly customers of the Gothenburg Company
manage to consume a very respectable sum total of
alcoholic liquor in the course of the year."

Bailie Lewis looked with somewhat sadder
eyes ; and this is what he saw :

" In the market-place there were no fewer than
three of these grog-shops, one of them having a front-

age of upwards of 50 feet. The mode of conducting the business appeared to me to be one of the most deadly description. In the first house which I visited, there were four active young women in addition to the wife of the man charged with the management of the place, all as busily employed as possible, every moment being required to supply the wants of their numerous customers. With the view of economizing time, a long row of glasses was arranged along the counter, filled with bran-vin, and which were every minute being emptied and as summarily replenished. In numerous instances, not a word was spoken. The money was laid on the counter, the glass drained, and, wiping his mouth, the customer departed in silence. While a brisk counter trade was thus being prosecuted with a promptitude and energy unsurpassed in any liquor-shop in Edinburgh, numbers were to be found in groups of two, three, and upwards, drinking at tables in different parts of the establishment. The quantity of liquor being sold and consumed in these public-houses was, indeed, startling. In the course of the seventeen minutes which I remained in the place referred to, no fewer than eighty-three persons were supplied with branvin ; and, when I left, nineteen others were being supplied. When about to leave, I observed a partially-sunk flat in the back part of the premises entering from a back street, and where an equal number, which I could not accurately estimate, appeared to be entering and getting supplied. This back entrance seemed to be a convenient adjunct, as I subsequently observed that those who entered from the back street seemed to be in more reduced circumstances, and less

presentable in their appearance. To show how successfully bran-vin competes with more nutritious and
less objectionable beverages, there were, out of the
eighty-three persons referred to, only four who partook of coffee, and all of them had it accompanied
by glasses of bran-vin. So astonished was I at the
number who frequented this one house, and keeping
in view that it was market-day, I paid it another visit
on the following Sunday evening, and found that no
fewer than 102 persons entered one door in the space
of twenty-five minutes."

Again, he says :

"After personal and minute observation on the
spot, I confess that I found the grog-shops of Gothenburg conducted with as great energy and efficiency
as those of Edinburgh. . . . . True, the law provides
that the premises shall be well lighted and ventilated,
and that no liquor shall be sold to persons who are
drunk. These provisions are not peculiar to Gothenburg. They are the statutory requirements of every
town in Scotland, and, generally speaking, so far as
Edinburgh is concerned, they are as well attended to.
. . . . Such persons are supplied by the company's
servants in Gothenburg. Of this I saw several
melancholy instances. One of them I may refer to.
On a Sabbath evening I saw one of the most wretched
victims I have ever witnessed. . . . . He stood before one of the company's grog-shops imploring those
who came out for money. Two well-dressed young
lads appeared to commiserate the unhappy object,
and gave him a few ore. The poor drink-cursed vic-

tim took hold of the rail and dragged himself up the few steps into one of those 'model public-houses'— the one so beautifully described in *Macmillan's Magazine.* I remarked to a friend, ' There goes the poor wretch for yet another glass ; surely he will not be supplied,' I added, remarking that I did not believe there were a score of publicans in Edinburgh who would give him more liquor. The 'customer' laid his six ore upon the counter, was supplied with his debasing drug, and soon afterwards returned to the street, and was again begging before the door, when I turned away with a feeling of unutterable disappointment and disgust."

Having included in Bailie Lewis' pictures these Sabbath-sights, we give "the system" the benefit of a statement we find in Mr. Balfour's letter :

" The company do not permit the sale of spirits in their premises on Sundays, nor after 6 P.M. on Saturdays ; but persons are allowed to take the customary dram before eating."

There is reason to fear (if the practice conforms to the theory) that some persons in Gothenburg must require " meals at all hours " on Sunday.

RESULTS.

We are now prepared to look at statistical results.

And first, there can be no doubt, if we look at the matter purely as a financial operation, the system "pays well" to the town of Gothen-burg. Before its inauguration, the town re-ceived annually from the sale of licenses about £7,000; the sum paid by the Bolag in 1874, was over £14,000; and the company having now acquired the Grocers' Licenses, it is estimated that the profits of last year (1875), which are payable to the town, will reach the sum of £35,000, or about one hundred and seventy-five thousand dollars. This is equivalent to a revenue of one million of dollars for the popu-lation of the city of Boston. And when we consider that this is derived from the *profits* on the sale mainly of the cheapest whisky, we get some idea of the immense consumption. There are but few, we trust, who will hesitate to join in the mild exhortation of Mr. Balfour to the Bolag:

"It is to be hoped that this large increase to the income of the town may be followed by a further diminution of the hours for selling spirits, and by a further curtailment of the inducements to managers to dispose of them."

I regret that I have no means of comparing the actual total sales of spirits in Gothenburg during the successive years of the Bolag administration with that of prior years. One thing is evident. It is admitted that the consumption is still enormous. It seems to be admitted that the *total* consumption of spirits (exclusive of malt liquors) in 1873, would average over six gallons for every man, woman, and child, if calculated upon the basis of the resident population of Gothenburg. It is but fair to say that Mr. Carnegie suggests that a considerable allowance should be made for the influx of rural visitors from a large area of practical prohibition.

As to the statistics of drunkenness, I append the table of arrests for this cause, for several years, together with the population, and the calculated per cent. the former is of the latter:

Years.	Population.	Drunkards.	Per cent.
1855	30,804	3,431	11.14
1856	33,424	2,658	7.95
1864	42,433	2,161	5.09
1865	45,750	2,070	4.52
1866	47,332	1,424	3.01
1867	47,898	1,375	2.87
1872*	55,986	1,581	2.82
1873	56,909	1,827	3.21
1874	58,307	2,234†	3.83

* I am not able to give the population of the intermediate

† Of this large number *only five were females.* All the authorities speak of the sobriety of the women of Sweden.

The table is instructive.

It will first be noticed that consequent upon the passage of the General Law of 1855, to which we have alluded, and the improvement in the tone of temperance sentiment which gave birth to it, there began to be a considerable reduction in cases even in Gothenburg; so that, in 1864, the absolute number had decreased more than one-third, and the percentage more than one-half.

It will be remembered that the operation of the Bolag commenced in October, 1865. The following year witnessed an immediate reduction of the cases of drunkenness of nearly one-third, and of the per cent. a little over one-third. A slight reduction continues to be shown for the two succeeding years, and then a standstill, followed by an upward tendency, balanced, however, by the increase of population, until, in the years 1873 and 1874, there is witnessed a large absolute and relative increase. This reaction is so clearly shown, that the fact is admitted, but what *Macmillan* (October, '73) calls

---

years. Some increase by enlarged area took place in 1868. The arrests during the omitted years did not vary much; they were respectively 1,320, 1,445, 1,416, and 1,531. I may add here that the table stops at 1874, because, as the British Under-Secretary of State remarked in the House of Commons as late as March 13, 1877, it is "the last year for which figures were obtainable."

"ugly and uncomfortable statistics," are explained away as due to the naughty grocers,
and not to the Bolag, and to the "good times."
As to the last, whatever may be the case in
Sweden, the Yankee believes in good times as
the normal condition of things ; and no invention which will not work in such seasons can
suit his demands. Nor is it seen how a little
exhilaration in the labor market can greatly affect the amount of drinking where the popular
beverage can be had for three farthings. As to
the suggestion that it is the grocers and not
the Bolag publicans who manufacture drunkards, it is purely hypothetical, and we must wait
for time to test it. The law vesting the complete monopoly in the hands of the Bolag, went
into operation October, 1874. Its friends say
(vide *Macmillan's Magazine*) :

" Here, then, at last, the system is about to have for
the first time a complete and decisive trial ; . . . . it
must be prepared to accept the responsibility as well
as the advantages of the new position of affairs, and
finally stand or fall on its own merits."

Mr. Balfour's pamphlet letter addressed by
permission to Mr. Gladstone, to which I have
frequently alluded, bears date January, 1876,
and embodies the result of his inquiries and observations in the autumn of 1875. In connec-

tion with the admission of the gradual increase of arrests for drunkenness in recent years, he has merely to express the hope "that when this further control has had time to produce its results, the arrests for drunkenness will again show a great falling off."

These hopes do not seem likely to be realized. In a very recent discussion in the House of Commons, upon a resolution offered by Mr. Chamberlain, M. P. for Birmingham, empowering Town Councils to become the proprietors and regulators of the liquor traffic after the manner of the Bolag, the Gothenburg experiment naturally came under discussion. Sir H. Selwin Ibbetson, the Under-Secretary of the Home Department, took occasion to say that he had that day received a letter from the British Consul at Gothenburg, "in which he said that the company had a good object in view when they established their system; but that it appeared to have proved a failure, owing to the way in which it had been carried out; that it was at present only a money-making concern, realizing a considerable amount annually; that drunkenness was great even among the better orders in Gothenburg, and that the lower orders looked upon the retail-shops as their privileged places of resort. That statement, accompanied by some figures which had been sent over by the same gentleman, furnished, he thought, very powerful arguments against the adoption of the plan which the House was invited to sanction." Instead of reproducing these figures I give an extract from the Gothenburg *Hændel's Tidning*, March 20, 1877. After calling the Consul's figures "misleading," it goes on to say:

" The figures for the year 1st October, 1875, to 1st October, 1876, which we lately gave, show a total sale of brän-vin 614,608 kans; of which on 'selling off' shops 357,445; therefore in public-houses 257,163 kans, or 11,000 more than the former year. The sale of spirits of higher class was 52,788 kans, or 1,000 more than last year." *

Then follows the old story of better times and rural visitors, as an explanation. But the editor is compelled to confess that "*doubtless it has been very difficult for Mr. Chamberlain to prove the benefit of the system by statistical figures.*"

COMPARISONS.

The claims of the Gothenburg system having been specially urged upon the attention of the citizens of Edinburgh, Bailie Lewis has shown that the average consumption of spirits in Scotland is only about two gallons for each person per annum; while in Gothenburg, the sale is

---

* This aggregates a total sale of over 400,000 gallons.

now nearer seven than six gallons *per capita* of the resident population.

The arrests for drunkenness in Edinburgh— including therein, for the sake of fairness, the seaport of Leith, therewith closely connected, and aggregating a population of 245,800—were in 1872 but 2,913, against 1,581 in Gothenburg, with a population of 55,986; whereas in the ratio of population Edinburgh should have had 6,944.

An intelligent correspondent of the *Alliance News* from Birmingham shows that the annual consumption of spirits there is only about two and a half gallons *per capita ;* and that while the arrests in 1875 for drunkenness in Gothenburg were one in about twenty-six of the population, in Birmingham they were only about one in one hundred and twenty.

And in the recent speech of Sir H. Selwin Ibbetson, to which we have referred, he says, in replying to Mr. Chamberlain :

"At least sixty-one towns out of seventy-one referred to in tables which the honorable member had himself drawn up, showed a less number of convictions as compared with the population than was the case at Gothenburg. Out of the seventy-one towns there were, perhaps, only three that compared very unfavorably with Gothenburg—namely, Tynemouth, South Shields, and Liverpool."

OBJECTIONS.

Having considered the nature and results of this scheme, let us now consider the weighty objections to it. And I shall pause to consider only those which *are* weighty and touch principles.

First. Its financial success is a great danger. *How* dangerous it is to connect revenue with the vices of a people only those can feel who have attentively watched the debates in the English Parliament when the question of encouraging or checking the opium trade in China or India was under discussion, or when some scheme was broached which might affect the twenty-six millions of pounds sterling which Mr. Lowe, the late Chancellor of the Exchequer, stated was derived by the Government from the liquor traffic.* And when this tribute is

---

* "Alcohol and the Exchequer." "That very revolution of fiscal policy which has contributed so much to the prosperity of the working classes has contributed, in fact, just as signally to the importance of the licensed victuallers. Their power is derived from their selling to the classes which have votes an article enormously consumed by them, under circumstances which enable the seller to influence the mind of the customer at moments of peculiar impressionableness and susceptibility. It seems startling that the modern republic established in 1867 proves to be guided from the bar and the public-house parlor, just as was the Commonwealth of Cromwell from the pulpit of Hugh Peters ; but one can not reason away the facts. Is, then, this enormous and increasing influence to be fortified by a conviction in the minds of states-

brought, as it were, to the very doors of the citizen by diminishing so apparently his municipal taxes, it is a bribe for active support, or, at least, passive endurance of evil, which is likely to greatly influence the average man. We are not surprised to learn that the intelligent workingmen of Gothenburg already realize this. Bailie Lewis tells us that upon putting the question to a large meeting of them, whether they would advise the introduction of " the scheme" into Scotland, the reply of " Nay," " Nay," came from all parts of the house ; and the reason afterward assigned was " that since the profits were paid over to the community large numbers of the trading and better classes did not care to have the public-houses put down, because now they were largely relieved from paying taxes."

The danger lies in the fact that, while the reduction in the tax bill is immediate and palpable, the loss to the whole community from wasteful expenditure, and the steady drain upon the physical, mental, and moral forces of

---

men that the most embarrassing financial difficulties may at any moment be occasioned by a diminution in the sale of strong liquor? One can not look without dismay at the prospect of the Chancellor of the Exchequer being mixed up with that quarrel between the publicans and the teetotalers at which the Home Secretary has burned his fingers."—*Pall Mall Gazette, April 10, 1875.*

the people, impairing the power of production, though fatally sure, is not so directly seen or felt.

Second. The drinking habits of men are not to be repressed or curtailed by removing the distasteful material or moral accessories of the dram-shop. Let the business create its own atmosphere—do not artificially purify it ; rather let its natural loathsomeness repel the yet young and pure. To make the grog-shop "well-lighted, roomy, airy, and clean ;" to allure with the security of pure liquors (*i. e.*, unadulterated poison); to furnish "respectable" bartenders and even "comely young women ;" to place the bar by the side of the family table, and to throw around the whole the double sanction of the State and a business corporation of the first citizens of the town—all this is but to aid the devil in the recruiting of his army of drunkards and to supply him with the choicest of stock.* No ! If the grog-shop is to exist, let it not become a reputable *institution*, nor even a commercial adventure in which the State

---

* A "Master Mariner" who recently visited Gothenburg, writes under date December 26, 1876 : "A gentleman told me that wherever a number of men are employed, the company open a drink-shop. His own words were : 'I have more trouble with my laborers than I ever had ; for now that the houses are cleaner, and the rooms more cosy and comfortable than they were in the old places, the men frequent them more.' "

(to use an expression of Cardinal Manning) is a "sleeping partner," but rather let it stand, like the brothel, a horrible excrescence upon our civilization, unconnected with any legitimate business or honest trade, unsecured by any police certificates, visited even by its votaries with a sense of degradation and conscious guilt.

Third. The eminent respectability of the Gothenburg Bolag is abundantly vouched for; and I have credited them with honest intentions to serve the public good. It is apparent that without these essential conditions no tolerance could be given in any community to this, even as a provisional scheme. In a town where drinking was so general as to justify the remark that "in almost no community were brutish coarseness or deep poverty more common," and where even now the consumption of spirits is greater *per capita* than in most other countries, it may be possible to find public-spirited persons who will undertake the task of running improved tippling-shops in the interest of temperance. But imagine a company incorporated to do this in Boston or New York! Let the reader select ten men of "property and standing," who are reputed to have "conservative" views upon the liquor question—ministers who believe in "moderate drinking," governors who veto stringent legislation, magnates of the ˉexchange who pride themselves upon their "public spirit" and their freedom from "fanaticism"—and ask them if they will organize as "The Grand Monopoly for the Retail Sale of Liquors," and so run the public-houses, the saloons, and the dram-shops generally, decently and discreetly, in the interest of public order, and of a "wisely-calculated temperance!" Would it be taken as a grim joke or a patent insult?

Fourth. And this leads us to a final and fatal objection to this scheme. It is absolutely repugnant to the moral sense and the enlightened conscience of our community. Even the better portion of the friends of license would revolt at such active support of, and such close connection with, so disgusting a traffic; while to men who view it as a crime in itself, as well as the prolific cause of crimes, such assumption of responsibility would be morally impossible. And those who do not feel this ethical difficulty must, at least, see that so long as the great mass of the temperance people do, a scheme which at once arrays itself against the sentiment and conscience of so large a part of the community, while it has to offer battle to one of the largest and the most powerfully-organized of the moneyed interests of the country, is one of the most impracticable of all projects.

CONCLUSIONS.

The lessons taught us from this survey we are now prepared to sum up as follows :

First. In the rural districts of Sweden, as elsewhere, entire or virtual prohibition of the liquor traffic has exhibited the happiest results.

Second. So far as the Gothenburg scheme has practically reduced the number of licensed places, it has reduced drunkenness and its sequences.

Third. When the reduction of licenses ceased, not only did all progressive amelioration cease, but, according to our latest statistics, the scheme is not able to prevent a slight progressive deterioration.

Fourth. Whether the explanation of its friends as to the cause of this is to be accepted, and whether the scheme will show a better record for the future, is a problem which is purely tentative, with the latest indications decidedly adverse.

Fifth. If any apparent improvement should again be shown, it must be greatly overbalanced by the permanent evils of the system, among which are especially prominent the subsidizing the public favor for the dram-shop by liberal contributions to the public revenue, and the deadening of the public conscience by its adoption as an institution of the State, bulwarked by the law, and sanctioned and recommended by "the respectability" which undertakes to manage it.

Sixth. The scheme being wholly opposed to the moral sentiment of our people, its administration here would be impracticable and its adoption impossible.

11*

CHAPTER XIX.

THE MILDER ALCOHOLICS.

MORE than a generation ago the question as
to the personal duty of the friends of the temperance reform and the policy to be pursued
by their organizations in regard to wines and
fermented liquors, was a subject of earnest consideration. The final result of the debate was
a settled and well-nigh unanimous conviction
that no distinction could be made in favor of
one class of alcoholic intoxicants over another.
As a question either of duty or of policy, that
conviction among the active workers in any
field of temperance effort has never been disturbed.

But as I address this discussion of the liquor
problem to a wider range of readers than those
technically known as temperance men, I shall
not rest the question whether the laws should
make any distinction between distilled and
fermented liquors upon opinion. Legislation
should follow the inductive method, and be
based not on theory, but on carefully-observed
facts ; and in this chapter, as elsewhere, I shall
appeal to history, to statistics, and to the

generalizations of thoroughly competent experts.

Although we are not treating the subject physiologically, but practically, it may be well to bear in mind, before we proceed to our practical inquiries, the elementary truth so well stated by Professor Miller, of Edinburgh, in his work on " Alcohol, its Place and Power ":

" All the varieties of spirits, wines, and malt liquors are the same as to their intoxicating quality : that invariably depends upon the presence of alcohol. . . . . A man is apt to draw a broad distinction, greatly in his own favor, between himself drinking beer and another drinking brandy as a daily habit ; but the truth is, that both are drinking the same thing, only in different guise and dilution ; chemically and practically there is much the same difference as between one who drinks spirits ' neat' and another who drinks his allowance of the same thing largely ' watered.' The one drinks alcohol slightly diluted ; the other drinks alcohol much diluted and somewhat modified by flavor, but both are drinking alcohol."

Or, as Dr. Richardson puts it in his " Diseases of Modern Life " (p. 210) : " In whatever form it enters, whether as spirits, wine, or ale, matters little when its specific influence is kept steadily in view."

It may also be well to recall the tables showing

the percentage of alcohol in different beverages. I cite certain of those given by Dr. Bowditch, in the Third Annual Report of the State Board of Health of Massachusetts, and credited to "Brande's Chemistry," except the American liquors, which were analyzed by Professor Wood, of the Harvard Medical School. It is well to notice the remarkable variations in some of the foreign wines. I arrange in the order of strength.

London small beer, ...	1.28 per cent.
London porter, ...	4.20 "
Boston lager, ...	5½ to 6. "
British cider, ...	5.21 to 9.87 "
London ale, ...	6.20 "
Brown stout, ...	6.80 "
Rhenish wine, ...	7.00 to 7.58 "
Burton's ale, ...	8.88 "
Vin ordinaire, ...	8.99 "
Champagne, ...	11.30 to 13.80 "
Burgundy, ...	12.16 to 16.60 "
Sherry, ...	13.98 to 23.86 "
Madeira, ...	14.09 to 24.42 "
Port wine, . , ...	14.27 to 25.83 "
American whisky ("worst"),	44.50 "
Kentucky Bourbon whisky, .	51.00 "
Brandy, . , , ...	53.40 "
Rum, ...	53.68 "
Gin, ...	57.60 "

WINES.

In regard to wines, the adulterations in the factitious liquors sold under this name in the

United States are somewhat fearful, and the reinforcements by distilled spirits still more so ; but if it were possible to procure them in their native purity, the evidence as to their evil, social tendency is abundant. It is clearly established that, in wine-producing countries the beverage leads to criminal intoxication, and so far from being a preventative, is a preparative to indulgence in the stronger liquors.

The Count de Montalembert, member of the Academy of Natural Sciences, said in the National Assembly of France in 1850 : " Where there is a wine-shop, there are the elements of disease, and the frightful source of all that is at enmity with the interests of the workman."

Of Switzerland, Dr. Guillaume, on behalf of the National Society for Penitentiary Reform, reports to the International Congress at London in 1872 :

" The number of criminals, small and great, abandoned to drunkenness, or who, at the moment of the Criminal Act, were under the dominion of drink, is by no means inconsiderable, forming, at least, fifty per cent. of the total number of crimes committed by men ; and this proportion is even higher among the correctionals. . . . . The number of misdemeanors occasioned by *wine* is considerable in some of the cantons, and the liberty of the *wine traffic*, pushed to its utmost limits, causes, in a number of these cantons (Neufchatel, for example), *the commission of one crime as the effect* of wine to every one hundred and four persons of the population," (p. 95).

So of Italy. When Mr. Delavan was in Rome some years ago, Cardinal Acton, then Supreme Judge, assured him that nearly all the crime in Rome " originated in the use of wine." And he pointed out to Mr. Delavan a part of the city which brought to his mind the " Five Points" of New York ; and upon visiting which Mr. Delavan made this record :

" I saw men, women, and children sitting in rows, swilling away at wine, making up in quantity what was wanting in strength ; and such was the character of the inmates of those dens, that my guide urged my immediate departure, as I valued my life."

And Mr. Hillard, of Boston, in his " Six Months in Italy," is compelled to say :

" In regard to temperance, I am inclined to think that the inhabitants of Southern Italy and the wine-making countries generally, enjoy a reputation somewhat beyond their deserts. . . . . If the proportion of cases of stabbing brought to the Roman hospitals, which occur in or near wine-shops, could be known, I have no question that it would furnish a strong fact wherewith to point the exhortations of a temperance lecturer."

And so Recorder Hill, in a paper furnished

for the Social Science Congress at Liverpool in October, 1858, said :

" With regard to the cause of crime in Baden and Bavaria, each of the governors (of State prisons) assured me that it was wine in the one country and beer in the other which filled their jails."

So a French writer on Criminal Statistics in the " Revue d'Economie Chretienne, Paris, 1862," says :

" The abundance of the harvest in 1858 diminished the poverty, and, by consequence, the crimes and offences to which misery impels ; but the abundance of the vintage, on the contrary, multiplied blows and wounds, the quarrels of cabarets, the rebellions, out-rages, and violence towards the police. These facts are found in all analogous circumstances." (Trans. by Dr. Lees in his " Condensed Argument," p. 37).

Did Charles Dickens exaggerate when he wrote :

" The wine-shops are the colleges and chapels of the poor in France. History, morals, politics, juris-prudence, and literature, in iniquitous forms, are all taught in these colleges and chapels, where profes-sors of evil continually deliver those lessons, and where hymns are sung nightly to the demons of de-moralization. In these haunts of the poor, theft is taught as the morality of property, falsehood as speech, and assassination as the justice of the people.

It is in the wine-shop the cabman is taught to think it heroic to shoot the middle-class man who disputes his fare. It is in the wine-shop the workman is taught to admire the man who stabs his faithless mistress. It is in the wine-shop the doom is pronounced of the employer who lowers the pay on the employed. The wine-shops breed, in a physical atmosphere of malaria and a moral pestilence of envy and vengeance, the men of crime and revolution. Hunger is proverbially a bad counselor, but drink is worse."

Can a civilized nation afford, under any theory of liberty, to tolerate such *a common school system of crime ?* For such it is ; if it were only a " college " or a " chapel " for crime, as Dickens calls it, it were more tolerable.

Nor is even the poor comfort left that the drunkenness is wine-drunkenness and the crime wine-crime alone. The mild does not banish, but invite the strong. I find it stated that Paris, *par excellence* the wine city of the world, excels in the consumption of distilled spirits — averaging, in 1863, seven gallons *per capita.* And it is in France that the deadliest of all alcoholics (absinthe) finds its chief consumption. Of this a writer in the London *Telegraph* says :

" The drinking of absinthe threatens to rank with the chief curses of France. Although she holds the first place among wine-growing countries, it is not wine, but absinthe, that, next to coffee, is becoming the favorite drink in her numberless cafés. To unaccustomed palates, the taste of the liquid is absolutely revolting—at once bitter, sickly, nauseous, like some foul decoction of the sick-room. But with constant use, the bitterness and the sickly odor become ambrosial elements. . . . . France, indeed, has more reason to dread absinthe than she has to fear Count Bismarck, and if the German statesman would but annex the villainous liquid, the dictates of patriotism would justify Trochu and Gambetta in thanking him for the service. Since so happy a stroke of robbery lies beyond the power even of the Chancellor, we must hope that some French Father Matthew will rise up to preach a crusade against the insidious destroyer. A victory over 'the devil in liquid form' would be as glorious to France as the defeat of Prince Frederick Charles."

The war with Germany had the effect not only to attract the attention of foreigners, through the correspondents of the press, to the horrible drunkenness of the French armies, but to reveal to the thoughtful statesmen of her own nation the extent of this national vice. In 1872 the Government appointed a "Committee of Inquiry" on the subject of drunkenness. The Secretary (M. Desjardines) in his report says :

" There is one point on which all the members of

the French Assembly thought and felt alike. They knew that, *to restore France to her right position, their moral and physical powers must be given back to her people. Being ambitious to restore the fortunes of the country, they ought also to make up their minds to its regeneration.* To combat a propensity which has long been regarded as venial because it seemed to debase and corrupt only the individual, but the prodigious extension of which has resulted in a menace to society at large and in the temporary humiliation of the country, is a duty incumbent on the men to whom that country has entrusted the task of investigating and remedying its ills."

We take from the *Constitutionnel*, a Paris paper, of the same year, this graphic picture :

"It is unanimously admitted that the habit of drunkenness has increased in France year by year since the beginning of the century. In all directions its increase is remarked, and complaints are made of the disastrous effects which it produces on public health as well as on public morality. The *habitués* of the taverns and the wine-sellers lose all inclination for work; they desert the workshop during several days of the week, and the gains of the other days are entirely devoted to the indulgence of their passion for drink. Family life is entirely neglected, all idea of saving is forever abandoned. Those drunkards who are married and fathers of families take no trouble to satisfy the most urgent wants of their wives and children. The money that should supply the household passes into the hands of the tavern-keeper, and where there might be comfort there is abject poverty and its demoralizing influence. If the wife complains, if she begs for a change of conduct, she is answered by blows, and the children see the terrible sight of the destruction of family ties. Often, indeed, the misconduct of the husband leads to the misconduct of the wife. Despairing of finding any comfort in her home, she seeks for some kind of compensation out of doors. As for the drunkard himself, it is fortunate if he becomes merely idle and neglectful of the most sacred obligations. His moral corruption often goes further. The tavern is a school of vice. It is from there that nearly all criminals emerge, and it is there that the great army of thieves and malefactors finds recruits. This is not all. The increase of drunkenness produces other evils not less fatal than the demoralization of numerous families. It is well known that the habit of drinking ruins the health, that it renders all diseases more dangerous, and is the direct origin of many of them. Observations made in the hospitals on this subject give startling results, and the germ of all these evils is hereditary. The drunkard's children are feeble and sickly, and the deterioration of the populations of the towns and districts in which drunkenness is most common is clearly perceptible. *The French race is deteriorating daily.* It is especially the drunkenness produced by alcohol which exercises a deplorable effect on the public health. The drunkenness caused by wine is less dangerous. *Unhappily the passage from one to the other is rapid. Men begin with wine, soon the palate is palled and asks for stronger excitement.* Alcohol is taken. In forty years the consumption of alcohol has tripled in France.   From 350,000 hectolitres in 1820 it increased to 620,000 in 1850, and to 976,000 in 1868.   These are the amounts on which duty was paid, and to these must be added all that escaped the customs' officers.   In 1869 the quantity taxed in Paris was 130,000 hectolitres. Divided among a population of 1,900,000 souls, this gives something over 6 litres a head, but the division per head is a fiction.   The number of those who participate more or less in the consumption of alcohol is estimated at about 300,000, which gives about 43 litres for each.   In 1839 the average annual consumption per adult was reckoned at 8 litres.   These figures show how rapid the increase has been.   Must we allow it to go on indefinitely?"

Surely the France of to-day feels that she has lessons to learn, and not to teach (except by examples of warning) to others.

Wherever we turn, the same truth as to wine forces itself on our attention.   Rev. I. S. Cochran, for many years a missionary in Persia, says of the people where he lives, that in the wine-making season " the whole village of male adults will be habitually intoxicated for a month or six weeks ; " and he calls " wine-drinking the greatest bane and curse of the people in the wine-making districts."   And the Rev. Mr. Labaree, another missionary in that country, says :

" If I had any sentiments favorable to the moderate

use of wine when I left America, my observations during the seven years I have resided in this paradise of vineyards have convinced me that the principle of total abstinence is the only safeguard against the great social and religious evils that flow from the practice of wine-drinking. . . . . There is scarcely a community to be found where the blighting influences of intemperance are not seen in families distressed and ruined, property squandered, character destroyed, and lives lost."

The fallacy of the wine-cure for intemperance is everywhere exhibited. Whether the culture of the grape makes wine abundant, or unwise legislation facilitates its use, the result is the same. Thus, under the mistaken policy of Mr. Gladstone's "Wine Act," not only were the direct results of the temptation by an enticing beverage deplorable, but it was followed by a large increase in the consumption of distilled spirits.

The same testimony comes from California in our own country. The editor of *The Pacific*, a San Francisco newspaper, who has traveled extensively through the wine regions, writes, under date April 15, 1872, as follows :

" Our impression is that the lowest, slowest, most illiterate, most unimpressible, most unimprovable, if not most vicious population, outside of the great cities, is found in the oldest wine districts of this

State ; and that the use of the product of vineyards has been the most active cause of this condition of the population ; that the increased production and consumption of wine on this coast, in the more recent years, has diminished the use of neither distilled liquors nor lager-bier, but rather increased the demand for both. We never hear of people who forsake liquors and beer for the sake of wine ; but we hear of many who never used an intoxicant till they learned to love wine, and then have abandoned wine for something more stimulating. In a word, we do not believe that wines reform anybody, and we do believe that they beguile many into drinking habits, and finally into drunkenness, who would never have drank a drop but for wine."

A State Convention of Congregational ministers, and delegates from their churches, in San Francisco, October, 1866, denounced the manufacture of wine as destructive to the highest political and religious interests of the Commonwealth. Rev. Dr. Stone, late of Park Street church, Boston, writes:

" The Convention struck a strong blow for the temperance cause, declaring in unequivocal terms against the manufacture and use of wine. This was a point upon which I will confess I had not previously a clear conviction. I had entertained a sort of hope that the manufacture of pure wines, and their introduction into general use, would crowd out the gross strong liquors and diminish intemperance.

I am now fully convinced that this hope was groundless and delusive. It is in evidence that full two-thirds of all the wine manufactured is converted by the manufacturers into brandy. It also appears that in the wine - growing districts intemperance is on the increase, extending even to the youth of both sexes. *There is no way but to take ground against the production of grapes for all such manufacture.* This touches a very large and growing pecuniary interest, and will provoke strenuous opposition, *but we must save this State, if it can be done, from such investment of capital and labor, and from the unavoidable result of drunkenness, profligacy, and crime."*

I close this division with the impressive testimony of a very competent and well-known observer. Says Mr. Nordhoff, in his work on " California " :

" I have now seen the grape grow in almost every part of California where wine is made. The temptation to a new settler in this State is always strong to plant a vineyard, and I am moved by much that I have seen to repeat publicly the advice that I have often given to persons newly coming into the State : *Do not make wine.* I remember a wine-cellar, ... and on a pleasant sunny afternoon, around these casks, a group of tipsy men—hopeless, irredeemable beasts, with nothing much to do except to encourage each other to another glass, and to wonder at the Eastern man who would not drink. There were two or three Indians staggering about the door ; there were swearing and filthy talk inside ; there was a pre-

tentious tasting of this, that, or the other cask by a
parcel of sots, who in their hearts would have preferred 'forty-rod' whisky. And a little way off there
was a house with women and children in it, who had
only to look out of the door to see this miserable
sight of husband, father, friends, visitors, and the
hired men spending the afternoon in getting drunk."

And, again, he says :

*"I advise no settler in the State to make wine. He
runs too many risks with children and laborers, even if
he himself escapes."*

BEER.

But it is the beer interest which, among us,
has been the most clamorous for relaxation of
restrictive legislation, so far as malt liquors are
concerned. And there have been symptoms in
many States of a disposition to make either the
legislation or the enforcement of the laws relating thereto exceptional.

The influence of the large German element
in our population may here be easily traced.
No class of emigrants have been more welcomed
by our people. They are nearly allied to us
in race, and what has given them, perhaps, still
more influence, they have been, in the main,
the political allies of the party so generally
dominant since the breaking out of the rebellion.
A *naive* declaration, in a published letter of a

representative in the Massachusetts Legislature, a few years ago, affords food for reflection : " I voted in the Legislature of 1870 for the Beer Law, as I believed in the interests of temperance *and the Republican party.*" But, as in most confessions, I fear the leading motive is put last. It is plain that no duty of the hour is more pressing than to so intensify the convictions of the friends of temperance of the dangers of the beer traffic, that politicians may be taught that the encouragement of that traffic does not promote the interest of their party.

ENGLISH EXPERIENCE.

" Experience," says Carlyle, " is the best of school-masters, but he takes dreadfully high wages." It is a sad fact in human history that we learn so little from what others have suffered.

In 1830 England tried the experiment of discouraging the " gin-palace " by the establishment of the free beer-shop. " The idea entertained at the time," says the London *Times* in 1871, " was that free trade in beer would gradually wean men from the temptations of the regular tavern, would promote the consumption of a wholsesome national beverage in place of ardent spirits, would break down the monopoly of the old license-houses, and impart, in short,

a better character to the whole trade. . . . .
The results of this experiment did not confirm
the expectations of its promoters. The sale of
beer was increased, but the sale of spirituous
liquors was not diminished."

Only a few weeks after its passage, Sidney
Smith, in his graphic style, wrote: "The new
Beer Bill has begun its operations. Everybody
is drunk. Those who are not singing are
sprawling. The sovereign people are in a
beastly state."

In later years, Recorder Hill, in one of his
charges from the bench, said that "the establishment of the beer-shop is *universally denounced as a curse upon the land.*"

Parliament has twice instituted, through com-
mittees, elaborate inquiries concerning the operation of this Act. The Committee of the
House of Lords in 1850 reported of the beer-
houses "that they are notorious for the sale of
an inferior article; that the absolute consumption of (ardent) spirits has, from whatever cause,
far from diminished; *and that the comforts and
morals of the poor have been seriously impaired.*" Among the testimony before that
committee was that of Chaplain Clay, whom
we have before cited as a well-known authority among all students of social science,
who said: "*I believe it impossible for hu-*

*man language to describe the misery and
wickedness added to the previous sum of our
moral and social ill by beer-houses."* In his
published life his son writes : " Drunkenness
is the main topic of his first and almost every
subsequent report. For some years it was
only the old-fashioned drunkenness of the public-
houses which he had to describe ; but after the
passage of the Beer Bill in 1830, and the consequent springing up of an enormous crop of
beer-shops, his fear of the great national sin
turned almost to *consternation."* In 1853, the
Committee of the House of Commons concurred
with the Lords' report, and declared that " the
beer-shop system has proved a failure."

Some modifications have been made in the
Act since ; but the nuisance is unabated. As
late as 1869, " the Lower House of Convocation of the Province of Canterbury," a body
having ecclesiastical supervision over a population of over 14,000,000, adopted the report of a
committee, who declare, after an elaborate investigation, that of " the direct causes of our
national intemperance, *one of the foremost and
most prolific,* as it appears to your Committee,
is the operation of the legislative Act which
called beer-houses into existence."

An appendix to this report contains a condensed summary of over 2,300 answers (each

being numbered) to different questions pro-
pounded to the clergy, judges, magistrates,
coroners, governors and chaplains of prisons,
masters of work-houses, superintendents of
lunatic asylums, and heads of the constabulary.
We might give many pages of these bearing
solely on the Beer Bill, but we can only select
a few at random:

"87. Beer-shops the curse of the country.

"88. Intemperance much increased since beer-
shops were introduced some years ago—especially
among young men."

"92. I gave £10 a year out of my own pocket (a
clergyman) to a man for giving up a beer-house."

"96. The beer-houses, as at present conducted, are
a social pest.

"97. An unmitigated nuisance."

"100. Intemperance decreased previous to, increased since, enactment of the Beer-Shop Act."

"103. I do not see how any thoughtful person,
who cares for the well-being of the poor, can feel
otherwise than that the State, by its encouragement
of the multiplication of beer-shops, commits a great
national sin, which must one day be punished by a
national retribution."

"109. I would sooner see a dozen public-houses in
a parish than one beer-shop."

"112. One of the most demoralizing acts of late
years."

"119. The sale of beer, to be drunk on the premises, has made many a happy home wretched, and been productive of the increase of crime."

" 128. The country beer-houses a e frequently the meeting-places of gangs for robbery, house-breaking, arson, sheep-stealing, etc., etc."

" 146. The low beer-shops a:e the great curse of the country."

" 170. Abolish all beer-houses."

" 179. The beer-houses are a frightful source of intemperance."

" 214. I would most certainly abolish beer-houses; you will, by this, save many young people by striking at these pest-houses, the root of all evil ; there . you find congregated the poacher, the tramp, etc."

" 220. The abolition of beer houses would be a boon to the workingman."

" 685. Three-fourths of the keepers of these beer-houses are the greatest drunkards, thieves, and everything that is bad. Such houses are the hot-bed or rearing-house and harbor for every crime. Boys of ten or twelve years of age begin to assemble there, and are encouraged in sin and crime."

" 1213. Among the 'General Remedies,' a special mission to the brewers who encourage low beer-shops to the destruction of all morality."

A similar, but less elaborate, report has been made by a Committee of the York Province Convocation. Among the legislative remedies it suggests are these : " Reduce public-houses to a minimum. *Entirely suppress* beer-houses." It is but fair here to say that one reason why the beer-house seems to the English mind a more intolerable nuisance than the tavern, is that the system of licensing the former is so lax that the most disreputable characters are among the proprietors. But I would suggest a consideration not always borne in mind, that the nature of the malt liquors invites the drinker to remain in the den, guzzling and tippling by the hour, where the stronger liquors would paralyze the senses quickly.

As to the English act, it would be wearying to multiply testimony from every source, or opinions from the public press ; and I close with the summing up of the *Globe :*

" The injury done by the beer act to the peace and order of rural neighborhoods, not to mention domestic happiness, industry, and economy, has been proved by witnesses from every class of society to have *exceeded the evils of any single act of internal administration passed within the memory of man.*"

MASSACHUSETTS' EXPERIENCE.

In spite of these sad lessons, Massachusetts, in the summer of 1870, at the behest of politicians, and with the aid of weaker brethren, in spite of the most earnest protests of the temperance masses, so altered her law of prohibition as to allow the sale of malt liquors in all places unless there was a local vote to forbid. The next year the law was so far changed as to require a vote in order to allow such sale. In 1873 this permissive law was swept from the statute-book by decisive votes, in accordance with the recommendation of the Governor of the Commonwealth, who said in his inaugural :

" If we are to accept the evidence of those who have had the most painful experience of the miseries produced by these places (beer-shops), they are among the greatest obstacles to the social and moral progress of the community."

A mass of testimony from the most reliable sources bearing upon every aspect of the question is at hand ; some impressive selections from which I proceed to give :

BEER A COVER.

The beer-shop is the rum-shop in disguise.

The Boston Chief of Police, in December, 1870, reported that out of 2,584 places in Boston where liquor is sold, *only seventeen sell lager-beer alone.*

The Chief Constable of the Commonwealth, under date October 3d, writes :

" That *not exceeding five per cent.* of the retail dealers *who pretend* to sell ale, porter, strong beer, and lager-beer, confine or limit their trade to malt liquors only. The service of the search-warrants almost invariably discloses the fact that 'lager-beer saloons,' so called, keep and sell more or less distilled liquors."

In reply to letters of inquiry addressed to District Attorneys, generally uniform answers on this point were received.

The District Attorney of Essex writes :

"According to the evidence which I have, beer-shops where nothing stronger is kept or sold are as scarce as men entirely without sin."

The District Attorney of the Western District :

" I believe, wherever beer is sold, strong liquors are also sold."

The District Attorney of the Northwestern District :

" The difficulty is that the beer traffic should be used as a cover for rum-selling. That it is so used can not be denied."

The Attorney of Worcester County :

" The exemption of beer affords a cover under which to sell spirituous liquors."

So a like testimony is borne by the justices of police and similar courts. We select a few :

Chelsea : "About every beer-saloon is a rum-shop." *Worcester :* "In saloons where the sale of beer is permitted by law, there spirituous liquors can usually be obtained." *Springfield :* "All sorts of spirituous and intoxicating liquors are sold under cover of such license."

To multiply evidence on this point is needless. It is clear that the Governor was amply justified in declaring in his Message that "a beer-shop, so called, has come to mean generally a place where all kinds of intoxicating liquors are furnished."

BEER A NULLIFIER.

This is a corollary from the last proposition ; but it is capable of being made more impressive from independent proof. The Police Commissioners of the State, in their First Annual Report, say :

" The ale and beer law is a veil that covers much that is vile, and it is one that is difficult for the officers to lift or see through ; and, under its protection, every vile compound that ever poisoned the human system may be sold almost with impunity."

In his last report, the present Chief Constable said :

" While it is the sole duty of the force to execute the laws, I may be permitted to say that the authority

12*

now given for the sale of ale embarrasses and hinders the force in their attempts to prosecute for the sale of liquors forbidden by law."

One of the most intelligent and active of the deputy State Constables writes :

" I believe it is almost useless to attempt to enforce the law against spirituous liquors while all persons are allowed to sell malt liquors."

The District Attorney of Worcester County says :

" I have no doubt that the beer traffic is adverse to the enforcement of the liquor law. I do not well understand how the friends of that law can hope to enforce it when the exemption of beer affords a cover."

The Justice of the Police Court of Springfield says :

" I think licensing the sale of ale and beer much increases the difficulty of enforcing the prohibitory law ; " while the Mayor of the city of Worcester declares that " to permit the sale of beer by law is only a deceptive method whereby the sale of all kinds and qualities of intoxicating liquors is legalized and clothed with a kind of respectability which does not belong to that nefarious business."

Mayor Richmond, who has earned a reputation far and wide for the vigorous and thorough enforcement of the prohibitory law in New Bedford, said in his valedictory in 1872 :

" It will be remembered that, on the first Tuesday of May last, our city voted to allow the sale of ale and beer. The result has proved that the legalizing the ale and beer-shop has been a curse to our city, and carried misery to hundreds of homes in our midst. They are nothing but shields to cover the stealthy sales of all intoxicating drinks, and *are almost a thorough protection of the rum-seller against the enforcement of the prohibitory law.*"

The causes which render the detection and conviction of sellers of distilled liquors difficult where the sale of fermented liquors is lawful, lie upon the surface, and are not difficult to see. There are, however, two other causes which enfeeble the enforcement of the laws in such cases, not less important, but less obvious. They are the same which have fatally weakened every form of license law. There is, first, the ineradicable American sentiment of opposition to all monopolies or unjust discriminations. If, as Oliver Dyer puts it, " a German with his brain soaked in ˙lager-beer is as bad a brute as an Irishman with his brain set on fire with whisky," it is difficult to see why the German beverage is to be encouraged and the Irish proscribed. And in the second place, the evils of the beer traffic itself are so immeasurable that the friends of temperance have but little heart to labor for any reform which leaves these untouched. For myself, so intense is my conviction of the miseries which spring from the liquor traffic that I would use the most clumsy and inefficient means for the curtailment of any branch of it rather than to sit down in inaction; but these elements of discouragement can not be overlooked in the discussion of this problem.

BEER A STIMULANT OF CRIME.

Let a single case show how the beer-house is a recruiting-shop for the police court. In New Bedford, the records of that court prove, that in 1872, after eight months of free beer, there was, as compared with 1871, a year of strict prohibition, an *increase of sixty-eight per cent.* in the aggregate *crime*, and of over *one hundred and twenty per cent.* in cases of *drunkenness.*

Among many persons of some general intelligence, a notion prevails that fermented liquors rarely excite to crime. Such is not the judgment of those practically conversant with our criminal courts ; such is far from the testimony of criminals themselves. I am aware that a considerable deduction is to be made from the disposition of the latter class to give their drinking habits as light a shade as possible; but in such cases, even where a false statement is given, it is a clear testimony that in the opinion of the criminal (and who should know better?) the " few glasses of beer" caused sufficient mental disturbance to rationally and plausibly account for his crime. But with all possible deductions, there remains a vast, and, perhaps, preponderant number of cases where it is evident that fermented and not distilled liquors were the excitant.

The District Attorney of Suffolk County (which includes Boston) writes :

" My observation has not been sufficiently accurate to enable me to give an opinion as to how the responsibility should be divided between distilled and fermented liquors. Many, very many, perhaps most of those who, within the last two or three years, whether as witnesses or parties, have been obliged to confess their bibulous infirmities—how truthfully I can not venture to say—have designated beer as their usual tipple."

The District Attorney of Worcester County says :   •

" The testimony in our criminal courts is to the effect that a majority of the crimes there investigated are committed under the influence of beer or a stronger liquor sold under cover of the beer traffic."

The Police Justice of Haverhill states :

"Very few are brought before me for any crime who are not drinking men ; and but few of them, even in cases of drunkenness, ever admit that they have drunk anything stronger than ale or beer."

Weigh well the pregnant suggestion made by the District Attorney of Essex : ·

"I am inclined to believe that beer not only creates an appetite for something stronger, but that its immediate influence and effect upon crime is more dangerous to the community than the stronger liquors, in this way: *the excessive use of the stronger drinks is liable to make men drunk and helpless, unable to do much harm, while beer excites men to acts of violence, desperation, and crime.*"

Science points to the same fact. In the "Cantor Lectures," Dr. Richardson, in describing the stage of alcoholic action prior to the overpowering of "the superior brain centers," and the consequent loss of all muscular action and mental sensibility, says at this period :

"The cerebral centers become influenced ; they are reduced in power, and the controlling influences of will and of judgment are lost. As these centers are unbalanced and thrown into chaos, the rational part of the man gives way before the emotional, passional, or organic part. The reason is now off duty, or is fooling with duty, and all the more animal instincts and sentiments are laid atrociously bare."   ·

And as Professor Youmans has so admirably
shown in his treatise on "The Scientific Basis
of Prohibition," the law concerns itself with
alcohol because its specific action is that of a brain
poison, exalting the animal and depressing the
spiritual nature of man :

"Long before the speech thickens and the motions
falter, there is a firing of irascible passions which lead
to the commission of numberless offenses—from two-
edged utterances that wound the spirit to homicidal
thrusts that destroy the body."

And it is while the dose of alcohol is only
sufficient to produce this apparently stimulant effect, and before it cumulates into an
evident narcotic, that the tendency to crime
exists. In plainer words, a man excited by
liquor is under the influence of his lower nature,
and a peril to the community; a man dead-
drunk is harmless to society, if at home ; and
if in public, merely an offensive nuisance to be
wheeled off by the police. If I were to add my
own testimony as a criminal magistrate to that
of others, I could fill this chapter with accounts
of grave offenses where there seemed no reason
to believe that the excitant was other than fermented liquors.

The indirect influences of the beer-house in
generating crime, though less obvious, are

hardly less deplorable. It antagonizes the home; and whatever lowers the home life prepares the way for crime. An impressive testimony on this point was given by Dr. John Todd, of Pittsfield, who, though summoned by the friends of license at the hearing before the Legislature in 1867, could not restrain himself from declaring :

" I wish to say in regard to beer, that while I think it is not so intoxicating as other drinks, it *demoralizes awfully*. We have a large population of foriegners with us, and beer is their chief drink. It makes them besotted ; it makes them cross ; *it makes their homes unpleasant ; it prevents them from rising in civilization ;* it shuts them out from the influence of everything that is ennobling."

It is surely in such an atmosphere that crime has its natural growth.

BEER A SNARE.

Dr. Albert Day, who has had probably the largest experience of any man in the world in the treatment of cases of drunkenness, stated some years since that—

" *A large majority* of the 4,000 cases of inebriety which I have treated commenced their course of drunkenness by the use of what is termed light drinks, such as wine, beer, etc. I am fully satisfied that the use of these light beverages is the initiatory step to a life of inebriety."

Mr. Lawrence, who followed Dr. Day as Superintendent of the Washingtonian Home in Boston, adds his testimony :

" At the present time the appetite for strong drink is formed in early life by drinking the lighter drinks, such as lager-bier, ale, cider, etc., in the fashionable saloons."

While the Beer law was in operation in Massachusetts, the Rev. Mr. Coombs, one of the agents of the State Temperance Alliance for visiting the public schools, reported that—

" In one town, 75 pupils told me that they had been more or less intoxicated. In 12 cases where boys came into school drunk, or were found to be so in the school-room, I was told that six of them drank cider. Careful examination will show that 19 out of 20 of the pupils who have been intoxicated were under the influence of cider or beer."

Can the State afford to give to places of temptation the additional force of legal sanction, and by all the educating power of law teach the young that they may safely enter?

While the beer-shop is the primary school of intemperance, the multitude rest not there. Not only common observation, but the excise returns in Great Britain and our own country, show that the increased consumption of malt liquors, so far from checking, creates a fresh demand for distilled.

Nor is the "snare" less dangerous to those who have just turned their feet back into the ways of sobriety. Says the Superintendent of the Washingtonian Home in a late report:

"I must here take occasion to protest against ale, beer, and cider, as unqualifiedly hindering causes in the thorough reform of inebriates. A large proportion of backsliders stumble over these light drinks who would hesitate long before they would dare to meddle with stronger liquors."

THE TESTIMONY OF ANCIENT LAWS.

Legislation against an evil is both confession of it and testimony against it. And where the course of legislation is uniform and long-continued, the testimony is weighty.

And such we find to be the case in regard to the lesser intoxicants. In the *resumé* of the license laws of Massachusetts, in another chapter, I have called attention to the fact that from the earliest years wines, beer, and cider took their place by the side of "strong waters," or distilled liquors, as inhibited without license. And I am not aware that the laws of other States differed in this respect. Long before the tem-

perance pledge embraced abstinence from them,
the practical legislator had determined that fermented liquors needed the same measure of
restraint as distilled.

When our forefathers, more than two hundred years ago (1667), enacted that none be
allowed to sell any *"cyder* by retail without
license, and that none allow any persons to
spend their time by *tippling of cyder liquors* in
their houses" (Plymouth Records, Vol. XI.,
p. 218), I take it that they knew more of the
nature and danger of the fermented beverages
than the theorists of to-day.

But it is to be noticed that *practical legislation* still keeps its ground. Not only the prohibitory law, but the license laws of 1868 and
of 1875, in Massachusetts, provide in the same
words that the term intoxicating liquors shall
include "ale, porter, strong beer, lager-bier,
cider, and all wines, as well as distilled spirits."
The license laws of New York, and I suppose
of other States, have contained similar provisions.

Dr. Bowditch thinks that "we in New England have not only a great climatic law to contend against, but we have also the influences of
race, and of a race educated to drunkenness by
bad laws and by war." The climatic law he

states to be that the tendency to intoxication is greatest above the isothermal line of 50° average temperature.   Like most theorists, Dr. Bowditch exaggerates the importance of the tendencies which he calls "laws," and which even he has to admit are often "overridden" by other circumstances.   But whatever may be estimated as the degree to which the appetite for alcoholics is "overloaded" under northern climates and in the veins of the Anglo-Saxon race, I should differ totally in the practical conclusions I should draw.   For such a people, I should say the path of total abstinence was peculiarly the path of safety, and the only path. To attempt to appease such an appetite by indulgence, seems to me the height of folly.   If the allopathic doctor believes in the homeopathic theory, "*similia similibus curantur,*" I must at least insist that he follow the other part of Hanneman's doctrine, of *infinitesimal doses.*

And I think the lesson of abstinence is still more strongly enforced by that peculiarity of American climate, "at least that found along the Atlantic slope," which Dr. Bowditch recognizes when he says:

"The peculiarly stimulating nature of our climate excites the nervous system so much, that we should endeavor to be more temperate in this country than the nations living in Europe between the same iso-thermal lines need to be."*

It is not light wines and lager-bier that can operate as a prophylactic to save such a race from drunkenness, but a law of strict prohibi-tion, the outgrowth and bulwark of moral con-victions. We can point Dr. Bowditch to the northernmost State of New England, of almost pure Anglo-Saxon race, under the regimen of what *he* would call bad laws, and challenge him among the lager-bier States of the Union, or the lager or light wine countries of Europe, to find a country so free from drunkenness and its sequences as the State of Maine. He will there see "isothermal lines," climatic tendencies, race appetences, and war demoralizations all over-ridden by moral influences, supplemented and sustained by what the "inexorable logic of facts" demonstrates to be *good laws.*

The census of 1870 gives the population of Maine as 626,915, and that of California as 560,247.

The Report of the Commissioner of Internal

---

* In this connection he tells us of two Englishmen who, while traveling through New England, "continued the same amount of stimulants they had always used. They were quite astonished when, after a three months' trip, they were both about the same time seized with an attack of delirium tremens, which had never afflicted them in England."

Revenue for the year ending June 30, 1874, shows these facts:

Maine operates 3 breweries and 1 distillery.*

California operates 195 breweries and 177 distilleries.

Maine contributes as gross receipts to the United States Revenue from distilled spirits alone, $34,901.83.

California, $1,373,374.76.

Maine furnishes only .1540 of one per cent. of the national revenue from fermented liquors.

California, 2.8739 per cent.

Maine contributes to the revenue from distilled spirits .0752; that is, seven and a half one-hundredths of one per cent. of the whole national revenue from this source.

California, from the same, 2.7844 per cent., or *thirty-eight times* as much as Maine.

The people of Maine are not in a condition to need Dr. Bowditch's prescriptions at present.

---

* Now (1877) *none.*

CHAPTER XX.

THE HISTORY OF PROHIBITION.

IN the chapter on License Laws we have shown that the people of Massachusetts, after the repeal of what was known as the "Fifteen-Gallon Law," by action in their several counties, proceeded to refuse licenses. The first effort in the Legislature for a general law of prohibition was next made in 1848. Upon the petition of the venerable Moses Stuart, of Andover, and 5,000 others, a report was made by a committee, who unanimously agreed that "the present license law, in our judgment, has done, and is doing, incalculable mischief." They add: " Public opinion, we are happy to know, is in advance of this law, which appears from the fact that during the last year no licenses have been granted under it in thirteen out of the fourteen counties in this Commonwealth." (1848, House Doc. No. 52). They reported a bill providing for the appointment of agents in the several municipalities to sell liquors for "use in the arts and for medicinal and sacramental purposes," and forbade, under penalties, all other sales.

Machinery for the enforcement of the law was also provided. It was made penal to keep with intent to sell. Provisions were made for search and seizure upon legal process, and for judicial forfeiture of liquors kept contrary to law. There was also a section making it penal to let a building for illegal sales.* But the bill, though meeting with large favor, failed to become a law, and Maine was the first State to embody these principles and measures in a statute which has become so widely and justly known by her name.

In his testimony before the Canadian Parliamentary Commission in 1874, Governor Dingley gives this account of its enactment. (It may here be noted that so far as the mere prohibition of sales, as a beverage, Maine had taken this step as to *spirituous* liquors in 1846, and extended it to all *intoxicating* liquors in 1848) :

"What is popularly known as the 'Maine Law,' but which bears on the Statute Book of this State

---

* The bill was reported and ably advocated by Francis W. Emmons, of Sturbridge. Mr. Bishop says: "Whatever credit or disgrace attends the devising of this peculiar form of legislation, belongs, so far as it attaches to any person in modern times, not to any inhabitant of Maine, but of Massachusetts." ("Statutory Crime," § 988).

the title 'An Act to prohibit Drinking-houses and Tippling-shops,' was enacted in 1851, and with the exception of two years (1856 and 1857), has remained, with slight modifications, the law of the State to the present time.

" For about two hundred years prior to the enactment of this prohibitory law, first in the parent Commonwealth of Massachusetts, of which this State was formerly a district, and then in the State of Maine, the system of licensing the sale of intoxicating liquors had been tried and had been proved to be practically powerless in restraining the evils of intemperance.

" The temperance movement which commenced in this State soon after 1830, and which received a new impetus from the Washingtonian movement of 1840, soon after led to a discussion of the influence which more stringent legislation against the liquor traffic would have in supplementing moral suasion.

" This discussion, as early as 1846, carried the question of substituting the policy of prohibiting dramshops by law instead of licensing them into municipal and State elections ; and resulted in 1850 in the election of a Legislature favorable to prohibition."

The law enacted by Maine, though it was much more complex in its details and machinery, and contained some stringent and summary provisions to aid in its enforcement, was substantially the same in its principles as that reported in Massachusetts in 1848. It, however, added destruction to forfeiture, in cases of liquors illegally kept—a measure which, while it

13

did not increase the deterrent power of the law, was useful as an impressive exhibition.

To Neal Dow is correctly attributed the organization of a public sentiment which made its enactment feasible and the motive power which made it actual.

The subsequent history of the law in the State of Maine may as well be given here in the words of Governor Dingley, in the continuation of his testimony :

"Although public sentiment was reasonably prepared for the ' Maine Law ' when first enacted in 1851, yet an act which suddenly prohibited a traffic that had always been authorized, very naturally excited bitter opposition at the outset. In spite of violent opposition in every town ; in spite of the failure of many prosecuting officers, and even the jurors to discharge their duties faithfully ; in spite of an organized political opposition at the polls in 1852, 1853, and 1854, to secure the election of a Legislature favorable to a repeal, the law was well sustained and even grew in favor, and was having a perceptible influence in breaking up the liquor traffic and restraining the evils of intemperance. Unfortunately, in the early part of 1855, in dispersing a mob which had gathered in the city of Portland on the occasion of some procedure under the ' Maine Law,' one man was killed. The enemies of the law seized upon this to influence the public mind against the prohibitory system, and at the State election in September, 1855, succeeded in choosing a Legislature which in the winter of 1856 repealed the 'Maine Law,' and substituted the most stringent license law ever placed upon the statute-book. This license law, however, proved a failure ; and at the State elections in 1856 and 1857 legislators were chosen by a large majority, which in 1858 re-enacted the Prohibitory Law. Before it went into effect, however, the question of prohibition or license was submitted to the people, and the vote stood for prohibition, 28,864 ; for license, 5,912. The vote was very light:

" The beneficial influence of the re-enactment of the ' Maine Law ' was at once apparent, especially through the rural parts of the State. The opposition to it obviously grew weaker from year to year, and although there were frequent attempts to secure a Legislature favorable to its repeal, yet they always failed."

The present stability of the law and its results will be abundantly shown in another chapter.

To return to Massachusetts. What was now called the " Maine Law " was enacted the next year (1852) by her Legislature. In consequence of a decision made by the Supreme Judicial Court in 1854, which declared some of the provisions of the law as to the search and seizure of liquors to be unconstitutional, while fully affirming the theory of the law and the constitutionality of the object sought, the Legislature of 1855 chose to thoroughly revise the law ;

and availing themselves of the aid of eminent
legal talent, the result was the production of a
law (Statute 1855, chap. 215) which has stood the
sharpest test of judicial criticism. In the hundreds of cases that have been taken up on questions of law before the highest tribunal of the
State, there has been found only a single and
incidental defect, which was, however, substantially remedied by the general provisions
of law.*   Nor has the statute been found
difficult to work intelligently and efficiently.
Its enemies being judges, it is a well construct-
ed machine.   One of the ablest lawyers in
Massachusetts, in a report made to the Senate
in favor of a license law, said :

" This prohibitory statute, known in its earliest form
as the Maine Law, is the fruit of much experience,
avoids the practical difficulties discovered by hostile
lawyers in the earlier statutes, is minute, thorough,
and comprehensive, and is believed to be the only
criminal law where the Legislature has provided forms

---

* The 32d section enacted that persons convicted before justices
of the peace or police courts, and appealing, upon failure to give
bonds to prosecute the appeal, etc., should be committed to abide
the sentence of the court appealed *from.*   It was held unconstitutional to clog the right of appeal for jury trial with this condition ; but that this section being void, the general provisions of
law applied, and that a party might rightly be committed to
abide the final sentence of ·the court appealed *to.*   (Sullivan
vs. Adams, 3 Gray, 476).

of proceedings; in short, as those who administer it have testified, *it is as perfect as a criminal statute well can be*" (1865, Senate Doc. No. 200).

I shall therefore proceed to give an abstract of this Massachusetts statute without troubling myself to compare its provisions with similar laws of other States which are identical in substance, and to a great extent, I believe, the same in detail.

The statute is distinctive both as to its object and in the modes of its accomplishment.

The object of the statute is the suppression of the traffic in intoxicatiug liquors as a common beverage. It therefore declares it to be unlawful for any person to manufacture or sell any kind of intoxicating liquors (among which lager-bier and cider are specially enumerated) except as follows :

Manufacturers may be licensed by the County Commissioners of the several counties and the Mayor and Aldermen of the city of Boston, to manufacture such liquors at appointed places, to be sold " in quantities not less than 30 gallons, to be exported out of the Commonwealth, and to be used in the arts or for mechanical and chemical purposes in this Commonwealth, or in any quantity to duly authorized agents of towns and cities."

Importers may sell foreign liquors in the original packages, and in quantities not less than the quantities in which the laws of the United States require such liquors to be imported, and as pure as when imported.

Druggists may sell pure alcohol to other druggists, apothecaries, and physicians, known to be such, for medicinal purposes only.

Cider may be manufactured or sold "for other purposes than that of a beverage," and "unadulterated wine for sacramental purposes."

Agents to be appointed annually by the authorities of each city or town to sell intoxicating liquors "to be used in the arts, or for medicinal, chemical, and mechanical purposes, and no other;" to record all such sales, and to receive a fixed salary not dependent on the amount of their sales, and to give bonds with sureties to conduct their business according to the provisions of the law.

In order to prevent unlawful sales, two new and leading provisions were made: one declaring it unlawful to keep liquor for sale; and the other authorizing the search, seizure, and judicial destruction of liquor so kept, without legal authority.*

---

* "Differences of opinion will for a long time exist whether the general prohibition is wise or not; but assuming it to be wise, the forbidding of the keeping of the liquor with the intent

There were also provisions punishing the transportation of liquors by carriers or other persons, who had reasonable cause to believe that the same had been or were to be sold contrary to law.

There were the ordinary provisions punishing single sales and the common seller, only in both cases by this statute the punishment was to be both fine *and* imprisonment.

The statute was undoubtedly unnecessarily multitudinous in its details, and some of the weapons it furnishes against the traffic have scarcely been taken at all from the armory. We therefore content ourselves here with this enumeration. The total prohibition of sales for a beverage, the punishment of the keeping without proof of actual sales, and the confiscation of the liquors by a process *in sem*, were undoubtedly the three distinguishing and practically most effective features of the law. None of these provisions, it may be remarked, were novel in themselves, but only novel in their application to the liquor traffic.

At the same session of the Legislature a short statute was enacted, known as "The

to sell it, and the forfeiture of the liquor thus illegally kept, are legislative methods of reaching the end greatly in advance of what in modern times had been attempted before." (Bishop on Statutory Crime, § 988).

Nuisance Act," which has been sometimes designated as an "attachment" to the liquor law, and which has proved of great practical utility, and has since been adopted by other States. It declared "all buildings, places, or tenements used as houses of ill-fame, resorted to for prostitution, lewdness, or for illegal gaming, or used for the illegal sale or keeping of intoxicating liquors," "to be common nuisances;" and "any person keeping or maintaining any such common nuisance shall be punished by fine not exceeding one thousand dollars, *or* by imprisonment in the county jail not more than one year. It further provided that use of premises for any of the purposes enumerated by a tenant should make void his lease; also that any person letting a building for any such use, or knowingly permitting such use, should be deemed guilty of aiding in the maintenance of such nuisance, and be punished accordingly. This statute has never been repealed. The courts decided that it was unaffected by the passage of the License laws, although, of course, the definition of what should be an *illegal* sale or keeping was changed thereby. In 1866 (Laws, chap. 280, § 3) there was a change of penalties, but no other alteration has been made in it.

The procedure under this statute has been a favorite one with public prosecutors. The courts early decided that the offense was a single one—to wit, the maintenance of a common nuisance ; but the same count in a complaint or indictment might allege it to consist of all three unlawful uses—to wit, for gaming, prostitution, or illegal selling or keeping of liquor, and the prosecutor might obtain a conviction by proof of either.   In a certain class of cases these vices were always found in friendly groups.   Later the courts relieved the embarrassment of proving proprietorship of the establishment by a decision that, as by the common law all who participate or aid in the commission of misdemeanors are principals, it would be sufficient to prove that the defendant had the charge "even for an hour" of the premises, "as clerk or agent of the proprietor, and that during such period of control and charge intoxicating liquors were illegally kept or sold" with his assent.   (Commonwealth *vs.* Maroney, 105 Mass., 467, n. Same *vs.* Kimball, *id.* 465).

To return to the statute particularly known as the Prohibitory law.   The statute of which we have given an abstract made no provision for the supply of liquors to city and town agents, except to authorize licensed manufacturers to sell to them.   But by a subsequent statute of the same year (1855, chap. 470) the system of the State Agency was established, and after-

13*

ward followed in some other States. It was
provided that the Governor should appoint a
commissioner, who should be authorized to purchase and sell liquors of a pure quality to city
and town agents, such sales to be for cash, and
at a price not to exceed 5 per cent. advance on
the actual cost. The commissioner was required
to give bonds in the sum of $20,000 for the
faithful discharge of his duties, and was made
liable, in addition, to severe penalties for adulteration, for sales to unauthorized persons, or
at an authorized price. It may be conceded
that the practical working of this part of the law,
in relation to State and municipal agencies, was
attended with more embarrassment and difficulties than any other. The appointment of State
Commissioner was not always a fortunate one;
in some of the towns it was difficult to get judicious agents, or improper ones were appointed
through favor; and some of the rural places
felt that no agent was needed. Some important changes in this part of the system were
made from time to time. In 1858 the commissioner was required to have all his liquors analyzed by one of the State assayers, and to sell
none unless upon written certificate of purity.
Upon the reënactment of the Prohibitory law in
1869 (chap. 415) this part received an entire
revision, the most important theoretical change

being a provision that, "after the expiration of six months from the passage of this act, all liquor of foreign production kept or sold by said commissioner shall be imported by him, or under his direction." It was also left discretionary with towns containing less than 5,000 inhabitants, to dispense with the appointment of an agent to sell for permitted purposes.

I suppose persons of every shade of opinion will agree in this : that the liquor trade presents peculiar temptations to all engaged in it, and that all attempts at its regulation for any purpose whatever have been attended with insoluble embarrassments. The honest merchant, the revenue official, the police officer, the careful consumer, as well as the legislator, have all realized this. Without pretending, then, that the system in Massachusetts for supplying liquors for what are esteemed necessary uses was perfect either in theory or administration, I think it the rather remarkable that the scandal and abuse was as little as it was ; and I have no doubt that in the later years of its administration a purer and better article was furnished for medicinal purposes than was accessible to the average buyer in other States.

The criminal provisions of the law underwent no important change or addition until its repeal in 1868, except that the operation of its penalties was substantially affected by the passage of a general law in 1866 (chap. 280, § 1), which enacted that when any law made an offense punishable by fine and imprisonment, the " offender may, at the discretion of the court, be sentenced to be punished by such imprisonment without the fine, or by such fine without the imprisonment, in all cases where he shall prove or show to the satisfaction of the court that he has not before been convicted of a similar offense."

The non-enforcement of the law by the authorities of Boston led to an agitation for the establishment of a Metropolitan Police for that and the adjacent cities, in lieu of the then City Police, and to be appointed by State Commissioners. When such a bill had passed the Senate in 1865, and some of its readings in the House, Governor Andrew proposed as a compromise the establishment of an independent State Police. The substitute was accepted, and became a law (1865, chap. 249). In the second section it was enacted that the force " shall especially use their utmost endeavors to repress and prevent crime by the suppression of liquor-shops, gambling-places, and houses of ill-fame."

In another chapter some account of their work in suppressing the liquor traffic will be found. Three years after the prohibitory law was repealed, and a license law enacted, and the latter then repealed the following year, and the prohibitory law reënacted in 1869 (ch. 415). The only change of any importance, except in the provisions of the State Agency, was in the qualified exemption of cider, "where the same is not sold, or kept with intent to be sold, at a public bar, or to be drank on the premises" (sec. 29). The body of the law was a reënactment *in totidem verbis* of the 86th chapter of the General Statutes, which was in itself substantially the law of 1855. Some further modifications were made in favor of malt liquors in 1870, which were repealed in 1873.

As stated in the chapter on License Laws, this was again supplanted by a license law, with a sort of local option, in 1875, under which the State now is, and under the operation of which licenses are granted in only about one-quarter of the territory of the State. At the late session of the Legislature (1877) the old prohibitory law came very close to reënaction; and it is the general judgment of the friends of temperance that its restoration is near at hand.

VERMONT enacted the law of prohibition in 1852, and has steadily maintained and generally enforced it ever since.

NEW HAMPSHIRE enacted it in 1855, and has kept it unimpaired on the Statute-book, although its enforcement has not been as effective as in its sister State.

RHODE ISLAND first enacted the law in 1852. Certain provisions, in regard mainly to the machinery for search and seizure, having been declared unconstitutional, the Act was amended in 1853, submitted to, and ratified by the people. In 1863 this law was repealed, and a license law substituted; upon which, in 1865, "local option" was engrafted. In 1874 Prohibition was established, and, as we shall see in the next chapter, *enforced.* The contest was carried into the elections. After a sharp and close contest, the candidate of the license section, a wealthy manufacturer, secured the nomination of the Republican convention for Governor; and although the prohibitory men of the party bolted the nomination, and gave their independent candidate a plurality at the polls, yet the liquor interest and the Democrats coalesced in the election of members of the Legislature, and thus secured a license majority and the ultimate election of their Governor. The repeal followed in June, 1875.

CONNECTICUT enacted the law in 1854, enforced it but spasmodically and partially, and repealed it in 1872.

NEW YORK passed a prohibitory statute, with some imperfections, in 1855. The highest court of the State pronounced some of its provisions unconstitutional in 1856; and the Legislature in 1857, instead of amending, replaced it by a license law.

DELAWARE embodied the *principle* of prohibition in a law as early as 1847. It was, however, conditioned upon the popular vote, and so was adjudged unconstitutional. A statute, in its general features prohibitory, but lacking many of the provisions of the " Maine Law," was passed in 1855, but was replaced by the law of license in 1857.

MICHIGAN passed the law in 1853, and ratified it by popular vote. This being declared an unconstitutional mode of legislation, it was re-enacted, without the clause of submission, in 1855. The law was repealed in 1875.

The Constitution of 1850 providing that " the Legislature shall not pass any act authorizing the grant of license for the sale of ardent spirits or other intoxicating liquor," there was nothing left except to pass a " tax law," which is elsewhere alluded to. The Constitution of *Ohio* contains a similar inhibition.

Some of the other Western States have had at times some form of prohibitory law ; but, we believe, only that of IOWA remains. Her act was passed in 1855, and ratified by the people at the ensuing election in April. It has never been repealed; but was crippled in 1858 by the exclusion of fermented liquors from its prohibition.

As the adoption of Prohibition by so many States, whether by their Legislatures or by the popular vote, did not establish its wisdom or its beneficence, so neither has its repeal by several of them any tendency to establish the contrary. A detailed examination of the causes which led to such repeal, and of the lessons to be thence educed, is beyond the scope of the present work. A bare allusion to some of them must suffice. Some of them were enacted in the tide of excitement following the original "Maine Law," without a sufficient support behind them in a settled and educated public opinion; in some instances adverse judicial decisions upon parts of the machinery of the statute discouraged its friends; in other States the law finally fell, as the result of the demoralization arising, first, from the sudden influx of foreign immigration, and this followed by the civil war, unsettling the occupations, the habits, and the morals of so many. But beyond all these temporary adverse influences is the great fact, to be acknowledged and to be kept ever in mind, *of the immense power of the liquor interest and its sure allies.* Whether prohibition ruined, or only branded, the trade, it was thoroughly aroused, and watched its opportunity to strike. The decisive fact has been, that its votes have been far more sure to follow its interests than the votes of temperance men their consciences. As a natural consequence, political parties have obeyed its behests.

CHAPTER XXI.

PROHIBITION A SUCCESS.

"An ounce of Fact is worth a ton of Theory."

In considering the problem of the legal prohibition of the common traffic in liquor, as we
have seen various questions arise, some of these
are ethical and political, and such questions are
rarely susceptible of answers absolutely demon-
strative. We may think the weight of argument heavily upon our side; but still, able and
ingenious men may continue to offer plausible
suggestions on the other. But there are certain practical questions to which experience can
give positive and indisputable answers. Happily, these are, to the mass of mankind, the
most important. The theoretical objections to
prohibition, however subtly and even eloquently
put forth by such writers as John Stuart Mill,
are satisfactorily laid aside by the common-
sense of "the plain people," as Mr. Lincoln
used to call them, who are, after all, the practical arbiters of legislation in the long run.

Befog the question as you may, the average
American knows that the dram-shop is a public enemy; and the only question really open

before the mind of the conscientious citizen is, Will Prohibition most successfully suppress the conceded evil?

To the record the prohibitionist fearlessly appeals. Yet because the experiment of *enforced* prohibition has been tried in comparatively few localities, and for comparatively short periods, much remains to be done to bring the demonstrated results to the general attention of the public.

I am free to confess that I deem this and the following chapter the most important in my book, and I desire that the testimony should be so full and so reliable as to carry conviction to the candid reader.

Before coming to the operation of "the prohibitory law," so called, I desire, first, to call attention to the effect of temporary or partial prohibition obtained in other ways.

And, first, I turn to a country remote in its location, but instructive in its lessons.

SWEDEN.

In an elaborate paper prepared by the Chief of the Statistical Office in the Department of Justice in Sweden, and endorsed "as of the highest authority" in the Report of the Massachusetts Board of Health, a detailed account is given of the varying phases of legislation upon this subject, justifying the conclusion drawn by Judge Aldrich:

"Thus the nation rose and fell, grew prosperous and happy, or miserable and degraded, as its rulers and law-makers restrained or permitted the manufacture and sale of that which all along the track of its history has seemed to be the nation's greatest curse."

From the paper itself I give a single sentence:

"*A vigorously maintained prohibition* against spirits in 1753–1756, and again in 1772–1775, *proved the enormous benefits effected* in moral, economical, and other effects, by abstinence from spirits."

But happily the lesson has more modern teaching.

In the Letter recently addressed by permission to Mr. Gladstone by Alexander Balfour, which I have referred to in another connection, he says:

"What is essentially a Permissive Prohibitory Act has existed in Sweden for the last twenty years. So vigorously have the people outside of towns used their permission to limit and prohibit, that among 3½ millions of people there are only 450 places for the sale of spirits. . . . . This it is which has so helped Sweden to emerge from moral and material prostration, and which explains the existence of such general indications in that country of comfort and independence amongst all classes " (pp. 36–7).

All this we have explained in detail heretofore.

IRELAND.

In all ages and in all countries the same constant ratio between drinking-houses and drunkenness, and between these and vice and crime, has been observed.

John Wesley writes in his Journal under date of July 9, 1760:

"I rode over to Killikeen, a German settlement near twenty miles south of Limerick. In the evening I preached to another colony at Ballygarane. The third is at Court Mattress, a mile from Killikeen. I suppose three such towns are scarcely to be found again in England or Ireland. There is no cursing or swearing, no Sabbath-breaking, no drunkenness, *no ale-house in any of them.* How will these poor foreigners rise up in the judgment against those that are round about them!"

But at the present day some of the large land proprietors have power to exclude the drink traffic from large areas—a power which they have beneficially exercised.

BESSBROOK is so marked and interesting a testimony to the success of prohibition, even in a manufacturing community, that I am induced to give a detailed account of the settlement as contained in a letter to the London *Daily Telegraph* of date August 17, 1874:

"The Bessbrook Quarries were opened by the great flax-spinning firm in the vicinity, with the object, at once benevolent and enterprising, of giving employment to the males of families whose female and juvenile members are engaged in the operations of spinning and weaving. Bessbrook is, taken altogether, a place of extraordinary interest, and I was glad of the opportunity of seeing for myself an establishment concerning which I had heard so much, as the successful realization of ideas we are generally inclined, with too reasonable warrant of experience, to pronounce Utopian, and therefore impracticable. So I carried an inquiring mind into Bessbrook; and though I made no domiciliary visits worth mentioning, nor stopped any operative to search him or her for the secret bottle, I can truly report that the evidence was strongly in favor of universal and seldom broken sobriety — that is to say, of rigid and total abstinence from all stimulating liquor. The "patriarchal relations" between employers and employed are not maintained at any sacrifice of independence, nor are they enforced at all. Mr. Richardson, the eldest son of the proprietor of Bessbrook, and his acting representative in the control of the mill and all things relating thereto, frankly disclaimed all the sentimental motives and intentions which I will confess I was half prepared to hear of, *ad nauseam.*

"I went to Bessbrook for the sole purpose of seeing that Irish Saltaire, the industrial village, in order to gather the truth as to all the wonderful things said about it; and I was glad to find in Mr. Richardson a man as free from the crotchets and theories of what is called philanthropy as any mer-

chant prince I ever saw. I asked him how he met
the difficulty of strikes, and he said in reply that he
had no panacea for the evil ; that there was no in-
trinsic virtue in the social organization of Bessbrook
to prevent or cure any disaffection of work-people,
but that there were advantages in the residential
arrangements, and that, as a fact, the Belfast strike
had not touched Bessbrook. . . . .

" An isolated position is also in favor of Bessbrook;
for, not to speak of comfortable homes, the people
determined on quitting the place would leave it with_
out being able to go next door, as it were. And certainly when I came to look at the beautiful neatness
of the village, and saw the economic method of
trading, and the high order of management in the
co-operative stores, I could not avoid the conclusion
that a prudent man or woman would be loth to part
with benefits so real and, unhappily, so rare. Bessbrook has 4,000 inhabitants, many of whom are too
young for labor in the mill. One penny for each
child is paid weekly by the parents for schooling.
There is a shop of every necessary kind in the place ;
there is a temperance hotel, but there is no house
licensed for the sale of beer or spirits. It is also a
boast of Bessbrook that the pawn-office is neither
known nor missed in those prudent precincts ; and,
more wonderful yet, there is no police station.

" The village square has an old-fashioned Flemish
look about it, quaintly mingled with freshness, for indeed all hereabout is as good as new. Flowers there
are in abundance ; and a farm supplies the village
with all kinds of food. The elder Mr. Richardson,
who founded Bessbrook, is a considerable land-owner

in the neighborhood; and the very road leading to his industrial establishment is private property, made and maintained at his own expense. An old Quaker family is this which has quietly and unostentatiously made Bessbrook. About two-thirds of the people employed in the mill are residents of the village; and, as I have already intimated, these are of different creeds or sects, worshiping according to their conscience, and bound only in one thing, which is to educate their children."

TYRONE COUNTY.—Lord Claude Hamilton, one of the large land proprietors of Ireland, and a member of the English Parliament, recently said as follows at a public meeting:

"I am here, as representing the county, to assure you that the facts stated regarding the success of prohibition there are perfectly accurate. There is a district in that county of sixty-one square miles, inhabited by nearly ten thousand people, having three great roads communicating with market towns, in which there are no public-houses, entirely owing to the self-action of the inhabitants. The result has been that whereas those high-roads were in former times constant scenes of strife and drunkenness, necessitating the presence of a very considerable number of police to be located in the district, at present there is not a single policeman in that district, the poor-rates are half what they were before, and all the police and magistrates testify to the great absence of crime." . . . .

BELFAST.—This large commercial city, unfortunately, can not be cited as showing the
effect of a *régime* of prohibition, except for a
very limited time. And yet the lesson read to
us from the experience of 1872 is very significant. I quote from an English paper :

"During the recent distressing and disgraceful
riots in Belfast, the magistrates put the city under a
prohibitory liquor edict for ten days consecutively.
For days previously riot 'and carnage were the order
of the day and the night. 'Public-houses drove
a trade fabulous in its extent ; for just in proportion as the rioters were inflamed with the demon
drink, did their fears and better judgment leave
them, and the more drink they consumed the more
reckless they became.' The first week's experience
of prohibition had so convinced the magistrates that
drink had been the chief sustaining power of the
riots, that even when the town was quiet, and when
there was not the faintest indication of a renewal of
the disturbances, they dreaded the risk that would be
incurred if the people were exposed to the temptations offered by the sale of intoxicating drinks.
They therefore extended the prohibitory order for
three days more. The rioters gradually recovered
their senses, and order was restored. This was after
whole streets of houses had been laid waste, the hospitals filled with killed and wounded, and the police
cells and prisons, extensive as they are, were peopled
to overflowing. Who will say that Prohibition can
not be enforced, when, even under such very unfavor-

14

able circumstances, a mere magisterial order can put a sudden stop to liquor selling, and bring social order out of riot and anarchy ?"

ENGLAND.

We have alluded to the power of land-proprietors in Great Britain to suppress the liquor traffic. Of the exercise of this power a writer in the *Edinburgh Review* for January, 1873, says :

"We have seen a list of eighty-nine estates in England and Scotland where the drink traffic has been altogether suppressed, with the very happiest social results. The late Lord Palmerston suppressed the beer-shops in Romsey as the leases fell in. We know an estate which stretches for miles along the romantic shore of Loch Fyne where no whisky is allowed to be sold. The peasants and fishermen are flourishing. They have all their money in the bank, and they obtain higher wages than their neighbors when they go to sea."

But the Report of the Committee of the Lower House of Convocation of the Province of Canterbury (embracing a population of over 14,000,000) made in 1869, gives a most noticeable showing as to the number of parishes where, " owing to the influence of the land-

owner, no sale of intoxicating liquor is licensed."
The report goes on to say :

"Few, it may be believed, are cognizant of the
fact—which has been elicited by the present inquiry
—that there are at this time, within the province of
Canterbury, upwards of one thousand parishes (a list
of which, as returned by the County Constabulary, is
given in the appendix) in which there is neither public-house nor beer-shop; and where, in consequence
of the absence of these inducements to crime and
pauperism, according to the evidence before the Committee, the intelligence, morality, and comfort of the
people are such as the friends of Temperance would
have anticipated."

In the appendix to the Report, under the
head of "Good effects of having no public-
house or beer-shop," are given extracts from
replies of 243 of the clergy, and 11 of Chief
Constables and Superintendents of Police. They
are all condensed arguments for Prohibition :
"No public-house, no beer-shop—no crime."
"No public-house, no beer-shop—no intemperance." "In parishes where there are neither
public-houses nor beer-shops, the absence of
crime is remarkable."

It will be said that these are mostly small
agricultural parishes. True; but parishes in
every other respect similar, but where the drink-
factor is present, generate their harvest of crime

and pauperism, as this very Report abundantly shows. But let us look for a moment at the results of banishing the liquor traffic from communities having different industries.

SHAFTESBURY PARK ESTATE.—Mr. W. Fulcher, a resident on this estate for a year, writes to an English paper under date September 11, 1875, as follows:

" Here, as you are probably aware, no public-house or beer-shops exist. We have here some fourteen hundred houses, with a population of from three to four thousand, and yet it is a fact that the duties of citizens, of fathers and mothers, of neighbors, and of individuals are satisfactorily discharged, without its being thought necessary to call in the aid of the publican. During the period of my own residence on that estate I have seen only two drunken men, and they, moreover, were passing through the streets, not citizens. I have never heard a drunken brawl, never known but one case of a domestic disturbance, and that arose from a husband ' mildly correcting' a wife, who, before coming on the estate, had learned to be too fond of her beer. During the past summer, the streets which are broad and well kept, have been made beautiful by the splendid show of flowers in which the inhabitants have indulged, almost without an exception. I have never heard the song of a drunkard, but during the summer evenings I have often listened to the songs, etc., of the people from the open windows. We have a large lecture hall, where various entertainments are provided; and when the estate is completed we shall be in possession of coöperative stores, medical institute, large club-house, library, and reading room, but no public-house or hotel; and, strange as it may appear, the inhabitants, *though by no means exclusively teetotalers, are perfectly satisfied,* and do not wish that great institution, the beer-barrel, to be introduced. Now, sir, this puts to silence forever the parrot-cry as to the people's inability to do without a public-house. I declare that by my own personal experience I can prove to demonstration the folly of such a statement, and if any of your readers should question the accuracy of anything I have said, I invite him to pay us a visit, when, I am sure, he will be able to confirm anything I have said. We have had some very distinguished visitors since our estate has 'sprung into being.' The Right Hon. B. Disraeli came, saw, and was conquered. Earl Granville, Thomas Hughes, Esq., M. P., Hon. Evelyn Ashley, M. P., and other distinguished gentlemen, have endorsed all the Premier said'; and more, the happy faces of the children, the contented looks of the wives, and satisfaction beaming from the countenances of the husbands on that estate, stamp the fact of its success on the experiment, and transform an interesting theory into an incontrovertible fact—Prohibition is a success."

VILLAGES IN NORTHUMBERLAND.—Of these, Edmund Procter, Hon. Sec. of the Newcastle-on-Tyne Auxiliary of the United Kingdom Alliance, writes thus:

"The people of Northumberland have practically tried prohibition, and, as Lord Claude Hamilton declared of Tyrone, ' have tried it with complete success.'

" I visited this week the colliery village of Throckley, a few miles west of Newcastle, on the banks of the Tyne. The owners of the colliery closed all licensed houses in the village a few years ago, and I have it on the authority of the proprietors, which was confirmed to me by some of the inhabitants and others, that from that day to this not only had the results in the diminution of drunkenness and quarrelling been very material, but that no complaints of any kind had ever been made.

" In further confirmation of this, the canvassers for the petition to Parliament in favor of the Permissive Bill declared to me that almost the entire adult population had signed the petition; the fact being that, as far as the canvassers were aware, only five persons had declined to sign! There are three or four agricultural and mining villages within a mile or two of Throckley where the feeling is nearly as strong, and I am assured by those who know the district, that if the inhabitants had the power to carry out the same policy which the proprietors of Throckley Colliery have exercised, they would do so with something very nearly approaching unanimity.

" There are other villages in Northumberland where the land-owners have closed all licensed houses for several years. I have a report, written by the Superintendent of Police for the Morpeth district, in which he says, under date of June 6, 1874 : ' A case of drunkenness or disorder in a village without a public-house is a very rare occurrence. For example, reports of crime are very rare from Longhirst (near Morpeth), a large colliery, where there is no public-house. Several other public-houses—at Belsay, Cambo, and elsewhere—have been shut up in this district, and I may say that very few of the country gentlemen in this neighborhood will allow one to be on their estates."

Low Moor.—This is a settlement near Clitherve, founded by the Messrs. Garnett, one of the oldest and most respected firms of cotton manufacturers in Lancashire. Under date of February 27, 1871, one of the partners says:

" We send some account of the community at Low Moor, which we are happy to say still remains without a beer-shop or a public-house. Indeed, we are deficient of so many of the usual adjuncts of civilization that we occasionally fancy it is like no other place—certainly it is like none with which we are acquainted. It has neither doctor, lawyer, nor until lately parson nor magistrate, neither has it a constable or policeman. It has neither public-house nor beer-shop, dram-shop, pawn-shop, nor tommy-shop. It has neither stocks nor gaol nor lockup. We have a population of about 1,100. Our people can sleep with their doors open, and we have the finest fruit in the district, in season, in our mill windows (which are never fastened) without any ever being stolen. Our death-rate is perhaps the lowest in the kingdom; taking the average of the last twelve years, it is under sixteen in the thousand."

Saltaire.—This is a manufacturing settlement, near Bradford, Yorkshire, commenced by Sir Titus Salt, and still under the management of the Messrs. Salt. The population is now about 5,000. For many years the sale of all liquors has been forbidden except for the year 1867–8, when an experiment was tried of permitting the sale of " Table Beer," under very stringent regulations. But even this mild intoxicant, introduced under the most favorable auspices, proved such a disturbing and degrading element that the year's trial brought back the *régime* of total prohibition, which has ever since continued. Of its present condition, Mr. James Hole, in his " Homes of the Working-classes," says :

"One thing there is which is not to be found in Saltaire, and Mr. Salt deserves as much praise for its absence as he does for anything he has provided. Not a public-house or beer-house is there. And what are the results? Briefly these. There are scarcely ever any arrears of rent. Infant mortality is very low as compared with that of Bradford, from which place the majority of the hands have come. Illegitimate births are rare. The tone and self-respect of the work-people are much greater than that of factory hands generally. Their wages are not high, but they enable them to secure more of the comforts and decencies of life than they could elsewhere, owing to the facilities placed within their reach, and the absence of drinking-houses."

And if one would see how much of Paradise
may be brought down into the work-day world
of a manufacturing village where the intelligent
philanthropy of the capitalist is supplemented
by the sobriety and industry of the laborer, let
his eye rest on this picture of Saltaire, situate
in the midst of the "lovely scenery of the West
Riding, with thick woods around, near the river
Aire : "

"The immense factory, with its skyward chimney,
and long lines of mill windows; the streaks that tell
where the canal and the Aire are ; the two mansions
—one near Shipley Glen and the other near Baildon
—of two of the juniors of the Salts; Victoria-road
stretching straightly out through its 'Italian villas,'
and shops, and spanning rail and river with bridge
gigantic; institute, schools, and chapels, pointing
their spires into the ether; neat cottages run therefrom at right angles through clean and wide streets ;
trees form green oases in a by-no-means desert; the
great park is an added area of lawn and terrace; and
northward the background is one of wood and water,
of road and river, of bank and bosky dell. Saltaire
is a hive in green lanes ; an immense home of order
in Arcadia; a great industrial exhibition in green
fields."

" BRIGHT SPOTS ON THE MERSEY."—The full
significance of this expression can only be appreciated by calling to mind the horrible pre-
eminence in drunkenness and its concomitants

14*

which the great city of Liverpool, near the
mouth of this river, has held for many years.
The eye, in turning from the sad pictures of
this drunken city, is indeed gladdened by these
"spots." I cut from *The Alliance News* of
February 13, 1875, a description of them with
the pertinent reflections they suggest:

"It may not be generally known that over large
districts in and around Liverpool, public-houses are
prohibited by owners of land and houses on their estates. The following are the principal of these prohibitory districts with the present and estimated future populations upon them when the whole of the
land already laid out shall be built upon.—1. Prince's-
road : Number of houses built or in course of erection
about 3,500 ; estimated population about 18,000. 2.
Park-road : Number of houses about to be erected,
2,400 ; estimated population about 12,000. 3. Walton-
road : Number of houses built or in course of erection,
about 700 ; estimated population about 3,500. 4.
Hamilton-road, Everton : Number of houses built,
about 1,000 ; estimated population about 5,000. 5.
Sheil-road : Number of houses built, about 200 ; estimated population about 1,000. 6. The Brook :
Number of houses built or in course of erection,
about 600 ; estimated population about 3,000. The
Corporation leases prohibit public-houses in the neighborhood of Abercromby and Falkner Squares, also
around the parks. It would be difficult to estimate
the population on those leasehold tracts. There is
good authority for stating that Upper Parliament

Fields will be restricted from public-houses, as well as the land on the other side of Prince's Road. When this land shall be built upon, the population upon it will not be less than 20,000 persons. When the whole of the land laid out, or contemplated, is built upon, the total number of the population of Liverpool living under prohibition of the liquor traffic in these localities will not be less than 80,000, including the residents around Prince's Park and Selton Park.

"By these experiments the following facts have been clearly demonstrated:

"I. That, as a business speculation, builders find it a more profitable investment of their capital to exclude public-houses from the neighborhood of the people's dwellings. It has been found that a public-house depreciates the value of the surrounding property more than the extra rent obtained for the house itself; it attracts and creates rowdyism; rowdyism drives away respectable tenants, causes loss of rent, frequent removals, damage to property, and expensive cleansing operations after infectious diseases, to which the intemperate are specially liable.

"II. That residences in these prohibitory districts are much in demand, and people are willing to pay a higher rent for dwellings here than elsewhere. There has been no instance of a complaint from the *residents* in these districts of the absence of a public-house.

"III. The most common objections against the prohibition of public-houses are:—(1) That it would encourage the *illicit sale of liquor ;* (2) That the number of public-houses around the prohibited district would be increased ; (3) That the residents would crowd to the outskirts of the prohibited district and

there indulge in drinking habits.   Seeing is believing.
Any one interested may satisfy himself, by personal
inspection, whether such objections apply to these
districts; if not, then one fact is worth a thousand
objections, and we need not travel to Maine or Massachusetts, to Saltaire or Bessbrook, to witness the
prohibition in actual and beneficial operation.

"IV. *That all the residents in these districts are
not necessarily total abstainers, for many non-abstain-
ers prefer, for various reasons, residing in localities
where there are no public-houses near.*"

UNITED STATES.

Let us now read the lessons nearer home.
And, first, we will glance at the operation of
what are known as Local Option laws, producing
local prohibition in a few of the States.   We
do not pretend to give a complete exhibit, but
merely present the results in cases where we
have at hand full and authoritative accounts.

MARYLAND.—This State has recently enacted
a local option law,   Under it several counties
have been enabled to prohibit the traffic.   The
Report of the President of the Maryland Prisoners' Aid Society for the year ending March
31, 1876, gives these facts in relation to its
operation in different counties :

Harford.—It is a source of gratification to know
that Harford County has been redeemed from the

liquor traffic, and drunkenness curtailed throughout its districts.

Talbot.—At Easton the jail contains only one prisoner. The sheriff remarked that the Local Option law in their county had produced a very happy effect in the diminution of crime ; that during the court term, April, 1874, they had seventeen prisoners ; in April, 1875, only nine, and these were committed before the law went into operation. Since then one or two arrests were made for petty offenses, but not retained.

Somerset.—I understand that seven districts of this county experience the benefit of the prohibitory law.

Worcester.—At Snow Hill I found one prisoner. The Local Option law has greatly diminished crime in this county.

And finally he states, under the head of " Conclusion : "

" The Local Option law has produced the most favorable results. Of this I have the strongest evidence in the decrease of prisoners, which I noticed in my visitations to certain counties, and in such districts where the law has been enforced. I have made diligent efforts to procure information from reliable parties. I have examined the prisons and held special interviews with the sheriffs and other officers who were expected to know its effects, and am informed that it has produced the most decided and happy changes in promoting peace, safety, and quiet where formerly riot, noise, and disorder prevailed ; especially on public days and on Saturday nights after the workingmen were paid off."

PENNSYLVANIA. — For many years Potter County has had a special prohibitory law. Hon. John S. Mann, speaking of the law, says:

" There it stands, a shield to all the youth of the county against the temptation to form drinking habits. Under its benign influence the number of tipplers is steadily decreasing, and fewer young men begin to drink than when licensed houses gave respectability to the habit. There are but few people who keep liquor in their houses for private use, and there is no indication that the number of them is increased since the traffic was prohibited. The law is as readily enforced as are the laws against gambling, licentiousness, and others of similar character.

" Its effect as regards crime is marked and conspicuous. *Our jail is without inmates, except the sheriff,* for more than half the time. When liquors were legally sold, there were always more or less prisoners in the jail."

A Local Option law for the State was passed in 1873. Forty-one counties, embracing an area of 27,708 square miles, and a population of 1,404,603, voted against license.

The law was in full operation but a little over a year when the friends of the liquor traffic and the politicians repealed it. It is not necessary to multiply testimonials to its beneficent effects. The Commissioners of Public Charities of the

State in their report bore this emphatic and decisive testimony:

" The effect of prohibitory laws is strikingly shown by the comparatively vacant apartments in the jails of counties where the Local Option law is in force."

NEW JERSEY.—The city of Vineland stands here a solitary bright spot upon the dark background of a drinking State. Its singular history has given it universal notoriety; but a closer examination of it will repay the student of sociology. An article in *Fraser's Magazine* for January, 1875 (from which, mainly, the account we give is condensed), written by Mr. Landis, its founder, will be found both interesting and profitable. Mr. Landis emphasizes the fact that he began his colony as a business operation, and not as a scheme of philanthropy:

" In the first place, I decided to theorize and reason with nobody. . . . . I would make the fixed principles of my plans of improvement the subject of contract, to be signed and sealed."

He says that he is not a temperance man, in the total abstinence sense, but that he considered the question of the sale of liquor " solely as it would affect the industrial success of his settlement." His observation had led him to see that the tavern was the consumer of the industry of its patrons, and the enemy of their homes. His success, he felt, "depended directly upon the success of each individual who should buy a farm" from him; and so sobriety, and the "happy, cheerful homes" which it induced, were necessary to the success of Vineland. He

"Had long perceived that there was no such thing as reaching the result by moral influence brought to bear on single individuals; that to benefit an entire community the law or regulation would have to extend to the entire community."

What follows I prefer to give exactly in his own terse and frank words:

"After this conclusion was reached, the way appeared clear. It was not necessary to make temperance men of each individual; it was not necessary to abridge the right or privilege that people might desire of keeping liquor in their own houses, but to get their consent to prevent the public sale of it; so that people, in bartering, might not be subject to the custom of drinking, and might not have the opportunity of drinking in bar-rooms, away from all home restraint or influence. In short, I believed that if the public sale of liquor was stopped, both in taverns and beer-saloons, the knife would reach the root of the evil. The next thing to do was to deal with settlers personally, as they bought land, and to counsel with them as to the best thing to be done. In conversation with them I never treated it as a moral question. I explained to them that I was not a total abstinence man myself, but saw clearly the liability to abuse, when liquor was placed in seductive forms at every street corner; that it incited crime, and made men unfortunate who would otherwise succeed; that most of the' settlers had a little money to begin with, sums varying from two hundred to a thousand dollars, which, if added to a man's labor, would be enough, in many cases, to obtain him a home, but which, taken to the tavern, would melt away like snow before a spring sun; that new places were liable to have this abuse to a more terrible extent than old places, as men were removed from the restraints of old associations, and brought into the excitement of forming new acquaintances; that it was a notorious fact that liquor-drinking did not add to the inclination for physical labor. I then asked them, for the sake of their sons, brothers, friends, to help to establish the new system, as I believed it to be the foundation-stone of future prosperity. To these self-evident facts they would almost all accede."

The settlement, from its commencement in 1861, was under the voluntary *régime* of prohibition, although the law empowering the people to vote upon the question of license was not passed till 1863. The vote has always been against license by such overwhelming majorities as to amount to practical unanimity.*

* March 21, 1876, the vote was: for License, 57; against, 982.

This city of 10,500 inhabitants, manufacturers, traders, fruit-growers, and farmers, spent
in 1873 for police $50, and for the support of
the poor only $400. It would seem from the
report of Mr. Curtis, " *the* constable and Overseer of the Poor" for 1874, that there is a slight
increase in police expenses, for he says: "The
police expenses of Vineland amount to $75 a
year, the sum paid to me." But a community
which has "practically no debt, and taxes only
one per cent. on valuation," can stand this increase well, especially when the constable also
reports :

"Though we have a population of ten thousand
people, for the period of six months no settler or citizen of Vineland has received relief at my hands as
Overseer of the Poor. Within seventy days there has
been only one case, among what we call the floating
population, at the expense of $4.

"During the entire year there has only been one
indictment, and that a trifling case of battery among
our colored population."

This is what Prohibition does, be it observed,
not for a picked band of religious emigrants, or
a community of scholars, but for a miscellane-
ous company of laborers from all parts of our
own country, and "from Germany, France,
England, Ireland, and Scotland."
We have not space to devote to a notice of

other settlements, like Greeley in Colorado,
and Bavaria in Illinois, where results of the
same kind have been attained in the same way;
but we must pass to the consideration of the
working of the Prohibitory Law itself in States
where it has been adopted. We do not make
our selection arbitrarily, to make out the best
case, but give the results in all the States of
which we happen to have at hand reliable testimony.

NEW YORK.—Here the law had but a transient operation. It was enacted in 1855. As
soon as the cases arising under it could reach
the courts, some of the provisions of the law
were declared unconstitutional, its friends lost
courage, the liquor interest was too powerful,
and before it could be put in fair working order,
it was repealed. Yet of its brief existence
Governor Clark, in his Message to the Legislature, said:

" Notwithstanding it has been subjected to an opposition more persistent, unscrupulous, and defiant
than is often incurred by an act of legislation, and
though legal and magisterial influence, often acting
unofficially and extra-judicially, have combined to
render it inoperative, to forestall the decision of the
courts, wrest the statute from its obvious meaning,
and create a general distrust, if not hostility, to all
legislative restrictions of the traffic, it has still, outside of our large cities, been generally obeyed. *The*

influence is visible in a marked diminution of the evils it sought to remedy."

But although the result of nominal prohibition in this State is to a great extent unsatisfactory, yet it so happens that the metropolis itself affords a most striking example of the results of *enforced* prohibition upon the *Sunday* traffic. The Metropolitan Excise Law for New York and Brooklyn, passed in 1866, and suffered to live for 31 months, was one of absolute prohibition of Sunday sales, and the Board attempted its thorough execution. It "had the grip of prohibition," and for *this day* it did the work of prohibition. The Annual Report of the Metropolitan Police Commissioners, in 1867, shows that the number of arrests for offenses "directly attributable to the use of intoxicating liquors," on eight *Tuesdays* in 1865, under the old system, was 1,018; under the new, 1,203 (being about the natural increase from population); while eight *Sundays* similarly compared showed that 1,078 arrests were reduced to only 523 by the new law (p. 21). Similar results are shown in the Second Annual Report of the Board of Excise; while even of the Sunday arrests they say:

" A very large proportion are those of persons who, having left those cities (New York and Brooklyn) to indulge in the suburbs their passions for strong drinks, return tipsy and disorderly at a late hour, and compel the police to take them in charge."

CONNECTICUT.—This State enacted a Prohibitory Law in 1854, which remained on the Statute-book till 1873. At first it was fairly enforced, but in later years it was openly violated in a large part of the State. The testimony as to the result of its *enforcement* is unanimous and emphatic.

In 1855, in his Annual Message to the General Assembly, Governor Dutton said:

" There is scarcely an open grog-shop in the State, the jails are fast becoming tenantless, and a delightful air of security is everywhere enjoyed."

Governor Minor, in 1856, said:

" From my own knowledge, and from information from all parts of the State, I have reason to believe that the law has been enforced, and the daily traffic in liquors has been broken up and abandoned."

The testimony of clergymen, chaplains of prisons, and city missionaries might be cumulated. Let one suffice. Rev. David Harvley, City Missionary of Hartford, said—

" That since the prohibitory law went into effect his mission school had increased more than one-third in number. The little children that used to run and hide from their fathers when they came home drunk, are now well-dressed and run out to meet them."

I will only add the testimony of Rev. Dr. Bacon, of New Haven, who has since arrayed himself in conspicuous opposition to the law, but who can not efface his testimony as to *facts :*

" The operation of the prohibitory law for one year is a matter of observation to all the inhabitants. Its effect in promoting peace, order, quiet, and general prosperity, no man can deny. *Never for twenty years has our city been so quiet as under its action.*"

Lax as the administration of this law had become in later years, the change of legislation in 1873 immediately brought forth the fruits of license in an increase of drunkenness and crime.

RHODE ISLAND.—At a public meeting in Providence, in October, 1874, I had the pleasure of hearing Governor Howard, who is no theorist, but a wealthy manufacturer, of unusual intelligence and candor, bear this most emphatic testimony to the success of the prohibitory law enacted in the spring of that year. The report is from the *Providence Journal* of the next morning :

" It was agreed on all hands that if it was possible to stay the ravages of intemperance it ought to be done. Where, then, is the remedy to be found? that was the question. To one conclusion I arrived, namely, that the strong arm of the law must be invoked. In what direction, I was not prepared to say. Those of you who remember my message to the Legislature last winter will remember that while I advocated stringent and energetic legislation, I stopped short, without recommending particularly the prohibitory law. I did so because I was not fully convinced that it was the best remedy to be found; but the law was adopted. After a long time, we succeeded in selecting such a force of men as was needed to execute those laws; and now, ladies and gentlemen, I am here to-night especially for the purpose of saying, not from the stand-point of a temperance man, but *as a public man, with a full sense of the responsibility which attaches to me from my representative position*, that to-day, *the prohibitory laws of this State*, if not a complete success, *are a success beyond the fondest anticipation* of any friend of temperance, in my opinion.

" Prohibitory legislation in Rhode Island *is a success to a marvelous extent*. I have desired, I have felt it incumbent upon me to make that declaration, and I desire that it shall go abroad as my solemn assertion."

And it was precisely *because of this success* that the liquor interest rallied so energetically to defeat the law.

MASSACHUSETTS. —The history and effects of the changing phases of legislation here we have had occasion to revert to in other connections, and we must confine ourselves here to brief general views of the results of prohibition, with a few special illustrations.

The law was first enacted in 1852. The graphic description given by the Rev. Horatio Wood, for nearly a quarter of a century the Unitarian City Missionary in Lowell, of its operation in that place, will apply more or less to all the cities outside of Boston. In the rural districts the open traffic had mostly disappeared before:

" It was my good fortune then to see a picture which has delighted my memory ever since. The sale of liquor was stopped in Lowell, so that the City Marshal had occasion to say, in a letter which he wrote to me at that time, that there was not a single place in Lowell where liquor was openly sold. . . . . A great many persons, who had been accustomed to drink, gave up drinking entirely. There were some who would have liquor in their houses. They would go beyond the line of the State and get their liquor in New Hampshire. . . . . But then it required more money to buy the liquor in any quantity than poor people generally had, and they soon got sick of that. One after another they would say, ' Well, we know it is best for us.' The wife would say, ' Husband, you know it is best for you. You know we have been a great deal happier and a great deal more respected since this law was passed.' And I will say here— what I wish distinctly understood in regard to the poor of Lowell—that *there is not so much a desire on their part for liquor, but by the temptations around them they are led into it ;* and not only led into it, but they are cajoled and pressed in every way into the purchase of liquor." (Testimony—Mass. House Doc. No. 415, 1867, pp. 538–9).

As far as regarded our cities, however, the scene soon changed. The law became measurably inoperative. As Mr. Wood says :

" At first there was an idea that the law was going to be carried out, and it must be succumbed to; but after a while it began to be asked, ' What is Boston going to do in the matter?' And when that question was asked, it began to be said that Boston was going to sell; then some began to make themselves bold to sell, and one city after another of our principal cities fell into the sale."

There were other causes, concurring with the influence of the metropolis, to paralyze for some years the effectual execution of the law. To enter into a consideration of these would lead us from our special topic.

But in 1865, coincident with the establishment of the State Police, there was a revival of zeal in the enforcement of the law, which continued up to the election in the fall of 1867. During that year alone the work of the State Police resulted in 5,331 liquor prosecutions, 1,979 seizures, aggregating 92,658 gallons of intoxicants, and the payment in fines and costs of

15

$226,427.19. (See Second Annual Report of the Constable of the Commonwealth).

That the result was a great diminution of the traffic hardly requires proof. The same report gives 819 as the number of dealers who had discontinued the traffic during that year alone.

At a hearing before the Legislative Committee of that year, Judge Sanger, then District Attorney of Suffolk County, testified that the prosecutions had "a tendency to diminish, and had in fact diminished," the sale even in Boston — "that is clearly seen since the decision in Mrs. Sinnot's case, for quite a number have come to me since then, and said they would throw up the business;" and he added: "Men will not be likely to engage in a business when they are likely to have every-day seizures made of their stock in trade." (Testimony, pp. 74–76).

Finally the Constable of the Commonwealth, in his Report above cited, was enabled to say:

"Up to the 6th of November (1867) *there was not an open bar known in the entire State, and the open* retail liquor traffic had almost entirely ceased. The traffic, as such, had generally secluded itself to such an extent that it was no longer a public, open offense, and no longer an inviting temptation to the passer-by" (p. 14).

Let the extent of the claim be carefully noticed—not that *all* sales were suppressed—a large clandestine traffic is admitted, but only that the bar-room traffic was suspended. On this point I also cite the testimony of the well-known pastor of the Beach Street Presbyterian church in Boston, the Rev. Dr. James B. Dunn, then a resident of New York city:

"During the year 1867 we made several thorough examinations of Boston to see how the law worked. In North Street we counted 56 closed stores, with the significant words 'To Let' on the shutters, while in the other places where liquor had formerly been sold, honest and lawful businesses were carried on. In those dark and narrow streets of the 'North End,' once crowded with throngs of thieves, harlots, and the most degraded wretches—where the dram-shops, dancing saloons, and houses of prostitution pushed their nefarious trade—now quietness and sobriety reigned. In one night during the month of May we visited, between the hours of nine and twelve, many of the liquor, dancing, and gambling saloons on Brattle, North, Commercial, Hanover, Union, Portland, Sudbury, Court, Howard, Fleet, Clark, and Friend Streets, and in no place was there seen, nor could there be openly bought, one glass of intoxicating drink.

"On another occasion we visited in the evening the principal hotels, such as Parker's, Tremont's, American, and Young's, and there found the same state of things to exist — bar-rooms empty, some of them closed; and where they were open this significant notice was hung up, 'No liquors sold over this bar.' "

In Circular No. 46, issued in October of the same year, the Constable of the Commonwealth used this significant language:

"To us who are daily observers of the effects of these prosecutions, the fact is not to be winked at or argued out of sight, that very many of the liquor dealers are utterly discouraged, and were it not for the hope that the approaching elections may afford them some relief, they would at once abandon the traffic."

The election came in a few weeks. The liquor interest and their political allies carried the State. The law was at once, for all practical purposes, repealed, and nominally repealed by the next Legislature. Between the day of the election and the 1st of April ensuing, 2,779 new liquor-shops were opened (1868, Senate Doc. No. 170). I repeat what I said at the time:

"License laws have been repealed for their inefficiency; and therein lies their permanent weakness. The prohibitory law is to be repealed for its efficiency; and therein lies its strength for the future."

The experience under license I have noticed in another chapter. The next year the prohibitory law was re-enacted. A fatal concession was made to the beer interest in 1870, the result of which is noticed elsewhere. It was not until 1873 that we returned to the policy of entire prohibition, But even of the year 1872 the then Chief Constable, Capt. George W. Boynton, in his report, January, 1873, was able to say :

"In small towns, especially where the public opinion of the place has been right, this traffic has been entirely suppressed, and in most of the small towns of the Commonwealth a very great improvement has been made. In the large towns and cities the work is more difficult. The dealers constitute a large class ; they represent wealth and exert a great influence on public opinion, so that it is not easy, even with sufficient evidence, to procure convictions. Besides, under a system of vigorous prosecutions, the dockets of the courts become so encumbered with the cases, that with the utmost diligence on the part of the courts and the district attorneys, but a small proportional number can be tried. In such cases the most that can be done, at present, is *to compel the dealers from open traffic ;* by seizures and prosecutions *to make the business disreputable ;* and to prosecute to the extent of the law where convictions can be obtained and public opinion will sustain the efforts."

I submit that this modest statement shows yet a degree of success such as no license system ever approached; and even in localities where the success is least marked, I have indicated, by italicizing, results which I deem of far-reaching importance, and in and of them-

selves an adequate vindication of the policy
of the law.

An increasingly vigorous prosecution of the
law took place up to the fall election of 1874,
when the law was again overthrown. The
prosecutions for that year were 7,126; seizures,
5,912, aggregating 117,683 gallons; fines and
costs paid, $152,189.62; number sentenced to
the House of Correction, 820. Of the results
of this action on a single branch of the trade
during 1874, Mr. Louis Shade, the special agent
of the Brewers' Congress, says:

> "Had our friends in Massachusetts been free to
> carry on their business, and had not the State author-
> ities constantly interfered, there is no doubt that in-
> stead of showing a decrease of 116,585 barrels in one
> year, they would have increased at the same rate as
> they did the preceding year."

Again, we note that the law was repealed,
not because it was weak, but because it was
strong.

I close this rapid general survey of the State
with two marked instances of the special success of prohibition, secured in very different
ways.

The city of Boston has always opposed prohibition. Yet, at the time of the "Great Fire,"
in November, 1872, the order was given by

the city to close all the dram-shops. "The good effects of this course," say the State Police Commissioners, "were manifest in the quiet streets of the city by day and night, even when in the absence of gas they were shrouded in darkness." The Chief of the City Police reported that the number of arrests for 10 days before the order was 1,169; for the 10 days after, only 675. Even Boston was compelled to see the blessing of ten days' prohibition.

Sometimes, a single experiment carefully performed and critically watched does more to impress a scientific truth than wider, but less exact, observations. It is possible, therefore, that a valuable impression may be made from a consideration of some phases of the problem of prohibition as wrought out in New Bedford. This is a maritime city of Massachusetts, with a population, in 1870, of 21,320. Its business since the partial decline of whaling has been gradually diversifying itself, and is now largely manufacturing, though not predominatingly so. Under the nominal enforcement of the prohibitory law which had then become the rule in the cities, a Committee of the Legislature in 1865 reported (Senate Doc. No. 200):

" Liquor is sold openly in New Bedford, but not in front-shops—the bars are generally in the back-rooms. From an actual count, there appear to be 138 places."

The same year the State Constabulary was established to remedy the remissness of the municipal authorities. In 1867 the City Marshal testified that there " were no places where liquor is sold in public, but a great many places where it is sold privately." In December, 1869, a City Government was elected upon the issue of a strict enforcement of the law. During the years 1870 and 1871 the City and State Police worked together for this object with such success that the liquor traffic was driven to peddle from the person its contraband fluids. Mark the results. In 1869 there were 298 arrests for drunkenness, and 565 "lodgers" at the station-house. In 1870 there were 181 arrests for same, and in 1871 there were 188, and 348 lodgers, showing a decrease, comparing 1869 with 1871 of 36 per cent. in arrests for drunkenness, and of over 38 per cent. in number of "lodgers." The aggregate commitments to the House of Correction and the Work-house, for all offenses, fell from 270 in 1869 to 130 in 1871—less than one-half. So much for *enforced* prohibition. In the chapter on the Beer Law we see the lesson of relapse.

VERMONT.—Governor Peck, who has been a Justice of the Supreme Court, says :

" In some parts of the State there has been a laxity

in enforcing it ; but in other parts of the State it has been thoroughly enforced, and there it has driven the traffic out. I think the influence of the law has been salutary in diminishing drunkenness and disorders arising therefrom, and also crimes generally. . . . . The *law* has had an *effect upon our customs*, and has done away with treating and promiscuous drinking. The law has been aided by moral means, but *moral means have also been wonderfully strengthened by the law."*

The testimony of Governor Converse is :

" The prohibitory law has been in force about twenty-two years. . . . . I consider it a very desirable law. I think the law itself educates and advances public sentiment in favor of temperance. There is no question about the decrease in the consumption of liquor. I speak from personal knowledge, having always lived in the State."

But actual pictures affect most minds more than statistics or general statements of officials, and I shall enliven these pages' by a lively sketch of the village of St. Johnsbury, with its 5,000 inhabitants, from a letter by Hepworth Dixon, the English tourist, who thus writes of this " workman's paradise " to a journal of his own country in 1874 :

" No bar, no dram-shop, no saloon defiles the place, nor is there a single gaming hell or house of ill-repute. Once, in my walks, I fancied there might be

15*

an opening in the armor of these Good Templars. Turning from the foreign street, I read a notice calling on the passer-by to enter the sporting and smoking bazaar. Here, surely, there must lurk some spice of dissipation. But I find myself in a big empty room; the floor clean, the walls bright, with a small kiosk in one corner for the sale of cigars and cigarettes, at which a nice-looking matron waits for customers, who are slow to come. 'They suffer you to sell tobacco, madam?' 'Yes, sir, for the present. Some are bent on putting down the sale, like that of beer and gin; a lecturer was here some nights ago; and in a year or so they may obtain a clear majority of votes.' 'Your trade will then be gone?' 'Well, some one must be last in everything, I guess.' I leave her, with a full conviction that there lurks no large amount of wickedness in this sporting and smoking bazaar.

" Intoxicating drinks are classed with poisons, such as laudanum and arsenic; but as poisons may be needed in a civilized country, under a scientific system of medicine, laudanum and arsenic are permitted to be sold in every civilized State. Such is here the case with brandy, beer, and wine. A public officer is appointed by public vote. The town lays in a stock of brandy, beer, and wine, which is carefully registered in books and kept under lock and key. These poisons are doled out, in small quantities, very much as deadly nightshade and nux vomica are doled out by a London druggist. ' Can not you get a bottle of Cognac for your private use?' I ask Col. Fairbanks. 'I can send my order,' he replies, 'for a pint of Cognac; it will be sent to me, of course; but my order for it will be filed, and the delivery entered

on the public books for every one to see.' 'You find
that system rather inquisitorial, do you not?' 'Well,
no ; it is intended for the common good, and every
one submits to what is for the good of all. We
freely vote the law, and freely keep the law. But for
myself the rule is a dead letter, since no intoxicating
drink ever enters my house.'

" In going through the mills, I notice 500 men toil-
ing in the various rooms. The work is mostly hard ;
in some departments very hard. The heat is often
very great. From seven o'clock till twelve, from one
till six—ten hours each day—the men are at their
posts. The range of heat and cold is trying, for the
summer sun is fierce, the winter frost is keen. Yet
the men engaged in these manufactories of scales are
said to drink no beer, no whisky, and no gin. Drinking and smoking are not allowed on the premises.
Such orders might be only meant for discipline ; but
I am told that these 500 workmen really never taste a
drop of either beer or gin. Their drink is water ;
their delight is tea. Yet every one assures me that
they work well, enjoy good health, and live as long
as persons of their class employed on farms. 'These
men,' I ask, 'who rake the furnaces, who carry the
burning metals, and who stand about the crucibles—
can they go on all day without their beer?' 'They
never taste a drop, and never ask to have a drop.
There is a can of water near them ; they like the
taste of water better than the fumes of ale, and do
their work more steadily without such fumes.'

" In fact, I find that these intelligent craftsmen are
the warmest advocates of the prohibitive liquor law.
They voted for it in the outset ; they have voted for

it ever since. Each year of trial makes them more
fanatical in its favor. Party questions often turn on
this liquor law, and these intelligent workmen always
vote for those who promise to extend its operations.

" 'You see,' says Col. Fairbanks, 'we are a nervous
and vehement race. Our air is dry and quick; our
life an eager and unsleeping chase. When we work,
we work hard. When we drink, we drink deep. It
is natural that when we abstain, we should abstain
with rigor.'

" 'Are there no protests?' 'None or next to
none; as year and year goes by, more persons come
to see the benefits of our rule. The men who formerly drank most are now the staunchest friends of
our reform. These men who used to dress in rags
are growing rich. Many of them live in their own
houses. They attend their churches, and their
children go to school.'

" Should a tipsy stranger be taken in the street, he
is seized like a stray donkey, run into a pound, and
kept apart until he has slept away the fumes of his
abominable dram. An officer then inquires where he
got his drink. On telling, he is set free, and the person who sold the liquor is arrested, tried, and punished for the man's offense. The vender, not the
buyer, is responsible for this breach of moral order."

The United States Internal Revenue Report
for 1874, shows that Vermont enjoys the honor
of furnishing the smallest revenue from spirits
of any State in the Union except Delaware,
which has less than thirty-eight per cent. of

her population, and more than makes up for her slight difference in the spirit tax by a large excess in fermented liquors.

Let us contrast two New England States. Vermont, with a population (census 1870) of 330,551, pays $14,969.75 on spirits and $3,301.45 on fermented liquors; Connecticut, with a population of 537,454, pays $277,295.98 on spirits and $59,447.51 on fermented liquors. A calculation will show that the license State pays over ten times the tax *per capita* for liquors that the prohibitory does.

CHAPTER XXII.

MAINE A CRUCIAL TEST,

WE devote a separate chapter to the experience of the State of Maine, because it seems to us that it is well entitled to be considered by candid friends and foes as a crucial test of the utility of enforced prohibition. It has been on her statute-book for a quarter of a century; it has had the general support of the Administration; it is a State of large area, with many considerable cities, and with very diversified industries. It has, therefore, the general conditions requisite for a satisfactory experiment. And although the friends of the law might speak of some special hinderances and embarrassments in the way of its perfect operation, yet if no decided and manifest gain is to be found, we shall have to confess that, however excellent the theory of the machine may be, it must be thrown aside as of no working value.

We accept the test. Why should not our opponents do the same?

The testimony as to the result is full and authoritative. We shall seem to many to cumulate unnecessarily. But the substantial agreement of many men of different positions, temperaments, and views adds greatly to the impressiveness of the evidence.

And, first, let us look at

MAINE AS SHE WAS.

The enactment of a law prohibiting the sale of intoxicating liquors as a beverage, always supposes the existence of a pretty active temperance sentiment; and when the observer sees the sobriety, good order, and prosperity of a community under such a system, the query arises whether the state of society is due to the law, or the law to the state of society. And, indeed, it is not possible to separate the two into an invariable antecedent and an invariable consequent. Each are both. The public sentiment begets the law; the law solidifies and increases the public sentiment. But the net gain from the law, both direct and indirect, may be seen from comparing the state of things before and after. And I have been surprised to learn the extent to which Maine formerly suffered from drink.

I call a few, but thoroughly competent, witnesses to this point.

Neal Dow, in a letter to the *Alliance News*, writes:

" In every city, town, village, and rural district in the

State, every tavern was a 'rum hole' and every grocery was a groggery.   The immensely valuable pine
timber, with which the State abounded, was sent in
great quantities from all our ports to the West Indies,
and the returns were almost nothing else than West
India rum, and molasses to be distilled into New England rum, and these products of the lumber trade
were consumed by our people; and so our grand for-
ests went down their throats in the form of rum !

"The distilling business here was very large.   In
Portland alone were seven distilleries, often running
night and day, and at the same time cargoes of West
India rum were landed at our wharves.   I think I
have seen nearly an acre of puncheons of West India
rum at one time on our wharves, just landed from
ships.   All this time seven distilleries running night
and day !   Now I will venture to say that we have
not had a puncheon of West India rum imported here
in five years, yes, I will say ten years, and there is but
one distillery in the State—not that running, I think;
but, if it runs, it is laid under $3,000 bonds to sell no
spirit except for medicinal or mechanical purposes, or
for exportation.   In those old times, every grocery
in Portland, whether a wholesale or retail shop, sold
liquors of all sorts ; now there is but one where liquors
are supposed to be kept.   There are low, base, Irish
shanties there, keeping 'tabaccy' and other small
matters, where liquor is sold more or less, in violation
of law ; but our groceries are strictly free from the
trade.

"Now these are mostly general declarations as to
the improved state of things in Maine.   I have spoken of a wonderfully diminished production and im·

portation of alcoholic liquors, but rather in a general
way. Let me go a little into particulars as to the
diminished consumption of them, a sort of treatment
of the matter that may be more satisfactory to out-
siders. I know well the town and village of Gorham ;
it is nine miles from my house ; the village is a ' corner,' a ' cross-roads,' as such places are sometimes
called. The town is a rural district of country—a
beautiful farming place. At the ' Corner ' were numerous shops—' Variety Stores,' as they were called—
keeping all sorts of goods for the country trade, from
salt, bar-iron, ox-chains, mill saws, and grindstones, to
all kinds of common ironmongery, common crockery,
common drapery, common haberdashery, and groceries, including liquors of all sorts. Every shop in Gorham had such a stock, larger or smaller in quantity and
assortment, according to the capital of the trader.
These shops bought their supplies in Portland, and
all the farmers for many miles about came there ' to
trade,' exchanging their farm products. for ' store
goods,' including always a large supply of rum ; and
the balance of the trade against them, which was generally considerable, was charged to their account, and,
after a few years, was secured by a mortgage on the
farm.

" Now there is not a rum-shop in that whole town.
The habits of the people have been entirely changed ;
they spend no more money for rum, and their farms
are freed from mortgage. At one time, a Gorham
man told me, three-fourths of the farms were mort-
gaged for ' store debts,' which would not have been
contracted but for the rum. I am familiar with all
this, having often visited a cousin there, on a noble

farm which he had purchased of a trader, who had it
by foreclosure of a rum mortgage! In the old time
the farmers were all poor, their farms and farm buildings were neglected and dilapidated, and everything
about the country as well as about the towns had
decided marks of the presence of the drink demon.
Now all that is changed, and we have no more thrifty
citizens than the farmers of Gorham. I have myself
a beautiful farm in that township, with a noble mansion upon it, now in perfect order, that I remember in
the old time as bearing marks of the general neglect.
This farm, like almost all others in Maine in the old
time, has a chequered and melancholy history, connected with the decay and final running out of the
noted families who formerly owned it. All through
the State are towns almost innumerable, whose his-
tories, as affected by drink and the drink traffic, are
precisely like that of Gorham. I could fill up a column
of your paper with the names of country towns well
known to me personally, which could be substituted,
and the picture would be a faithful one all the same."

I next call Hon. William P. Frye, at present
one of the delegation in Congress, and ex-
Attorney-General of the State. In a letter to
the *Chicago Advance* (March 19, 1874) he says:

"Twenty-five years ago, the most of our grocery
stores, all druggists, all hotels, both in city and country, sold liquors, and, in my opinion, the majority of
grown men used them as a beverage. Poverty, crime,
suffering, and ignorance prevailed; our jails were full,
our farmyards empty, the landlord rich, his neighbors

for miles around poor; his house well painted, glazed,
and blinded, and full of comfort; theirs unpainted,
the windows stuffed with rags, the rooms full of nothing but sorrow."

He adds: " *When the law was enacted, I have no
doubt two-thirds of the people were at heart opposed to
it ; now they could not be induced to repeal it.*"

Ex-Governor Perham, in his testimony before
the Canadian Commission, on this point says :

" Forty years ago intoxicating liquors were sold as
freely in this State as the necessaries of life.   It is
notorious at that time, and later, nearly every country store and tavern was a dram-shop.   I happened
to have statistics gathered in 1834, in the then rural
town of Waterville, in a neighboring county, when it
appeared that nearly every store and tavern sold intoxicating liquor by the glass, the sales of liquor in
that year being four hundred hogsheads."

My only other witness upon this point shall
be the Hon. Woodbury Davis, ex-Judge of the
Supreme Court.   Speaking of the time after
the old Temperance reform and the Washingtonian movement had each successively reached
its climax, he says :

" Notwithstanding all the good that was done in
reforming the habits of the people, there were still
large numbers accustomed to use intoxicating liquors;
and there was really no legal restraint upon the sale.
It was permitted in almost every town ; nearly every

tavern, in country and in city, had its 'bar;' at almost
every village and 'corner' was a grog-shop; and, in
most places of that kind, more than one, where old
men and young spent their earnings in dissipation;
men helplessly drunk in the streets and by the way-
side were a common sight; and at elections, at military trainings and musters, and at other public gath-
erings, there were scenes of debauchery and riot
enough to make one ashamed of his race." ("Maine
Law Vindicated," p. 7).

Now for

MAINE AS SHE IS.

And as we desire to cover the whole ground,
let us commence with recalling the last witness,
and let him tell us of the results of the law up
to the time of his testimony. He resumes:

" What has become of this mass of corruption and
disgusting vice? It seems so much like some horrid
dream of the past, that we can hardly realize that it
was real and visible until twenty years ago. The
Maine Law has swept it away forever. In some of
our cities something of the kind may still be seen;
but in three-fourths of the towns in this State such
scenes would now no more be tolerated than would
the revolting orgies of savages. A stranger may pass
through, stop at a hotel in each city, walk the streets
in some of them, and go away with the belief that our
law is a failure. But no observing man who has lived
in the State for twenty years, and has had an opportunity to know the facts, can doubt that the Maine

Law has produced a hundred times more visible improvement in the character, condition, and prosperity of our people than any other law that was ever enacted.

" I have always resided in this State. At the bar I assisted in conducting to a successful result scores, if not hundreds, of prosecutions against liquor-sellers, under the statutes of 1846 and 1851. Having since 1855 served for nearly ten years as one of the associate-justices of our Supreme Court, I have tried many cases, against common sellers, in different counties, from one extreme of the State to the other. And notwithstanding the unfaithfulness or timidity of Temperance men, the difficulties of enforcing the law, the inadequacy of its penalties, and the effect of the war in retarding its execution, I am convinced, by what I have seen, that it has accomplished an incalculable amount of good. Of our four hundred towns and cities, making the estimate below what I believe the facts would justify, I am satisfied that in more than one hundred the law prevents any sale of liquors whatever for a beverage. In at least two hundred of them it is sold only in the way that Doctor Bacon calls ' on the sly,' just as, in the same towns, there are persons guilty of lewdness and other crimes.

" In most of the other one hundred towns liquors are sold probably without much restraint. But in these the traffic generally shrinks from the public gaze, conscious of its guilt and shame. And though the law is but partially enforced, prosecutions under it are numerous and constant even in places where large quantities are sold. The condition of things, therefore, even in such places is far better than ever it was under the license laws " (*id.*)

We now proceed with more recent testimony, showing still greater improvement.

First, we will hear from the Governors of the State for a succession of years :

GOVERNORS.

" BRUNSWICK, MAINE, *June* 3, 1872.

" The declaration made by many persons that the Maine Law is inoperative, and that liquors are sold freely and in large quantities in this State, is not true. The liquor traffic has been greatly repressed and diminished here and throughout the State, and in many places has been entirely swept away. The law is as well executed generally in the State as other criminal laws are.

" Many persons think that there is not one-tenth so much liquor sold in the State as there was formerly. While we prefer not to certify to any particular degree of repression of the traffic, we say without reserve that if liquors are sold at all, it is in very small quantities compared with the old times, and in a secret way, as other unlawful things are done.

" JOSHUA L. CHAMBERLAIN."

(General Chamberlain was Governor from 1867 to 1871, and is now President of Bowdoin College).

" EXECUTIVE DEPARTMENT,
" AUGUSTA, MAINE, *June* 3, 1872.

" MY DEAR SIR :—In answer to your inquiry in regard to the effect of the Maine Law upon the liquor trade in this State, I think it safe to say that it is very much less than before the enactment of the law— probably not one-tenth as large. In some places liquor is sold secretly in violation of law, as many other offenses are committed against the statutes, and the peace and good order of society; but in large districts of the State, the liquor traffic is nearly or quite unknown, where formerly it was carried on like any other trade.

"Very respectfully yours,

"SIDNEY PERHAM,

"TO GEN. NEAL DOW.   *Governor of Maine.*"

HON. NELSON DINGLEY, JR., Governor from 1874 to 1876, writes to the editors of the *Chicago Advance* (March 19, 1874):

"We have had twenty-three years' experience of the policy of prohibition, and the results have been, on the whole, so far greater than those secured by any other system of legal restraint that the prohibitory policy is accepted as a settled fact in this State, and no considerable body of men favor its repeal. In more than three-fourths of the State, particularly in the rural sections, open dram-shops are almost unknown, and secret sales comparatively rare. In some of the cities and larger villages, where public sentiment on the temperance question is not so well sustained as in the rural districts, the law is not so effectively enforced as to prevent open sales to some extent, although, even in such places, prohibition is not without some influence for good. Statistics show that under the influence of our prohibitory system and the indispensable moral efforts which have been put forth to increase its efficiency, the sale and use of liquor in this State have very largely decreased ; that drinking habits have ceased to be fashionable; and that total abstinence has come to be a common virtue instead of, as formerly, a rare exception."

The present Governor, General CONNOR, thus alludes to the subject in his message, (1876) :

"I have no official information to present to you with regard to the working of the laws prohibiting the sale of intoxicating liquors. It is a matter of common knowledge that they have been very generally enforced, especially in the cities and large towns, where the traffic is most persistently attempted to be carried on in defiance of them. The law as a whole fairly represents the sentiment of the people. The opposition to it presents in appearance a strength which it does not in reality possess.

"Maine has a fixed conclusion upon this subject. It is that the sale of intoxicating liquors is an evil of such magnitude that the well-being of the State demands, and the conditions of the social compact warrant, its suppression."

It so happens that the certificates of three other Governors to the same effect, appear under other heads in this chapter—Crosby (Governor from 1853 to 1855), Hamlin (1857), L. M. Morrill (1858 to 1860).

In this connection it may be a significant fact to notice that among the "planks" in the platform of the Republican Convention of 1875, was this:

"Temperance among the people may be wisely promoted by prohibitory legislation, and it is a source of congratulation that the policy of prohibition always upheld by the Republicans of Maine, is now concurred in by a vast majority of the people of the State."

A similar resolution was adopted at the late Convention in August, 1877.

I believe the "Democrats" ·have ceased to "resolve" against it; and, indeed, such a resolution introduced at their last Convention was decisively rejected.

CONGRESSMEN.

The following certificates give the judgment of the entire delegation in Congress from the State—Messrs. Hamlin (formerly Vice-President) and Morrill being the Senators, and Messrs. Blaine (then Speaker), Frye, Peters, Hale, and Lynch, the Representatives.

"WASHINGTON, D. C., *May* 29, 1872.

"MY DEAR SIR:—Your favor of the 26th instant, containing an inquiry as to the effect of the Maine Liquor Law in restraining the sale of liquors in our

State, etc., is before me; and in reply, while I am unable to state any exact percentage of decrease in the
business, I can and do, from my own personal observation, unhesitatingly affirm that the consumption of
intoxicating liquors in Maine is not to-day one-fourth
so great as it was twenty years ago; that, in the country portions of the State, the sale and use have almost
entirely ceased; that the law of itself, under a vigorous enforcement of its provisions, has created a temperance sentiment which is marvelous, and to which
opposition is powerless. In my opinion, our remarkable temperance reform of to-day is the legitimate
child of the law.

" With profound gratitude for your earnest and persistent efforts in the promotion of this cause, I am,
very respectfully, your obedient servant,

"WM. P. FRYE, M. C., of Maine,
" And ex-Attorney General of same State.
" HON. NEAL DOW."

" I have the honor unhesitatingly to concur in the
opinions expressed in the foregoing, by my colleague,
Hon. Mr. Frye.   LOT M. MORRILL.
" UNITED STATES SENATE, *May* 29, 1872."

" I concur in the foregoing statements; and on the
point of the relative amount of liquors sold at present
in Maine and in those States where a system of license
prevails, I am very sure, from personal knowledge and
observation, that the sales are immeasurably less in
Maine.   J. G. BLAINE."

"SENATE CHAMBER, *May* 29, 1872.

" I concur in the statements made by Mr. Frye.

In the great good produced by the Prohibitory Liquor Law of Maine, no man can doubt who has seen its result. It has been of immense value.

"H. HAMLIN."

"HOUSE OF REPRESENTATIVES.

"We are satisfied that there is much less intemperance in Maine than formerly, and that the result is largely produced by what is termed prohibitory legislation.

"JOHN A. PETERS, M. C., of Maine.
"EUGENE HALE, M. C., of Maine."

"I fully concur in the statement of my colleague Mr. Frye, in regard to the effect of the enforcement of the Liquor law in the State of Maine.

"JOHN LYNCH, M. C., of Maine."

I have before me a similar declaration, made by most of the above in 1875, with the substitution of J. H. BURLEIGH, who succeeds Mr. Lynch. Mr. Burleigh "concurs in the opinion that the Maine Law in operation in this State has proved to be most expedient and wise."

I pass to the testimony of those whose official duties have made them familiar with the liquor traffic :

"THE SUPERVISOR OF INTERNAL REVENUE, *May* 31, 1872.

"In answer to your inquiry, I have to say, that in the course of my duty as an Internal Revenue officer, I have become thoroughly acquainted with the state and extent of the liquor traffic in Maine, and I have no hesitation in saying that the beer trade is not more than one per cent. of what I remember it to have been, and the trade in distilled liquors is not more than 10 per cent. of what it was formerly.

"WOLCOTT HAMLIN, Super. of Int. Rev.,
"Dist. Maine, New Hamphire, and Vermont.
"To GEN. NEAL DOW."

PROSECUTING OFFICERS.

The Report of the Attorney-General for 1874 contains reports from many of the county attorneys in relation to this subject. I make room for a portion.

The attorney for *Aroostook* (on the north-east frontier of the State) says:

"The Sheriff has been very diligent in looking after the violators of the law. It is a noticeable fact that the cause of temperance is prospering in this county, and especially in the town of Houlton, to a degree never before witnessed. The enforcement of the law has diminished the number of dram-shops and driven the traffic into secret places."

Cumberland (includes Portland).—"The amount collected (fines and costs) in the Superior Court is larger than that collected in any previous year, and, I think, is more than sufficient to pay the expenses of prosecution. I have met with no difficulties in prosecuting persons indicted for violations of the liquor law, which do not attend the successful prosecution of other criminal offenses."

Hancock.—"Almost all of the liquor traffic in this county is carried on in Ellsworth. There is hardly any other town where public sentiment gives it any countenance. In Ellsworth we have not suppressed the traffic wholly, but in no place is liquor sold openly. Every possible precaution is taken by the sellers to protect themselves against the law."

Lincoln.—"The liquor traffic in this county has been confined chiefly to the towns of Waldoboro', Damariscotta, and Wiscasset. Several attempts have been made to open and run rum-shops, but they have in every instance been nipped in the bud and stopped. In Waldoboro' and Damariscotta, and also in Bristol, the work has been very successful, and the temperance people seem well satisfied with the results; but in Wiscasset the work has not been so successful in closing up the business. At the last October Term every rum-seller in that town was indicted and paid his fine of $100 and costs. I am satisfied that some of them will stop, and some will doubtless persist."

Androscoggin (which includes the large manufacturing city of Lewiston).—"I think I am justified in saying that at this time there is not an open bar for the sale of intoxicating liquor in the county."

York.—"During the present year, signalized as it has been by a prolonged effort to suppress the traffic by force of law, crowned as this effort has been by success much exceeding our most sanguine expectations, the people of this county have marked the contrast between free rum and total prohibition. The absence of petty crime, the peace and good order in the community, are most gratifying.

"In the city of Biddeford, a manufacturing place of 11,000 inhabitants, for a month at a time not a single arrest for drunkenness and disturbance has been made or become necessary."

MAYORS AND OTHER OFFICIALS.

"PORTLAND, *May* 28, 1872.

"In reply to your request to us to state our impression as to the diminution of the liquor traffic in the State of Maine, and particularly in this city, as the result of the adoption of the policy of prohibition, we have to say that the traffic has fallen off very largely. In relation to that there can not possibly be any doubt.

"Many persons, with the best means of judging, believe that the liquor trade now is not one-tenth as large as it was formerly. We do not know but such an opinion is correct, but we content ourselves with saying that the diminution of the trade is very great, and the favorable effects of the policy of prohibition are manifest to the most casual observer.

"BENJ. KINGSBURY, JR., Mayor.

"W. M. THOMAS, ex-Mayor.

"AUG. E. STEVENS, ex-Mayor.

"J. T. MCCOBB, ex-Mayor.

"JACOB MCLELLAN, ex-Mayor."

"We are sure that the liquor trade is greatly diminished.

"JOSEPH HOWARD, ex-Mayor.

"D. W. FESSINDEN, } Clerk of all the Judicial Courts for Cumberland Co.

" EBEN. PERRY, Sheriff of Cumberland Co.
" WM. E. MORRIS, Judge of the Municipal Court.
" WM. SENTER, ex-Alderman."

"We are of the decided opinion that the liquor trade is not one-tenth of what it was prior to the adoption of the Maine Law.

> " EBEN. LEACH, Register Cumberland Co.
> " H. J. ROBINSON, City Clerk.
> " H. W. HERSEY, City Treasurer.
> " M. D. LANE, Judge Sup. Court.

" To GEN. NEAL DOW."

Augusta is the capital. We append the testimony of officials there :

"If we were to say that the quantity of liquors sold here is not one-tenth so large as formerly, we think it would be within the truth ; and the favorable effects of the change upon all the interests of the State are plainly seen everywhere.

> " J. J. EVELETH, Mayor of Augusta, Maine.
> " JOSHUA NYE, Augusta, late State Constable.
> " G. G. STACY, Secretary of State.
> " B. B. MURRAY, Adjutant-General."

Let us hear from a rural district :

" DIXFIELD, OXFORD CO., ME., *June* 4, 1872.

"I am thoroughly acquainted with my own county (Oxford), and do not hesitate to say that there is not now a gallon of liquor sold where there was a barrel before the Maine Liquor law of 1851.

"At our last term of the Supreme Judicial Court,

in March, not a single indictment for any crime was
found.　Our [county] jail is empty, our work-house
greatly reduced, and the improvement wonderful.

"E. G. HARLOW,
"Member Exec. Council in Maine."

To this additional letter of ex-Mayor PUT-
NAM, who was elected by the Democrats of
Portland at a time when, as a party, they open-
ly opposed the law, I invite careful attention:

"PORTLAND, MAINE, *May* 29, 1872.

"MY DEAR SIR:—In reply to your inquiry, although never yet able to approve the principles of
Prohibitory Liquor Laws, I must in candor state:

"I have had good opportunity to observe the condition of this State in the matter of the use and sale
of intoxicating liquors for several years past, as compared with some other States where there are no prohibitory laws, and am certain that the rural portions
of Maine are, and have been, in an infinitely better
condition with reference to the sale and use of such
liquors than similar portions of other States referred
to; and are, and have been, moreover, comparatively
free from both the sale and use; and this must fairly
be considered the result of prohibitory legislation.

"In the large towns and cities I have not observed,
for the most part, any substantial difference in the
above respects between this State and other States.

"At the present time, however, the law is probably enforced even in large towns and cities as thoroughly, at least, as any other penal statute.

" Any discussion as to whether as much could be accomplished by some other system, to my fancy more in accordance with that of a Republican people, is not called for by your inquiry.

" Very truly,   WM. S. PUTNAM.
" HON. NEAL DOW."

We now give the testimony of Bangor officials :

" MAYOR'S OFFICE, CITY OF BANGOR, *May* 30, 1872.

" SIR :—Your note is received, asking my opinion of the effect of the Maine Law upon the liquor trade in Bangor and in the State generally. . . . .

" Last year the law was seldom enforced in our city ; this year it has been.

" The records of our police courts show only about one-fifth the number of cases before it as compared with last year. For a portion of the year the *weekly* number of commitments to the station is about the same as the *daily* was last year.

" The law is being enforced throughout the State as never before, and with wonderful success.

" No resident of our State can have any doubt that the liquor traffic has been greatly repressed and reduced.

" It is safe to say that in our city not one-tenth part as much is sold now as in years past, when the law was not enforced.

" Your obedient servant,

" J. S. WHEELWRIGHT, Mayor."

16*

" We fully concur in the foregoing statement.

" W. C. CROSBY and ⎰ Aldermen for 1871 and
" CHAS. HAYWARD, ⎱   1872.

" JOHN H. HAYES, City Clerk.

" ALPHEUS LYON, ⎰ Recorder of the Police
⎩ Court of Bangor.

" A. G. WAKEFIELD, ex-Mayor.

" JOHN E. GODFREY, Judge of Probate.

" JERE. FENNO, ⎰ Collector of Internal Reve-
⎩ nues, 4th District, Maine."

CLERGYMEN.

Eleven clergymen of the city of Portland, representing seven distinct denominations, appended their names in 1872 to a declaration, as follows :

" We say without hesitation, that the trade in intoxicating liquors has been greatly reduced by it ('the Maine Law ').

" In this city the quantity sold now is but a small fraction of what we remember the sales to have been, and we believe the results are the same, or nearly so, throughout the State.   If the trade exists at all here, it is carried on with secrecy and caution, as other unlawful practices are.   All our people must agree that the benefits of this state of things are obvious and very great."

The venerable Enoch Pond, Professor in the Bangor Theological Seminary, expresses his concurrence with the certificate heretofore given, from the officials of that city.

"The pastors of Free Baptist churches in various parts of Maine, assembled at a Denominational Convention in Portland in 1872, unanimously agreed to a declaration 'That the liquor traffic is very greatly diminished under the repressive power of the Maine Law. It can not be one tithe of what it was.'"

The census of 1870 gives us another glimpse at what the progressive enforcement of this law has done for Maine. Thus the number of persons convicted of crime in 1860, is given as 1,215, while in 1870 the number had fallen to 431. So the number of paupers in 1860 was 8,946; in 1870, only 4,619.

And the Overseers of the Poor in Portland in 1872 united in this declaration :

"The favorable effect of this policy is very evident, particularly in the department of pauperism and crime. While the population of the city increases, pauperism and crime diminish, and in the department of police the number of arrests and commitments is very much less than formerly."

The editor of the *Chicago Advance* (the leading Congregational paper of the West), in 1874 wrote to prominent citizens of Maine for "their opinion of the efficacy of the Prohibitory Law, formed from their personal observation of its working." In publishing their replies in full the *Advance* remarked :

" Their testimony is shaded according to individual'
acquaintance with the operations of the law, but will
be found *to agree for the most part in the main points
of interest.*"

Most of the letters were from public men,
whose testimony we have given. The most
discouraging one is from the Rev. John O.
Fiske, D.D., one of the most "conservative"
of men, residing in Bath. This is a sea-faring
community. According to his account, the law
at that time had lax enforcement. He says :

" In the leading hotels the free sale of intoxicating
liquors is notorious, at the same time that the proprietor of one of them has given his bond not to sell
any. I often meet with drunken men in the streets,
and there is no doubt that drinking alcoholic liquors
in places of public sale, as well as private houses, is
very common. What is true of Bath is true of many
other places of equal importance in the State."

Yet, he goes on to say :

" The law is all that the best friends of temperance
can desire ; only there is wanting in many places the
needed public sentiment properly to enforce it. In
many small country places almost no liquor at all is
sold by the glass ; and this happy condition of things
is attributed, whether with justice or no, I can not
say, to the force of the Prohibitory Law.
" It seems to me to be very well and right to brand
by law, as illegal and criminal, a traffic which is act-

ually disgraceful and exceedingly dangerous. It is well at any rate to have good laws, and to prohibit what is so obviously and largely detrimental to the public interests, even if we can not hope by such legal prohibition actually and entirely to suppress it. I am inclined to think that the influence of the law, on the whole, is decidedly beneficial in helping to. maintain a proper tone of public sentiment. The sale of liquors is kept out of sight as an illegal business, and probably less liquor is sold than would be if our system of prohibitory legislation was repealed."

The testimony of clergymen has *special* significance only so far as they are accustomed to that kind of religious work, which brings them to the homes of all their people. We close our evidence, therefore, with a letter from the Rector of St. Stephen's Episcopal Church in Portland. It is evident that he knows whereof he affirms :

"PORTLAND, MAINE, *June* 4, 1872.

"MY DEAR GENERAL :—I was surprised to learn from you that the cause of temperance is damaged in England by an impression that it has been retarded here from the Maine Law and similar enactments.

"That the contrary is true I feel sure, and am certain that it is, within the sphere of my observation for the past fifteen years.

"Many, in the humble classes of society particularly, have correct views, and form good resolutions, which they carry out successfully when not solicited to drink by the open bar.

"Mar.y wives have assured me of the improved condition of their families through the greater restraints put upon their husbands.

"Families whose homes are in drinking neighborhoods, or in streets where formerly were many drunken brawls, have gratefully acknowledged the happy change wrought by the due administration of the law suppressing tippling-shops.

"To make this law a still greater blessing all that is needed is to enforce it as faithfully in the future as at the present time.

"Truly yours,   A. DALTON.

"HON. NEAL DOW."

U. S. OFFICIAL STATISTICS.

The United States Census Report for 1870, and the last Internal Revenue Report which I have at hand (1874), supply proof of a different kind, tending to the same result. Let us compare Maine with two other States under license laws, one in New England, and the other in the Middle States, and selected not as the worst of their class, but as nearly related in population:

	Population.	*Distilleries.*	*Breweries.*	*Retailers.* (a)	*Liquor Revenue.* (b)
Maine	626,915	1	3	843	$ 49,237.77
Connecticut . .	537,454	68	23	3,353	336,743.49
Maryland. . . .	780,894	43	65	4,285	1,285,700.15

(a) The number in Maine, of course, includes the town agencies.

(b) These sums are the aggregates of all revenue collections on spirits and fermented liquors, as given in report for 1874, pp. 78, 79.

To all this weight of evidence of various kinds I should have said, until recently, that Mr. Murray, the British Consul, stands opposed. For he has been annually writing to his Government upon the strength of the police reports of Portland, which, as it is a seaport town where the law has been variously and spasmodically enforced, show a considerable number of arrests for drunkenness, that "the Maine Law is a failure." But I learn from an English paper that his report for 1875 contains this important admission :

" As regards the town and villages there can be no manner of doubt that the law has been nearly successful."

Well, if that were all, the towns and villages, the homes of the major part of the people, and the nurseries of all that is ultimately great and powerful in the cities, were well worth the saving. But we have seen that the law is not without beneficent action in the cities.

In view of what has been accomplished since the testimony above given was obtained, and of the recent action under the more stringent penalties of the law of 1877, I shall seem to our friends in Maine to have made an understatement of their present condition ; but the case will bear it, and I leave it without addition.

From the testimony we have now adduced, it would seem that the Committee on the Judiciary of the House of Representatives of the United States were justified in- saying in their Report upon the Commission of Inquiry, made in January, 1874, through their chairman, Judge Poland, as follows :

" For a considerable number of years the general opinion of those most interested to break up and suppress the use of intoxicating drinks has been that the only sure and effectual mode was by prohibiting their manufacture and sale, and thus cut off the means of supply of those disposed to drink. In many of the States such laws have been passed, and more or less rigidly enforced. That they have ever been, or ever will be, enforced so strictly that no intoxicating liquors will be used, probably no one believes or expects ; but *that their effect has been greatly to lessen the consumption in all the States having such laws, the committee believe will be conceded by every candid man living in such States.* It is often asserted that the use of liquor has increased in such States ; but the allegation is uniformly found to come from persons who are hostile to a prohibitory law."

CHAPTER XXIII.

SECRET DRINKING.

THE assertion is frequently made at random, that the diminution of the open traffic in intoxicants under a *régime* of prohibition is balanced by an increase of secret indulgence. The assertion seems to me so reckless and unreasonable, that I should hardly think of devoting a chapter to its refutation, had I not found, by a recent letter from a clergyman of intelligence and candor, that it was possible for him to query whether, " While public drinking has been reduced by prohibition, has not secret drinking been the re-action ? "

I answer, first, that the alleged increase of secret drinking is entirely supposititious, and not supported by proof.

But more than this, it is negatived by the evidence heretofore adduced, showing, by the internal revenue returns, very greatly reduced sales in Maine and other prohibitory States.

So also all the evidence adduced to show under prohibition a diminution of the *sequences* of drinking, intemperance, pauperism, and crime is conclusive proof of the abatement of drinking itself, whether it be open or secret.

And the result is entirely in accordance with the reason of the thing. It is not, of course, intended to deny that, in some individual cases, the repression of open drinking will be followed by secret indulgence. But all that is claimed is that the amount of the latter is not nearly sufficient to replace the former.

It is necessary, again, to call attention to a proposition, the truth of which we have already had occasion to consider.

This is not a case where a natural demand calls for and creates a supply, but where a tempting supply creates an unnatural demand.

Nor is drinking generally *willful.* In the outset, it is rarely so ; and even among sots there are a large class who "feel the body of the death out of which they cry hourly, with feebler and feebler outcry, to be delivered."

Prohibition, at the least, gains time for the struggling soul—and time is sometimes victory for sobriety ; it prevents the " *look* upon the wine-cup when it is red," which inflames desire ; it substitutes for the glare and glamour of a fashionable traffic the ghastly surroundings and the secrecy of a criminal occupation ; it lifts up the warning finger of the law to the yet unfallen, pointing out that this way danger lies.

In the "Editor's Easy Chair" of *Harper's Monthly* for August, 1869, George William Curtis gives us this suggestive incident :

"A law, even when public sentiment is not exactly ready for it, if its intention is supported by the public conscience, if its operation naturally leads to better order, to greater happiness and lower taxation—has a certain victory. Unquestionably the Maine law had it. It was said, indeed, derisively, that a man could get as much liquor to drink as ever in Maine or New Hampshire, or wherever this outrageous inquisitorial statute prevailed. And so he might, but not agreeably. 'The Easy Chair' proved it upon various occasions. It proved it on the State of Maine itself. A vague intimation, consisting of a wink, and a smile, and a nod, conveyed the possibility of ' getting a drink' even in the capital city of the temperate Commonwealth. Following the wink, like a convict, the turnkey and the ' Easy Chair' passed through the corridors to a door, which was unlocked ; then down a narrow staircase into a cellar—and hotel cellars do not always stimulate the imagination ; then to another door, which, being duly unlocked, and closed, and re-locked upon the inside, revealed a dark, dim room—a cell in a cellar—with half a dozen black bottles and some cloudy glasses. This cheerful entertainment was at the pleasure of the convict. The turnkey pours out a glass of something, and offers it to his companion. It was better than Father Mathew. 'No, thank you ; not upon these terms.' The turnkey looked amused. 'Wa'al, it isn't exactly gay !' and he swallowed the potion ; and leading the way, furtively

opened the door again and locked it; and the two
revellers, with the jollity of conscious malefactors,
stole back again into the light of day."

Can the force of prejudice go so far as to induce any one to say that a traffic pursued and
hunted down into such quarters as these can
be as dangerous to public virtue or private
morals as the flaunting and fashionable saloons
of New York?
Drinking follows the same law as that which
governs the prevalence of analogous social
vices.   Public tolerance, facility of gratification,
open temptation,* tasteful and enticing acces-

---

* Upon analogous matters, the daily press of our cities talks
sensibly.   Thus the Boston *Globe* of July 29, 1875, after con-
demning the laxity of the police, says : " It is perhaps not necessary to dwell on the evils which spring from this disgraceful state
of things, and yet people seldom think how great a proportion of
these might be prevented by driving this iniquity into its hiding-
places, and preventing it from coming forth to lure its victims
from among the unwary and comparatively guileless.   Few young
men who are worth saving, or are likely to be saved to decency and
virtue, would seek it out if it were kept from sight.   But when
it comes forth in gay and alluring colors, it draws after it a pro-
cession of our youth on that path which hath an awful termina-
tion.   Nor does the evil which springs from an easy toleration
of the open way in which this vice carries on its traffic of destruction fall only on men.   A sad proportion of these 'strange
women' is made up from shop-girls and those who are not so
infatuated at the start that they would plunge into a life of prostitution if it were strictly under the ban and kept widely separated
from the world of decency.   But it intrudes itself upon them.
Its temptations and opportunities are before their eyes, and the
way is made easy for their feet to go down to death."

sories increase, while the opposite of these diminish indulgence.

And this law is generally recognized. The good sense of our Anglo-Saxon race teaches us that outlawed vice is much less dangerous to the public weal than legalized vice. Because secret prostitution is alarmingly prevalent in New York, no moralist proposes to license it as in Paris, or to allow it to advertise itself at the windows of palatial residences, as in some quarters of European cities. Because behind barred doors in Boston the gambler shakes his dice, we do not propose to assign him elegant and well-lighted apartments on Washington Street with the coat-of-arms of the Commonwealth of Massachusetts on a license to be hung over his doorway. Others have tried the costly experiment for us of old and of late. I cut this instructive paragraph from the Boston *Evening Transcript:*

" *How Licensed Gambling Worked in Louisiana.*— The evil effects of the license system, as applied to gambling, form a subject for general discussion at present, and various papers having alluded to the disastrous workings of it in New Orleans, the Louisiana press hastens to confirm the testimony. The 'speckled' Legislature, as the Southerners call it, tried the experiment of a license law, but were obliged to repeal it at the end of a year. Within a month after it was put in force, New Orleans was transformed into a vast gaming saloon. A local paper speaks of it as follows:

" 'Anywhere for half a mile along one of our great streets a man could stand at a corner and pitch a rock into half a dozen saloons. Outside were crowds roping in strangers and the inexperienced ; within was a dense mass of men and boys, thick clouds of smoke, a din of balls, dice, and cards, much profanity and loud talking, a great rattling of glasses, and a formidable guzzling of villainous and nauseating compounds. The beast of Bengal was fought with fierce onslaught all night and all day, and the street was in an everlasting uproar.' "

It may be noticed, finally, that the objection that forbidding open sale of intoxicants increases private indulgence, applies to laws of restriction as well as of prohibition, in so far as in any case they do practically prevent public sale to any class, at any hour, or upon any day. This fear of home drinking has been constantly appealed to in the recent debates upon the "Sunday Closing Bill for Ireland." It was deprecated years ago, as an expected consequence of the Forbes Mackenzie Act in Scotland. But the Royal Commissioners' Report on the Licensing System of Scotland showed that it was groundless. (I cite an extract as given in Dr. Lees' "Condensed Argument," p. 53) :

" Evidence was adduced to us from all classes of persons of the benefits which have arisen. The improvement in large towns has been *most remarkable*. Whereas, formerly, on Sunday mornings, numbers of persons in every stage of intoxication were seen issuing from the public-houses, to the great annoyance of the respectable portion of the population on their way to church, the streets are now quiet and orderly, and few cases of drunkenness are seen. . . . . We did not obtain any evidence to prove that the practice of drinking to excess in private houses prevails to a greater extent among the lower orders now than it did formerly ; and with regard to ' shebeens,' it may be noticed at present, that to attribute to them anything like the amount of intemperance which the closing of public-houses has put down, is to ignore the evidence as to the decrease of Sunday convictions, and the increased regularity of attendance by the laboring classes at their work on Monday."

And yet it is to be observed that a law which permits every facility and every temptation for drinking on six days, and shuts down the dramshop on the seventh, only thus aiming, not at the gradual eradication, but the arbitrary suppression, of an abnormal appetite, would be the more likely to induce home drinking.

CHAPTER XXIV.

LAW AS A TEACHER.

" Law and government are the sovereign influence in human society ; in the last resort they shape and control it at their pleasure ; institutions depend on them, and are by them formed and
modified ; what they sanction will ever be generally considered
innocent ; what they condemn is thereby made a crime, and if
persisted in, becomes rebellion."—THOMAS ARNOLD, D.D.

I AM aware that the very idea of government
becoming in any sense a school-master is repulsive to those who attribute to it no higher function than that of a policeman to knock on the
head the rascal who is pilfering a purse.   But
to most men government has nobler and wider
functions, and is among the beneficent institutions ordained by the Great Lawgiver for
the promotion of human welfare ; and if human
welfare depends primarily on moral conduct and
character, then government, in the discharge of
its proper duties, should not only frame its laws
so as (to quote Mr. Gladstone) " to make it as
hard as possible for a man to go wrong, and as
easy as possible for a man to go right," but it is
bound to set before him a true ethical standard.

Reverence for law is a sentiment of force
among both the lower and the higher classes
of society.   Coarser natures are impressed by

the power it represents and the force which exe-
cutes it ; while the higher feel toward it something of that chivalric loyalty which found expression in the well-known sentence of Hooker,
in which he declares of Law as an idea that
"there can be no less acknowledged than that
her seat is the bosom of God, her voice the
harmony of the world ; all things in heaven and
earth do her homage, the very least as feeling
her care and the greatest as not exempted from
her power." The educational influence of the
laws of a country, though silent, is yet constant
and most powerful, because not merely of their
external authority, but because of this strong
instinct of reverence.

Every student of the philosophy of history
has noted how influential have been the laws of
a people in fixing their moral standard. An expression at first of the high or low state of the
average private conscience, they have re-acted
upon that conscience and served to intensify
and perpetuate the state of mind and heart
which gave them birth.

This idea was forcibly expressed and perti-
nently illustrated by Judge Sprague nearly thirty
years ago in his speech before the committee of
the Massachusetts Legislature :

" It is a profound observation that the morality of
no people can be maintained above the morality of

17

their laws. Their institutions are an index of their sentiments. Reason, observation, and history, all teach this. While gambling-houses were licensed in Paris and New Orleans, that vice could not there be made disgraceful; and where prostitution, even, has been licensed, as in some parts of Europe, it has been · there viewed in a very different light from the abhorrence with which we regard it. Where polygamy is lawful, a plurality of wives is reputable. If we recur to the history of Rome, we learn that public brothels were there tolerated with the inscription, '*Hic habitat felicitas*,' glaring upon their front, as may even now be seen in the ruins of Pompeii; and at the same time public exhibitions of mortal combats by gladiators, and of human victims thrown to wild beasts, were common amusements of the people. And what was the effect upon morals and manners? A combination of the extremes of luxurious licentiousness and ferocious barbarism. The laws of a country may reconcile public sentiment to crimes, even the most abhorrent to our nature, to murder itself; nay, to the murder of one's own offspring. Where infanticide is allowed, people look on and see parents destroy their own children, not only without remonstrance, but without emotion."

Our own country supplies a forcible illustration of the extent to which the influence of a legal sanction to a moral crime may debase and deaden the public conscience. Slavery as a creature of the law was bulwarked by the law. It rose to the dignity of an institution. Not

only those who were educated under it respected it, but the men of the North did it reverence
because of its conformity to law and its protection by Constitutional guaranties. When Henry
Clay, in the Senate of the United States, attempted to sneer the Abolitionists out of the
arena of debate as visionary fanatics, and im-
patiently exclaimed, " What the law declares to
be property *is* property ! " it did not shock the
conscience of the average American ; although
to Lord Brougham and his countrymen " the
doctrine of property in man was a wild and
guilty phantasy." It may well be hard for the
young men of to-day (and it will be still harder
for the young men of to-morrow) to realize
that not a generation ago a system which allowed one man to live upon the compulsory
and unpaid toil of another, and then to eke out
a support for his vices by selling the children
of the man whose life was spent in such toil, or
even his own by a slave-mother, was held to be
anything but infamous. And yet the law which
allowed it so debased public opinion, that the
brave men who attacked it bore the stigma of
infamy rather than those who merited it.
Strange as it may seem, the law was able to
make slavery respectable.

Judge Sprague well adds to what I have
quoted above a most suggestive thought :

" Extraordinary efforts or the impulses of a particular occasion may, for a time, carry up public
sentiment to an elevation above that of legal institutions; but the laws must either be changed to come
up to public sentiment, or public sentiment will be
brought down to a level with the laws."

The truth of the last remark was painfully
apparent to the earnest men who had awakened
the public conscience and touched the public
heart at the time of the great temperance reformation in this country.   Said Dr. Humphrey,
of Amherst College, in 1833:

" It is plain to me, as the sun in a clear summer
sky, that the license laws of our country constitute
one of the main pillars on which the stupendous
fabric of intemperance now rests."

In the same year, the honored Frelinghuysen,
of New Jersey, expressed himself thus :

" If men will engage in this destructive traffic, if
they will stoop to degrade their reason and reap the
wages of iniquity, let them no longer have the law-
book as a pillow, nor quiet conscience by the opiate
of a court license."

Dr. Justin Edwards, in his " Sixth Report of
the American Temperance Society," used this
language :

" The point to be decided by Legislatures of these
United States—to be decided for all coming pos-

terity, for the world, and for eternity—is, shall the sale of ardent spirit as a drink, be treated in legislation as a virtue or a vice? Shall it be licensed, sanctioned by law, and perpetuated to roll its all-pervading curses onward, interminably, or shall it be treated as it is, in truth, a sin?"

Let us look a little closer at the educational work of different laws in relation to the liquor traffic. License laws carry to the popular mind the implication that although the traffic in intoxicants is an exceptional one, requiring some unusual safeguards, yet that there is a legitimate public demand for such liquors as an ordinary beverage, which the State is bound to allow adequate means to supply. The correlative of regulation by the State is moderate drinking (or what he imagines to be such) by the individual.

On the other hand, prohibitory laws as plainly declare that the sale of intoxicating liquors as a beverage supplies no legitimate want, and is fraught with such dire evils to the State as to justify and require its suppression. What is so dangerous to the State can hardly be deemed safe to the citizen; and the natural* sequence of prohibition is total abstinence.

---

* Observe, I say, the *natural*, not the *inevitable;* for on this point I quite agree with Prof. F. W. Newman, who recently wrote thus to the *Alliance News* of England: " I think it is full twenty

Suppose, instead of license or strict prohibition, the State adopts some "half-way measure." If, for instance, under a system of "local option," what is criminal in the country becomes innocent in the city, does it not tend to the confusion of moral distinctions? Will it not inevitably lead the thoughtless to practically feel, if not to theoretically believe, that in other things, as well as in drinking, a different standard of conduct is permissible in the one place from that in the other? Or suppose the law undertakes to discriminate between the different kind of alcoholic beverages, allowing, for instance, the sale of malt liquors and prohibiting that of distilled spirits, is there not, plainly, beyond the enticement offered to the use of the beers by their free public exposure and sale, a most impressive, and, at the same time, as we believe, a most dangerous advertisement of them by the

-----

years since I heard Lord Harrington (the first nobleman who joined us) say, ' I like a glass of wine, and think it does me good: and as long as I think so, and can get it legally, I mean to drink it. But I see that there are tens of thousands whom our drink traffic, as now conducted, frightfully ruins ; and sooner than let this go on, I will, when that proves necessary, give up my glass of wine.' To me the man who so speaks seems not only to be consistent and sincere, but to have a merit which none can claim who hold that alcoholic drink is in itself bad for all men. The latter class (to whom I belong) make no sacrifice in renouncing drink, and do not renounce it for the sake of others, but for their own sake."

State itself as harmless beverages? The force of these considerations as to the weight which law has in the popular mind, in matters of opinion and conduct, will be more and more apparent to the reader upon reflection.

It may be that the influence of law in the formation of opinion, and the regulation of human conduct in matters beyond its domain of positive rule, is excessive. It is true that a right and wise-minded man will find a more unerring external and internal standard for the regulation of his moral belief and conduct than that of statute law; but it is a profound remark of George Eliot that "to judge wisely, I suppose we must know how things appear to the unwise; that kind of appearance making the larger part of the world's history."

Soon after the enactment of the present license law in Massachusetts, I was holding a term of court, when a deputy sheriff said to me one morning: "I have just seen a sad sight—a fellow persuading a reluctant comrade to enter a grog-shop. 'Come along,' said he, 'this is now as respectable a place as any; the Commonwealth of Massachusetts says so.'"

But this immediate application of the statute law to override moral tastes and convictions, is the coarser and less dangerous kind of the educational influence which bad laws exert.

The greater danger is in the slower and more insidious influence which such laws exert in familiarizing us with public vice ; in accustoming us to its public tolerance ; in repressing the natural force of moral indignation,* and in inducing a faithless acquiescence in the inevitableness of moral evil.

And, on the other hand, it is in accordance with both philosophy and experience, that the effect of prohibitory laws should be surely, if slowly, to discourage the formation of drinking habits. It is a mistake to suppose that men often rush into evil courses in a spirit of moral defiance ; when the State writes " criminal " over the doorway of the most elegant drinking-saloon as well as over the lowest grog-shop ; when it places at the bar of justice the tempter by the side of his victim, and when it stamps every package of liquor as a dangerous beverage, meriting destruction as a public nuisance, it has done much to warn the young and unwary, and to turn their feet aside from the downward path.

* Even so stern a moralist as Albert Barnes recognizes this. He says : " An evil always becomes worse by being sustained by the laws of the land. . . . . This fact does much to deter others from opposing the evil, and from endeavoring to turn the public indignation against it. It is an unwelcome thing for a good man ever to set himself against the laws of the land, and to denounce that as wrong which they affirm to be right." (Sermon on " The Throne of Iniquity," p. 4).

As a matter of fact, the influence of such laws has been recognized, and recognized most clearly where the law has been most continuously enforced. Hon. William P. Frye, M.C., formerly Attorney-General of Maine, says of the law in that State :

" It has gradually created a public sentiment against both selling and drinking, so that the large majority of moderate respectable drinkers have become abstainers."

So Governor Dingley, in his testimony before the Commissioners of the Canadian Parliament, declared that " the influence of the law as a temperance educator, even when only partially enforced, was marked."

The Hon. Woodbury Davis, ex-Judge of the Supreme Court of Maine, testified in this emphatic manner before the legislative committee of Massachusetts in 1867 :

" My opinion has been from the first, and has been continually strengthened by my observation and personal connection with the enforcement of the law, that one of the most valuable results of it is, it has an effect on·the public sentiment in making it disreputable to drink, and in restraining men from a practice in which they could not indulge, except by doing it secretly, which they do not like to do ; and,

17*

therefore, aside from its direct influence, perhaps its most valuable work was on the point you suggested, making the use of liquor disreputable, and thereby restraining the young from the habit." (House Doc. No. 415, p. 734).

CHAPTER XXV.

ENFORCEMENT.

" Admiral Dupont was once explaining the reason why he failed
to enter Charleston harbor with his fleet of iron-clads. He
gave this reason, and that reason, and the other reason; and
Farragut remained silent until he had got through, and then
said: 'Ah, Dupont, there was one more reason.' 'What is
that?' ' *You didn't believe you could do it.*' "

THE problem of the Enforcement of Prohibition troubles so many minds, that I ought not
to close this discussion without giving to it
some consideration.*

But it is to be noticed at the outset, that *it is
not a problem peculiar to the policy of prohibition.* Frame what laws you will; as experience
has shown, if they are laws operating in any
way *against* the liquor traffic, they encounter
at *the point of pressure* about the same amount
of resistance.

And, beyond this, if we have proved anything
in this argument, it has been that, under equally favorable conditions, *the law of prohibition
has been far better enforced than the law of
license.*

Impatient reformers must learn to check

their tendency to think nothing has been accomplished till everything has been accomplished. There are natural limits to the perfect
execution of any human law; especially is this
true of laws which antagonize great pecuniary
interests, and deeply-rooted sensual appetites,
and which may be violated in secrecy. We
may indeed hope for a progressive success in
the execution of these; but it must be by a
steady, persistent, and patient pressure which
shall not only repress outward acts, but gradually deflect capital from a perilous and wan-
ing market, and eradicate, or at least weaken,
a diseased appetite. Let us take Goethe's
motto: " Without haste—without rest."

Neither is it always best to be hunting up
new machinery. I remember to have been
very much impressed years ago with the remark of a wise man, when some new " attachment" to the prohibitory law was under discussion, that "what was needed, rather, was more
head of water than new machinery." " There is a
time for all things ; " but there is a pretty constant call for more

WATER POWER.

The time ought to come, and for the safety
of American institutions it must come, when
there shall be only a contest over the enact-

ment, and none afterward over the execution of the laws. But it is not so now. There may be force enough to keep the law on the statute book, but not force enough to execute it, or to execute it firmly. Any weakening of public opinion, that great power in a republic, is immediately followed by a relaxation in the arm of the executive and the judiciary ; the police are enervated ; prosecuting officers become timid and compromising ; juries are demoralized, and courts are weakly lenient. If it requires moral force to obtain the law, it requires more to retain it and make it a terror to evil-doers. Every turn of the screw, up to the point of assured conquest, develops new power of resistance. If, therefore, as we have shown, moral teaching culminates in law, so law in turn necessitates, at least in its struggling stages, stronger moral teaching for its sustentation. But in addition to this, *it demands self-sacrificing and organized political action* at the hands of its friends. Of all expressions of public opinion that at the ballot-box is the clearest and most effective.

It is, in turn, an encouraging fact that the successful enforcement of the law tends to strengthen public opinion ; and while it awakens the resistance of its enemies, it arouses the enthusiasm of its friends, and develops an interest in those who at first opposed it from theoretical objections, prejudice, or lack of faith in its practicability.

MACHINERY.

Wherever and whenever there is a public opinion developed, which calls for still more effective machinery to enforce the prohibition of the liquor traffic, it can be supplied.

The attention of students of Penology, both in England and America, has of late been specially attracted to the relations of capital and crime. Without here entering upon the general subject, it is apparent at first thought, how dependent the mass of liquor-sellers are upon owners of real estate. A lawyer who had in the course of his life a large experience in the administration of criminal justice, appeared some time since before a committee of the Legislature of Massachusetts, and suggested that if landlords were made liable for leasing their premises for unlawful selling, that it would root out the traffic. He was unaware that the Legislature had already gone beyond this. By the statute of 1855 (chap. 465), not only is the owner who knowingly lets a tenement for the unlawful sale of intoxicating liquors, liable to a fine or imprisonment, but any such use by a tenant annuls his lease, and gives the landlord an immediate right of entry, and if after notice of such use by his tenant he omits to take all reasonable measures to eject him, he is made liable as for an original letting. But this law had slumbered so deeply upon the statute, that an intelligent lawyer knew not of its life. But imagine a prosecuting officer and a Grand Jury having the courage in our large cities to "due presentment make" of the offenders against this statute! They will do it the very day that public opinion calls for it. And when these "eminently respectable" owners of real estate are arraigned by the side of the low criminals whom they aid and abet, a great progress will be made in the execution of the laws.

The general mode in which the criminal law seeks to prevent offenses to the State, is by punishment of the offender; but in one kind of misdemeanors, embraced under the extensive head of nuisance, the law combines remedial with punitive justice, and after punishing the offender, removes the offense. The order for abatement of a nuisance after conviction is familiar to English and American jurisprudence; and the order of abatement is flexible and adapted to circumstances; thus, if the evil is not in the physical thing itself, but in the use of it, and the latter is separable, that alone is to be abated. When by the statutes of several States all places kept for the illegal sale of intoxicating liquors were declared to be common nuisances, a long step forward was taken which drew after it many remedies peculiar to the law of nuisance, the application of which awaits a developed and aroused public sentiment.

The State of Illinois, which treats unlicensed dram-shops as common nuisances, has a recent statute (1874), which provides that "it shall be a part of the judgment (in case of conviction) that the place so kept, shall be shut up and abated until the keeper shall give bond with sufficient surety to be approved by the Court, in the penal sum of one thousand dollars, payable to the people of the State of Illinois, conditional, that he will not sell intoxicating liquors contrary to the laws of the State." The statute is drawn crudely, and is capable of evasion, but it points the way to effective legislation hereafter.

The remedy, by injunction, to stay a flagrant nuisance until more formal proceedings ripen into a judgment, is very familiar to the civil side of our courts, and is not unknown in criminal practice. In the latter case, however, it must rest upon special statute law. Thus it is provided in Massachusetts: that "the Superior Court or a justice thereof, in term time, or vacation, may, either before or pending a prosecution for a common nuisance affecting the public health, issue an injunction to stay or prevent the same until the matter shall be decided by a jury or otherwise; may enforce such injunction, according to the course of proceedings in chancery; and may dissolve the same when the Court or one of the justices shall think proper." (General Statutes, chap. 26, sec. 13). In 1864, a Committee of the Massachusetts Legislature reported a bill extending these provisions to liquor nuisances, and in their report they say:

"Certainly few nuisances can be conceived more prejudicial to the public health than the class under consideration, and none *as* injurious to the whole circle of interests, pecuniary, social, and moral, of the State. The faithful application of this remedy (by injunction), antecedent to verdict, and according to the practice of the Court, to remain till acquittal by the jury, or other cause shown for its dissolution, will prove an important practical auxiliary to existing laws."

The bill which contained this provision passed both branches of the Legislature; and a bill containing the same provision was passed in the following year; but neither became a law, both bills being vetoed by Governor Andrew on the ground of other provisions which he deemed objectionable.

Such exercise of the preventive jurisdiction

of the courts is not attended with the delays and uncertainties which are often inseparable from the punitive. The right to a technically faultless complaint or indictment, to a trial by jury, to the revision of the highest judicial tribunal of every trivial question of law, are all secured to a defendant before he can be *punished ;* but when the question is presented of protection against a continuing nuisance, the State may step in with a prompt and vigorous hand and arrest the evil *pendente lite ;* and any violation of an injunction is a contempt of court, to be speedily disposed of by the magistrate.

ENGINEERS.

It is a truism to say that after you have secured an adequate motive power, and obtained the most approved machinery, you must have for success not only a competent, but a well-disposed engineer. And where the result is encouraging in one quarter, and discouraging in others, is it not well to look to the engineer? Wendell Phillips put this felicitously some years since:

" Boston has five or six trains of railroads. . . . . All of them run locomotives where they wish to. Suppose that, on the Fitchburg Railroad, one locomotive, for a year, never got further than Groton, what do you think the directors of that road would do? Would they take up the rails beyond Groton, or would they turn out the engineer? There is a law of the Commonwealth of Massachusetts thoroughly executed in every county but ours, and here the men appointed to execute it not only do not want to, but you can not expect them to. They were elected *not* to execute it, and they say they can't execute it. Shall we take up the rails, or change the engineer? Which?"

When will men learn to conduct philanthropic politics with the same good sense with which they conduct their business affairs? What man of sense would expect a difficult business to prosper if its management were confided to a superintendent who had no faith in its designated modes, or who was in the pay or interest of parties who had a direct pecuniary interest in its failure? And yet, over and over again the friends of temperance have struggled strenuously to obtain the law of prohibition, and have then entrusted its execution to men who had no faith in it, to men who would be glad to see it fail, and to men who had an eye to the liquor vote. And so here again we come upon the necessity of organized political action. The officers who are to enforce the law against strong, antagonistic pressure, must feel no divided allegiance; they must be men *elected to do it.*

CHAPTER XXVI.

THE OUTLOOK.

"The ultimate issue of the struggle is certain. If any one doubts the general preponderance of good over evil in human nature, he has only to study the history of moral crusades. The enthusiastic energy and self-devotion with which a great moral cause inspires its soldiers always have prevailed, and always will prevail, over any amount of self-interest or material power arrayed on the other side."—PROF. GOLDWIN SMITH.

AND here our discussion of the problem is brought to its natural close. We have sought to show that the Liquor Traffic is the enemy of the State and a foe to all the objects for which the State exists; that it requires the intervention of law, and that moral suasion, educational and religious instrumentalities, are all inadequate without the aid of legislation; that it is within the legitimate province of law and the rightful sphere of government to interfere with it to whatever extent the public good demands; that attempts at its regulation have proved failures, and of necessity always will; that distinctions in the law as to different alcoholic beverages have proved impracticable, unwise, and unsafe; and that society can be adequately protected only by the suppression of all; that prohibition has proved a success in proportion to the thoroughness and persistency of its enforcement; and that the law itself has been a pervasive and persuasive moral teacher.

It can not be denied that many, who will admit the force of the argument, are yet distrustful as to the practicability of securing such legislation. They are appalled at the power of the traffic. They see that it has uncounted wealth at its command; that it is organized and unscrupulous; that it has the support of a fierce appetite behind it and the alliance of every evil lust; that it is able to bribe or intimidate the great political parties. All this is true; but still it is not to be the final victor. It has all the elemental moral forces of the human race against it, and though their working be slow, and their rate of progress dependent on human energy and fidelity, the ultimate result is as certain as the action of the law of gravity in the material universe.

Wealth may be against us; rank may affect to despise us; but the light whose dawn makes a new morning in the world rarely shines from palace or crown, but from the manger and the cross.

Before the aroused conscience of the people, wielding the indomitable will of a State, the ministers to vice, the tempters of innocence, the destroyers of soul and body shall go down forever.

I speak of the future day of triumph; I do not underrate the severity of the struggle. I would not ignore the years of hard toil and persevering effort that lie between us and it.

Meantime, what better can be done than to fight the battle openly, courageously, persistently, and upon a basis of principle? Such a contest is the most effective mode of educating the people. Such a contest is a process of self-education in some of the noblest traits of manhood—trust in Divine Providence, faith in humanity, courage, fidelity, philanthropy. By one of those grand and beautiful laws of "the Spiritual Harvest" which God has established, he who works for others, works most truly for himself.

We have sought to follow the discussion of our subject in these pages calmly and dispassionately, suppressing emotion, and appealing rather to logical conviction than to the moral sympathies; but if we are right in the conclusions to which we have arrived, the heart may well arise at the thought that in working for the suppression of the liquor traffic we are in that grand line of effort for the development of humanity which seeks to set forth the glory of God by the moral elevation of His children. Such a work is the noblest characteristic of our Christian civilization.

www.ingramcontent.com/pod-product-compliance
Lightning Source LLC
Chambersburg PA
CBHW032338280326
41935CB00008B/372